Illustrated Guide to
WOOD STRIP CANOE BUILDING

SUSAN VAN LEUVEN

Schiffer
Publishing Ltd

4880 Lower Valley Road, Atglen, PA 19310 USA

Back Cover: Photo *Courtesy of Howard Van Leuven*

Library of Congress Cataloging-in-Publication Data

Van Leuven, Susan.
  Illustrated guide to wood strip canoe building / Susan Van Leuven.
    p. cm.
  Includes bibliographical references.
  ISBN 0-7643-0537-9 (hardcover)
  1. Fiberglass canoes--Design and construction--Amateurs' manuals. 2. Wooden boats--
Design and construction--Amateurs' manuals. 3. Laminated wood--Amateurs' manuals.
  VM353.V35   1998
  623.8'29--dc21   98-22943
                                                        CIP

Designed by Bonnie M. Hensley
Layout by Randy L. Hensley
Typeset in Korinna BT/Times New Roman

ISBN: 0-7643-0537-9
Printed in China

Acknowledgments

The production of a book demands much more than just a writer knowing how to do something, such as build a canoe. The making of this book was very much influenced by, and dependent on, the help of other people. I want to express thanks to Steve Penberthy, owner of Woodcrafters, and his staff and customers, for opportunities to teach (and learn) the art of strip boat building at their Portland, Oregon store. I am also grateful to Hal Lindstrom and Jan Gano for their help in refining the first draft of the book. I very much appreciate their generosity in spending the time to identify areas needing more work, volunteering additional construction tips, and in many cases, offering suggestions for clarifying presentation. Joann Jenny deserves special recognition for her willing assistance in solving computing problems, and for lending me computer equipment. The good humor and patience of other friends and family members were invaluable in providing encouragement through all phases of this project. One friend and family member was by far the greatest sponsor of this effort. This work probably would not have begun, and certainly could not have been completed, without the unwavering support of my husband, Dick Jenny. Creative people who have understanding and supportive spouses are most fortunate, and I belong to that set. Finally, a large measure of appreciation must go to all of the people who have shared their boat building (and related) expertise so that other people, including me, can learn and enjoy this craft. Most humble acknowledgment goes to those craftsmen who first developed the method of wood strip boat construction, and then wrote of their experience.

Published by Schiffer Publishing Ltd.
4880 Lower Valley Road
Atglen, PA 19310
Phone: (610) 593-1777; Fax: (610) 593-2002
E-mail: Schifferbk@aol.com

In Europe Schiffer books are distributed by
Bushwood Books
6 Marksbury Avenue
Kew Gardens
Surrey TW9 4JF England
Phone: 44 (0) 181 392-8585; Fax: 44 (0) 181 392-9876
E-mail: Bushwd@aol.com

Please write for a free catalog.
This book may be purchased from the publisher.
Please include $3.95 for shipping. Please try your bookstore first.
We are interested in hearing from authors with book ideas on related subjects.

Contents

Introduction

A Wee Lassie model solo canoe, built by the author from plans by Feather Canoes, Inc. *Photo courtesy of Howard R. Van Leuven.*

Wood strip canoe building is enjoying ever more interest as a hobby, and some folks have found it so engrossing that they've gone on to make a full-time occupation of it. Building with wood strips allows you to make a boat of very high quality without specialized, expensive tools. As a hobby boat builder, you can enjoy luxuries often unavailable to the professional builder. When building to please yourself, you can choose whatever materials you want, and finish the craft to your own standards. Since you are building this boat to meet your needs, your own priorities and standards determine the amount of time and money applied to the project.

Amateur and professional builders favor wood strip construction for a variety of reasons. This type of construction lends itself to practically unlimited variations in smooth, graceful hull shapes. Modifications to existing designs can be readily made to suit individual tastes. Canoe manufacturers often make new prototypes out of wood strips, which are then used under "real-life" conditions for the purpose of testing the prototype for performance. Strip canoes built strictly for utility purposes can be put together very quickly. On the other hand, these canoes are suited to treatment as three-dimensional artwork, and a perfectly functional craft can also have the appearance of fine furniture.

The strength and weight of a wood strip canoe can be varied according to the needs of the user. One quality is usually gained at the expense of another. For example, more strength is generally obtained at the price of more weight, but these craft have a well-deserved reputation for being light for their strength. Well-made strip canoes compare favorably to factory-made canoes in this respect; very few commercially produced canoes can outdo cedar strip canoes here, and you can build your own strip canoe for a lot less money than it will run you for a light weight production model.

As noted above, price can be a major motivator for building your own boat. The cost of materials for a wood strip canoe is much less than the purchase price of a comparable quality commercially manufactured canoe.

The greatest cost in creating a strip canoe of your own is the time and labor that is required to complete the project. A common inquiry is, "How many hours does it take?" Because there are so many variables that affect the progress of such a project, a number figure in hours would be meaningless. Although it is possible to put such a canoe together in as short a time as a two or three weeks (under ideal conditions, and that doesn't include varnishing), most first-time builders working on their own need a more generous time frame. For example, when I built my first canoe, a 17-1/2 footer, I had to learn all the building techniques and how to use the tools as I went along, and I was only able to work on the canoe on weekends. It took me thirty-two weekends to finish the project. You can adjust that figure to suit your own situation, depending on your level of woodworking and boat building experience, the amount of time you have available during the week, the size of the craft, and your attention to cosmetic features. For sure, the details that don't necessarily affect the function of the canoe, but which reflect the craftsmanship, really take up the time! Even if you are only proposing to build a "utility grade" canoe, you need to be able to enjoy the building process. That requires some patience, otherwise, you would be better off making a canoe of plywood—plywood boats go together faster.

Most of the material in this book can be found elsewhere, but it is scattered over a range of sources. Some of the innovations are my own, although it's possible someone else may also have come up with the same idea and I don't know of it. Early in my canoe-building experience, a common problem was not being able to find information I needed, when I needed it. Beginners often find that sources of information give first-time builders credit for more knowledge than they actually have. While this is quite flattering, it has left me in a situation of having to work my way through certain stages of construction by a process of trial and error, sometimes leading to marginally acceptable results.

With this book, it is my intent to provide all the information needed to build a wood strip canoe of the highest quality. Since aesthetics are important to me, I have allotted a sizable amount of space to details that will give you the finest results, as well as the basic techniques required for producing a good, functional canoe. For those who are not as particular about the final appearance as I am, I have attempted to indicate where you can afford to cut corners and still end up with a good canoe, in terms of performance.

The information in this book is drawn from my own experience, and also the experience of other established professional builders whose work I respect. Where I have decided not to include information that may be interesting to some readers, but probably not a majority, sources have been provided in endnotes. It has not been such a long time since I was a beginning builder, and since I remember the difficulties I encountered then, it is my primary objective to be as complete, accurate, and specific as I can. Some readers will find that more information is provided than they really need. While I hope experienced builders will find this book to be of value, I have written the book for people who have no boat building experience and limited woodworking experience. I have talked to a number of capable crafts people who have become mired in a frustrating problem, and often it turns out that a specific, critical detail of information is all they need to be able to resume progress. Recognizing that these details are important to someone, I have chosen to include them.

For any given step in the construction of a wood strip canoe, there usually is more than one way to get the job done. Sometimes, the results are equally good no matter which route you go. In this book I describe different ways to accomplish the same objective, with emphasis on those that I have tried and found to give good results. In some instances I mention proven methods that I have not tried myself. Since I hesitate to describe in detail methods that I have no experience with, I have used endnotes to refer readers to sources for more details on these methods. All the hobby builders I know like to pick and choose means of construction that suit their individual tastes and abilities. With that in mind, this book is designed to offer options to help you build what you consider to be a masterpiece of good craftsmanship and taste, as well as a serviceable canoe that is a joy to paddle.

Steps in the Construction Process: The Itinerary

One of the major attractions of strip building boats is that the builder can develop the skills needed to get the job done as the project progresses and still end up with a decent boat. In other words, you don't have to be a skilled boat builder to produce a good wood strip craft. The skills involved in strip construction are:

Basic woodworking skills
Basic skills in application of plastic resin and fiberglass
Finishing (varnishing and/or painting) skills

As with any other creative process, practice makes perfect, and prior abilities that you have acquired will serve you well. If you build more than one canoe, each successive boat will reflect refinements you make as a result of your previous experience, plus knowledge you glean from other sources. Having said all that, I still contend that patience, persistence, and attention to the work are more influential in successfully constructing the strip canoe of your dreams than sheer expertise.

The process of taking the boat from concept to completion can appear more complicated than it actually is. The whole business can be distilled as follows:

1. Study the plans and read through the instructions for construction.
2. Make the mold.
3. Construct the hull of wood strips, over the mold. (You need to mill the strips first, if you didn't buy them pre-milled.)
4. Fiberglass the outside of the hull.
5. Remove the hull from the mold and cut the sheer to shape if necessary.
6. Fiberglass the interior of the hull.
7. Make and install gunwales, bulkheads (if called for), and decks.
8. Make thwart(s) and seat(s).
9. Install seat risers, if indicated in plans.
10. Varnish (or paint) the interior of the canoe.
11. Install thwart(s) and seat(s).
12. Varnish (or paint) the exterior of the canoe.

Shaping, scraping, and/or sanding is involved between and during just about every step. The amount of this you do is determined largely by the balance point between your affection for sanding and the desired appearance of the canoe.

A good way to ensure success with a boat building project is to study the plans (which for a strip canoe are very simple) and at least read through the building instructions before reaching for those tools. Canoe plans are straightforward, but not all designers do everything the same. Also, some plans come with instructions, while others do not. If the instructions you get are sketchy, or perhaps nonexistent, dread not. This book was made to fill those voids in information. Reading ahead often clears up questions that arise as you go along. There usually is a choice of different ways to do a given operation, but some of them limit your future options more or perform better than others, and you will want to know about those matters before you get there.

If this is your first canoe, give yourself a break and think of it as a series of small projects instead of one large (potentially overwhelming) project. Post a list of the twelve steps, and mark them off as you complete them. Celebrate each one with a little party, if you want. And remember that you are getting more than a canoe out of this. You are also acquiring some very useful and valuable skills. It won't hurt your pride either, when you take this craft of yours to the water and people remark on the beauty of your canoe and register amazement that you actually created such a thing.

A slightly modified Micmac model tandem canoe, built from plans in David Hazen's book, *The Stripper's Guide to Canoe-building*. Building your own canoe provides an opportunity to learn new skills, and rewards you with a high-quality craft that will give many years of performance and pleasure.

Chapter One

Terms Defined

Batten—a long, narrow, flexible piece of wood. A strip makes a good batten, for the purposes of this project.

Bias—diagonal to the weave of fiberglass cloth. A bias cut crosses all the intersecting fibers at a 45 degree angle. Cloth cut on the bias is more flexible and able to conform to contours than cloth cut parallel to the run of the lengthwise fibers.

Blush—a waxy residue that forms on the surface of epoxy as it cures, especially during humid weather. It is a combination of a byproduct of the curing epoxy with moisture from the air.

Breasthook—a triangle-shaped structural piece similar to a deck, that holds the sides of the canoe together at the stem. The breasthook serves most of the same purposes a deck does. The difference is that a breasthook is fastened directly to the inside of the hull, rather than to the inwales.

Bright finish—a clear, usually gloss or semi-gloss finish such as varnish, on wood (or transparent fiberglass and epoxy over wood) which enhances and protects the natural appearance of the wood (or fiberglass, if applicable).

Bulkhead—a piece that is installed crosswise inside the hull for the purpose of strengthening the hull, and usually to create a sealed air chamber for additional flotation.

Carrying yoke—a specialized thwart designed to fit the shoulders of a person carrying an overturned canoe by him/herself.

Centerline—the exact midline running lengthwise of a boat. This term is often used interchangeably with keel line.

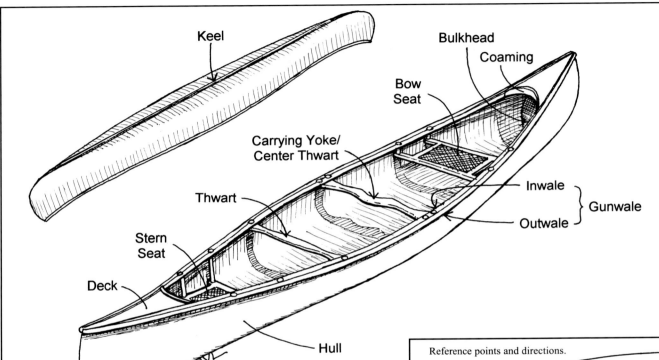

Anatomy of a canoe.

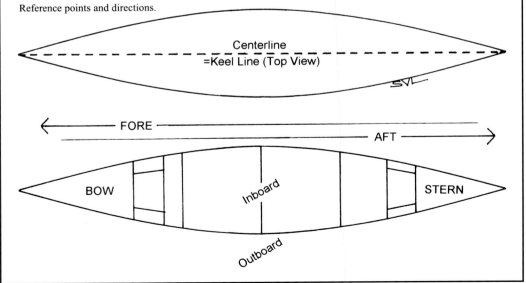

Reference points and directions.

Boatbuilding, like any other worthwhile pursuit, includes its own parlance. Sometimes terminology, or jargon, can serve as a barrier to novices. It is important to recognize that these terms come into use in response to a need for streamlining cumbersome descriptions. So while new terms may seem to complicate learning initially, the actual goal is to simplify and clarify discussion of the subject.

Since this book is designed to help people whose expertise lies outside the realm of canoe construction, lay terms are employed extensively. In the interest of clarity and conciseness, however, it is necessary to use some boat building terminology. Because these terms are indispensable, I encourage you to make yourself familiar with the contents of this chapter before immersing yourself in the rest of the book. Descriptions of particulars and processes will be more meaningful, and the book will therefore be of more value, if you have a grasp of the language used.

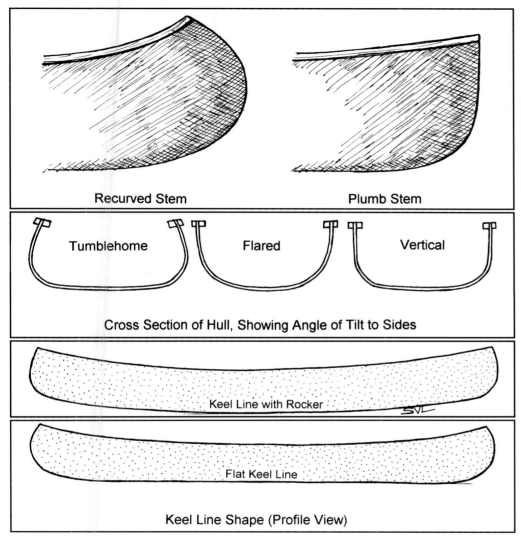

Recurved Stem   Plumb Stem

Tumblehome   Flared   Vertical

Cross Section of Hull, Showing Angle of Tilt to Sides

Keel Line with Rocker

Flat Keel Line

Keel Line Shape (Profile View)

Left: Canoe shapes. The shape of the internal structural member known as the stem has a direct effect on the profile of the end of the canoe. Because the outward appearance of the canoe effectively duplicates the shape of the stems, the term "stem" is often also used to refer to the leading and trailing edges of the craft. The terms "flared" and "vertical" describe the sides of the canoe, whereas "tumblehome" applies to the inward tilt of the sides. Similarly, the keel line either *has* rocker or doesn't.

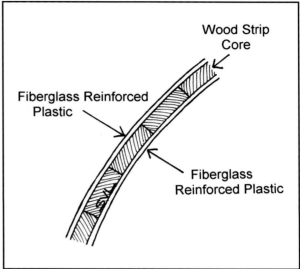

Wood Strip Core

Fiberglass Reinforced Plastic

Fiberglass Reinforced Plastic

Cross-section of a wood strip hull, showing the laminates that form the structure of the hull. The strips, viewed end-on here, are glued together over a mold. The next step is bonding fiberglass cloth to the outside of the wooden hull with resin, in this case epoxy, which cures to a plastic solid. Then, the hull is taken off the mold, and fiberglass cloth is applied to the interior. This produces a balanced laminate that is much stronger than the wood core would be alone.

Coaming—a vertical wooden piece attached to the inboard edge of a deck. Its purpose is to deflect water running off the deck into the canoe, and to give the deck a more finished appearance.

Core—the inside layer(s) of a laminate. In the case of wood strip canoes, the strips form the core of the laminate produced by bonding to the inside and the outside of the wooden hull.

Dart—a slit cut in the edge of fiberglass cloth in order to make the cloth lie flat, with the cut edges overlapping each other.

DA sander—dual action sander, which is also commonly called a "random orbit sander." The head of the sander spins on its own axis, and that axis revolves around another axis, producing an action that is superior to that of an ordinary disk sander for smoothing and fairing the hull of a boat.

Deck—a piece that covers the end of a canoe, bridging from one gunwale to the opposite one. Decks on canoes can be very short, extending just a few inches inboard from the ends of the craft, to structures that close over most of the topside. They can be of structural importance, supporting the hull, or lightly built decorative pieces designed to exclude water and improve the canoe's appearance.

Deck plate—a removable hard plastic cover (or lid) that can be installed in decks or bulkheads to permit access to a chamber that is sealed off when the covers are fastened in place. The whole deck plate unit amounts to a ring (with threads around the inside hole) which is fixed to the boat, plus a round "lid" which threads into the ring.

Design—a specific hull shape, including length, width, and contours. The contours can be defined by sets of coordinates at established intervals along the length of the hull. For strip canoes, plans include a series of outlines, which replace the numeric coordinates, at given intervals. These outlines represent the shape of a cross-section of the hull at a particular point along its length.

Dozuki saw—a traditional Japanese dovetail and joint-cutting saw, which cuts on the pull stroke. This hand saw makes very precise cuts.

End grain—the exposed ends of wood fibers in a piece that has been cut directly across the grain. Growth rings in wood are most easily recognized in the end grain.

Entry—the cutting action of the leading edge of a canoe as it moves through the water. Fast canoes which readily cut through the water have long narrow ends, referred to as a "fine entry." Wider, more buoyant canoes that tend to ride up over waves do not have this.

Fair—the smoothness or evenness of a surface or line. This term is usually used to describe the shape of the hull. Sometimes it is applied to the line defined by a strip attached to the mold for the purpose of checking alignment of mold parts. A hull that is fair is flat where it is supposed to be flat and smoothly curved where it is supposed to be curved.

Fiberglass—glass fibers that are spun into strands, and then woven or otherwise treated for use as the reinforcement part of a fiberglass/resin matrix. Fiberglass used in wood strip construction is woven into a cloth, which is available in a variety of coarser or finer textures and widths. The term fiberglass is often used more loosely to refer to the entire glass cloth and resin composite after it has been applied, or as a verb meaning the act of applying fiberglass (with resin) to a wood surface.

Flared—hull sides having an outward tilt, from the bottom up.

Grain—the lengthwise orientation of fibers. This term is applied to both wood and fiberglass cloth in discussing handling and working characteristics.

Grit—the coarseness or the texture of sandpaper. Fine grit sandpaper has smaller grit particles more densely distributed, so has a higher numbered designation, such as 220-grit. Coarse grit paper has larger particles, more widely scattered, as in the case of 60-grit paper. The number denotes the number of particles per square inch of paper.

Gunwales—a set of lengthwise structural members attached to the hull along the upper edge (the sheer). The gunwale of a canoe consists of two parts: the inwale, attached to the inboard side of the sheer; and the outwale, attached to the outboard side of the sheer. The gunwales are also sometimes called the rails.

Hardener—an agent that causes resin to cure to a solid condition. Different hardeners produce a range of different characteristics in the handling ability of the resins they are mixed with. Suppliers often have several different hardeners for use with a single type of resin.

Hull—the most basic, essential part of the boat; the bottom and sides, which are in contact with the water when the boat is afloat. A canoe is the simplest of boats in that it is no more than a hull plus whatever framework is needed to hold the hull in shape.

Inboard—the inside of the canoe. When the term is used as an adjective to describe direction relative to something else, it means toward the middle of the inside of the boat from the point of reference.

Inwales—lengthwise structural support pieces attached to the inside of the hull along the sheer. These make up one half of the support system known as the rails, or gunwales.

Jig—an apparatus that holds canoe parts in place while they are being assembled or worked on. The mold is a jig for assembling the strip hull over, and other jigs are used for cutting, shaping, or gluing pieces.

Keel—an external lengthwise piece located along the centerline of the hull. The keel may be wide and flat, or a fairly narrow fin-like projection. Its purposes are to improve the canoe's ability to travel in a straight line and to protect the bottom of the canoe. Sometimes additional keels, called bilge keels, are placed to either side of the main keel, usually to afford more protection to the bottom of the hull.

Keel line—the line defined by the position of a keel. Since the keel (if there is one) is placed on the centerline of the boat hull, the term keel line is used almost interchangeably with the term centerline in this book. The location indicated by either term is the same.

Layup—the composite of fiberglass bonded with resin to a surface. In more complex fiberglass applications, the layup consists of a specific sequence of layers of fiberglass products applied according to a time schedule to take advantage of specific stages of resin cure during the process.

Leveling—as applied to a finish such as varnish, it refers to the ability of the liquid varnish to flow so that differences in coating thickness equalize. In other words, the marks left by a brush either do or don't disappear in the varnish, depending on the leveling ability of the varnish.

Outboard—outside of the canoe or hull. Sometimes the term is used to indicate a location away from the middle of the inside of the canoe (relative to some other thing).

Outwales—lengthwise structural support pieces which are attached to the outside of the hull along the sheer. The outwales make up part of the rails, or gunwales.

Plans—a set of drawings and written specifications which contain enough information to build a boat from.

Plumb—vertical. This term may either be applied to the shape of the end of the canoe or stem piece, viewed in profile, or the shape of the sides of the canoe (the sides may tilt inward, outward, or be vertical).

Pot life—the length of time that mixed resin retains its "runniness" and workability, before it begins to gel.

Recurve—the shape of the end of a canoe or stem piece, where the end of the canoe forms a rounded curve when viewed in profile.

Resin—a liquid that can solidify into a rigid plastic once mixed with the appropriate hardener. There are many kinds of resins, but the best one for strip boat building is epoxy resin. This term is often used more loosely to mean resin that has been mixed with a hardener, but which has not gelled yet.

Rocker—the slightly curved shape of the bottom of a canoe (if it has this feature), when viewed in profile. Hull bottoms may be perfectly straight from end to end, or have a slight to fairly pronounced convex curve. Rocker improves maneuverability of a boat in fast water.

Scuppers—holes, usually for water drainage, in a railing. These are cutout openings in the edge of the rail that is fastened to the boat hull or deck. In strip canoe building, this type of railing is often used for inwales.

Sheer—the upper edge of the hull of a boat, when viewed in profile.

Sheer line—the line defined by the shape of the sheer.

Stem—structural piece located at the end of a canoe, which the ends of the strips are attached to. The shape of the stem, either recurved, plumb, or some other shape, determines the outward profile of the end of the canoe. For that reason, the term "stem" is sometimes used to indicate the area of the extreme end of the canoe, not just the structural piece itself. Stems are only in the "pointed" ends of boats, so a square-sterned canoe would have only one stem, while all other canoes have two. Depending on how a canoe is constructed, the stem may be a single unit inside the end of the hull, or it may be a two-part unit made up of an inside stem piece and an outside stem piece, the latter of which is visible on the outside of the hull. The meaning of the term "stem" in use depends on the context.

Stem band—a narrow metal band that is sometimes attached to the extreme outside ends of a canoe along the centerline to protect the hull from abrasion and impacts.

Thwart—a structural framework member that is placed crosswise to the centerline of a canoe, connecting the gunwales of both sides of the canoe to each other.

Tooth—a roughened texture on a surface, which affords a better grip for subsequent coatings.

Trim—the attitude of the canoe as it rests in the water. The optimum trim is usually level for best handling, but there are situations where it is better to have the bow ride a little higher than the stern. It is almost never beneficial to have the bow lower than the stern.

Tumblehome—a term describing the inward tilt (from the hull bottom up, toward the sheer) of the sides of a canoe hull. Not all canoes have this feature; it is most common in the more traditional hull designs.

Turn of the bilge—the area of transition where the bottom of the boat meets the sides.

Waterline—the location of the water surface if it were marked on the side of a floating canoe. Most canoes are designed to handle best when the hull is loaded so that it settles 4 in. deep in the water. For that reason, most study plans show the 4 in. water line of the specific model under consideration.

Wet Out—to saturate fiberglass with resin, so that the fibers are encased in resin and air has been displaced from the cloth. This does not mean that the cloth is flooded with epoxy; the texture of the fiberglass is still readily apparent even after it has been properly wet out.

Chapter Two

Workspace and Equipment

Facilities

While we thing makers love to fantasize about spacious, well designed, and well equipped workshops, reality finds us pressing into service workspace that was generally intended for some other use. Garages, basements, living rooms, and patios become boat shops wherever exploitable space is identified by prospective builders and access is granted by the reigning authority of the residence.

Considering all of this, what follows is a list of features that a work area must have to be suitable for building a strip canoe.

Space

At a minimum, a space as long as the finished canoe plus another six feet (more is better) all the way around will be needed. Otherwise, the inconvenience of moving around the boat with long, floppy wood pieces, electrical cords, and so forth will present difficulties that might dampen your enthusiasm for the work. In addition to the jig that you will build for assembling the hull over, another space-consuming item is the long workbench you will need for working on gunwale pieces before attaching them to the canoe. The workbench can be improvised of plywood or 2 x 8 in. lumber supported by sawhorses, as long as it is flat, at least 6 in. wide, and no more than a couple feet shorter than the full length of the gunwale pieces. A bench that is as long as the gunwales frees you from having to scoot the pieces back and forth as you rout or plane the corners off. If you plan to rip your strips and gunwale stock yourself, you will need room enough to feed the lumber you saw the pieces out of completely through the saw in a straight line. That means however long the lumber is, you need twice that distance plus some room for the saw and space to move around at both ends. (This is also true for planing the strips and shaping the edges of the strips with a router, if you choose to do those things.) These strip milling operations are best done outdoors if the neighbors will tolerate the noise and the weather is amenable. In that case, sufficient space is usually not hard to come by. If working outdoors is not a good alternative and milling indoors is out of the question, the solution is to buy your wood strips pre-milled or hire someone you know to do it. So, you can still build your canoe even if you lack the space to rip strips.

Access

While this point would hardly seem to bear mentioning, I have heard enough stories of boats being built in places they could not be extracted from that a comment is warranted. Make sure that once built, you can get your creation out of your shop space and to the water! I have a relative who once had to remove a window from the family home to get his newly built craft out of the basement. Another fellow I know had to tear down part of his shop to get his sailboat out. That individual is presently considering his options for getting the same boat down a curving, tree-lined driveway for the trip to the launching site. The boat, a trimaran, is wider than the driveway. A canoe is considerably smaller than a sailing trimaran, but it still won't go around a corner in a tight stairway.

Temperature Control

Most glues, epoxy resins, and varnishes dry or cure best at about 65° to 75°F. The warmer it is, the faster they cure. It is possible to get epoxy formulations that will cure at any temperature above freezing, and it is also possible to get epoxies specially made for use in hot climates. There are glues readily available that dry well at temperatures below 65°F, too. However, varnishes demand conditions that permit drying while still retaining leveling characteristics. If you can't regulate your workspace temperature, consider what environmental conditions will exist when you are working at various stages of the construction process. If you are assembling the hull and fiberglassing when the temperature is about 55°F, you can adjust for that in your choice of glue and epoxy resin. If temperatures are rising, by the time you're ready to varnish, the temperature may well be within the desired range for varnishing. (If you're building in 90°F heat, you will probably want to wait until temperatures have dropped to varnish.) Obviously, it is advantageous to be able to adjust workspace temperature as needed. This is not an absolute necessity though, if one has the option of waiting for cooperative weather.

Light

It is essential to have good light to produce a first-class piece of work. A combination of natural and artificial light that allows you to see all parts of your project is most desirable. Speaking from experience, if you build a bright-finished boat under poor light conditions, you will surely get a surprise the first time you bring it out into the sunshine. By then it will be too late to go back and sand all those scratches out of the cedar hull because it is covered with fiberglass, not to mention all those coats of varnish (that probably have some flaws you didn't notice before).

Flooring

When you build boats, you get stuff on the floor. While sawdust is readily removable, other materials are not. Epoxy resin, when added to fiberglass cloth, cures to produce a wonderfully tough coating that is integral to the strength of a wood strip hull. That same epoxy, when added to the living room carpet, produces a far less desirable result. Make sure that whatever is on the floor or ground under your project is expendable.

Shelter from Airborne Contaminants

Outdoor boat construction is not only enjoyable, but the sole option in many circumstances. During sanding operations and while milling strips, it is certainly more sensible to leave the volumes of dust and piles of chips outside. Besides, people who build and use canoes appreciate a good excuse to get out in the fresh air.

There is, however, a hitch. In my part of the world anyway, the air is often full of things that hinder my canoe-building efforts. Rain complicates sanding and gluing bare wood, and doesn't mix well with any of the materials I put on the wood to make it waterproof. At times pollen from the fir trees leaves a visible yellow coating on anything left outdoors for more than a few minutes. Both the maples and the firs produce a fine "rain" of sap during the summer. And there are hordes of winged insects whose purpose in life apparently is to immortalize themselves by permanently installing themselves in wet epoxy and varnish. On top of that, applying fiberglass to a bare wood hull in direct sun is likely to compromise the finish, since the heating of the wood usually causes it to continue to release air bubbles into the epoxy resin after the resin has set too thick to permit the bubbles to escape.

Based on the assumption that your part of the world has some or all of these factors and maybe more, I recommend that you obtain at least overhead shelter. Walls that have doors and windows that close and have screens are a plus. This is especially important if you work on your canoe in the evening hours with the lights on, and every bug on the planet wants to come in and join you, or if the wind carries dust into your work area. Of course, a building that can be closed up also makes it possible to control the temperature as needed. You can still exercise your option of working outdoors if you make your jig portable by placing it on a platform with casters, or have a friend help you carry the sawhorses or cradles and canoe to your spot of choice.

Proximity to Power

Most builders these days find power tools indispensable. Whether your tools are powered by compressed air or electricity, see that appropriate power is available to the proposed workspace. At least two outlets will prove helpful, since sometimes two tools, or one tool and an extra light will be used for a given operation.

A place to build a canoe. There are plenty of power outlets, adequate light sources, good access, a concrete floor, and the place can be closed up to keep out airborne pests. Temperature can be regulated by means of a thermostat-controlled furnace. Most importantly, there is enough room for a canoe and its creator to coexist comfortably for at least a few quality hours at a stretch.

Tools

The building of a strip canoe can be undertaken using ordinary shop tools. For those who are often engaged in woodworking projects, most of the tools needed will already be on hand. If it is necessary to purchase tools for canoe building, the expenditure can be readily justified by the anticipation that the same tools can be used for other projects later on.

There are situations during the course of the project where different tools can be used to achieve the same result. For example, most of the cutting I do with a jigsaw could also be accomplished with a band saw. This section contains a list of the tools I used in making the canoe shown in this book. The list should be taken as a suggestion, not as a list of required equipment. If, due to equipment availability or user preference, a builder chooses a different tool for a given task, the only criterion for evaluating the choice is how well it works. If the alternative tool does what is required, then use it. If not, try something else. The ones listed are known to work.

Tool quality can sometimes make a big difference in how much pleasure you get from the building process. In the tool list, there are instances where I name specific manufacturers of tools, because their product gives good results; usually significantly better than others I have tried. That does not mean there are no other brands that are as good. Rather, the named brand should be used as a standard of quality for comparing others to. My intent is to save novices from the pain of trial-and-error experimentation with tools while learning how to build a strip boat.

Power tools deserve some special attention. I like hand tools because they are quiet, but there are certain power tools that I would not want to be without. The ones I use regularly are a table saw, drill, jigsaw, dual action (random orbit) sander, and vacuum cleaner. I also depend on a small angle grinder and a router to expedite some operations, but these tools aren't absolute necessities. I occasionally use a drill press, thickness planer, and belt sander. These tools are nice to have but are luxury items for this project.

Table Saw

The table saw is an item that sees frequent enough use that it is worthwhile to have one handy for the duration of the project. It is used for cutting pieces for the mold, ripping strips, cutting scarf joints, and making all the hardwood framework pieces such as seat frames, gunwales, and thwarts. None of this demands a top-of-the-line saw. In fact, the main requirements in a table saw are that the blade and fence stay locked where you want them, once adjusted; the entire unit be substantial enough to stay put while the saw is in use; and the saw deck be large enough to support long boards and plywood pieces such that they don't tip out of position during cutting. The deck on the saw I use is 27 x 41 inches.

Of more particular interest is the saw blade. An ordinary ripping or combination blade can be used, but a thin kerf carbide tipped blade is a much better choice. During the process of ripping strips, there is potential to waste one whole strip worth of wood for every two strips you produce using a blade that takes the usual 1/8 in. kerf. Considering that you will need fifty to eighty strips to build a canoe, the magnitude of the waste becomes alarmingly high, especially if you have spent your hard-earned money to obtain premium grade lumber in long lengths for the strips. A thin kerf blade that takes only 1/16 in. pays for itself in saved wood. Besides that, a good quality thin kerf blade gives smoother cuts, and that saves you work later on. A blade that has produced excellent results for me is a 7-1/4 in., 1/16 in. kerf, 36-tooth carbide tipped combination blade manufactured by Matsushita. I've run it on a standard 10 in. table saw with no problems, and it really is a precision tool.

Drill

A drill is another item that needs to be handy for the duration of the project. It is used in assembly and disassembly of the mold, cutting holes and recesses for hardware, installing some or all of the framework and trim pieces, and a variety of other optional steps like boring holes for dowels in seat frames. A 1/4 in. drive, variable speed, reversible hand drill is a versatile tool that will meet your needs for strip canoe building.

Strip boat construction calls for a variety of drill bits. A set of brad point bits ranging from 1/8 in. to 1/2 in. is essential. In addition, I used a 5/8 in. Forstner bit, two different adjustable countersinking drill bits, a countersink, and a hex shank Phillips screwdriver tip (actually went through a couple of them) to build the canoe used to illustrate this book. You may or may not need all of these, depending on how you decide to build your boat. These items will be mentioned in the narrative when appropriate.

Jigsaw

Some means of making curving cuts is a basic necessity. I use a jigsaw, but in all instances except one a band saw would work just as well. The one exception is when holes are cut in bulkheads to accommodate deck plates. Both bulkheads and deck plates are optional items, so if you don't want them, it doesn't matter that you can't make the holes with a band saw. Though a band saw would not work for cutting a round hole, a hole saw would, and even better than a jigsaw. So for practical purposes, the jigsaw and band saw are interchangeable, but you will need one of them. The main requirement for the ability to cut curves is in mold building. Other curvy parts are bulkheads, decks, and thwarts. A nice feature in a jigsaw is the capability of varying the operating speed. For cutting out the mold pieces and other finely controlled work, a smooth scroll cutting blade with ten teeth per inch is best. For cutting plywood and 2 x 4 lumber into sections, a coarser, faster cutting blade with six teeth per inch saves time.

Dual Action Sander

A dual action sander, also commonly called a random orbit sander, is just the ticket for smoothing up the wood strip hull before applying fiberglass, and also for smoothing the fiberglass and epoxy after application to the hull. The action of the sander gives really good results while affording excellent control for the user. A 5 or 6 in. variable speed sander with a 1/2 in. foam contour pad that takes self adhesive sanding disks will handle most of the sanding of the hull. I have a 5 in. model manufactured by Porter Cable, and it is an excellent tool. It is the most effective sander of any I have tried on cured epoxy, which is notorious for loading up sandpaper. Even though the dual action sander I favor is similar to a disk sander in appearance, its performance is so superior that there is ample reason to get this sander even if you already own a disk sander. The sanding disks are available in a wide range of coarseness; the ones used extensively in this project are 80-grit, 120-grit, and 220-grit.

Vacuum Cleaner

It may seem odd to list a household-type vacuum as a shop tool, but I use one often during the sanding steps, especially on the inside of the hull. If you do not have dust collection units attached to your tools, there is no better means of dust collection than a vacuum with a hose and brush attachment. Collecting the dust with a vacuum takes it completely out of circulation. If you varnish your canoe in the same area where sanding took place, you may find out what a nuisance circulating dust can be. The more thoroughly you can clean the hull, and the less loose dust there is in the shop, the better off you and your canoe will be.

Other Tools

A router is a handy item for making short work of rounding over corners on gunwales, seat frames, and thwarts. The same thing can be accomplished using a plane, spokeshave, or file, and sandpaper, so you don't have to have a router for this. A different operation that requires a router or shaper is milling the edges of the strips. This is a popular way to treat the strip edges, because it promotes tight fits between the strips without having to hand bevel each strip. Router or shaper bits that mill strip edges into interlocking shapes are available as two separate bits for the two matching shapes, or as a single bit that has both shapes. The combination bit is adjusted to the depth required to produce the desired shape. If a router is used to power the bit(s), then it needs to be mounted in a router table. There are a few alternatives if you don't have a router or shaper available and don't want to buy one. You can elect not to shape the edges; it is a fairly common practice to skip this step. (See the chapter on structural materials for more discussion.) You might decide to hire some other properly equipped individual to do the shaping work for you, or buy strips pre-milled.

A planer is nice to have for making the strips (and pieces of framework stock) the same thickness. Ripping strips with a high quality blade and a stable equipment setup will produce strips of fairly uniform thickness, but planing will eliminate any variation, and also residual saw marks, thus reducing the amount of effort put into sanding later on. This is probably not sufficiently important to justify the purchase of a planer, but if one is available, you may want to take advantage of it. The one I use is a portable 12 in. planer made by Delta, and is a respectable unit.

Most of the hand tools used in this type of construction are "everyday" shop tools. There are a couple that may need to be added to the regular complement, however. One is a longboard, which is indispensable for fairing the hull of a strip canoe. Stores that sell tools and supplies for auto body work offer mostly power-driven models. You can make your own hand-operated version from thin plywood such as paneling or door skins, plus two handles. The plywood is cut into a rectangular piece 16 to 20 in. long and 2-3/4 in. wide, with the handles attached at each end of one side. The handle at one end is usually a knob, while the handle at the opposite end is longer. (See photos in Chapter 7 for handle configuration.) The bottom surface, where the sandpaper is attached, must be smooth (no protruding screw heads below the handles). Dense foam padding may be bonded to the bottom of the longboard. A longboard 16 to 18 in. long will accept a single piece of power longboard paper (attached with feathering disk adhesive), which is convenient when purchasing and using the paper. The tool I use for a longboard is actually marketed as a type of safety push block, and it makes an inexpensive, durable, effective longboard.

The other "specialty" tool is a Dozuki saw that cuts on the pull stroke. These saws make very clean, precise cuts, and are easy to use. Such a saw is in regular use throughout the process of stripping up the hull, for trimming and fitting strip ends. The one I bought as an experimental tool was an economy version, and it has proven to be one my best tool purchases ever. You do not need a top-end Dozuki saw to get excellent results. The one I have makes better cuts that any other type of small hand saw I know of.

For working epoxy resin, squeegees (also called spreaders) are essential tools. They are actually expendable items, but are good for a few uses before they have to be replaced. Squeegees are not all created equal, so watch quality when buying. Make sure that the edges are smooth (no burrs), and that when the squeegee is laid on its side, it lies flat. Squeegees that have an arch to them do not spread resin evenly as required for this work. Another tool used in the application of epoxy resin, and also wood glue, is a syringe with a long, pointed tip. These are sold with either straight or curved tips, usually in pairs. Squeegees and syringes are both available from epoxy suppliers, and also auto body and craft supply stores.

Clamps of various sizes and types will be needed for all of the wood fabrication and installation work. The number of clamps needed varies depending on whether the builder assembles the hull using clamps or staples (or nails) to hold the strips in place while glue dries. To estimate the number of clamps needed in the former case, see the chapter on stripping the hull for photos showing how the clamps are arranged. Figure that one 3 in. C-clamp will be needed for each foot of canoe length (some of these can be medium-sized spring clamps), plus a web clamp for each foot of length. You may also need as many as six more C-clamps to hold the inside stem pieces on the mold during hull assembly; I say "may" because the inside stem is an optional item. Elastic shock cord can substitute for the web clamps. The C-clamps used here will be needed later for gunwale installation, so adding to your collection will pay off over the term of the project. The web clamps I use most can be made at small cost from lengths of 1 in. web strap material with plastic buckle clips (like those made by Fastex, for example). The receptacle end of the clip is sewn onto one end of the strap, while the pronged part of the clip is threaded onto the other end of the strap to provide for adjustment. Both the strap material and buckles can be purchased at outdoor sports stores that serve backpackers, climbers, and paddle sport addicts. (I use 24 to 30 in. of webbing per strap. If you need more length than that, you can connect two web clamps together end-to-end.) I also have a web clamp that has a ratchet for adjusting tension, and a set of 10-foot cargo tie-down straps with simple metal buckles that grab onto the strap and hold by friction. Both types find their way into use often. Spring clamps are convenient and useful. The medium-sized ones are best for most things, but two to four small ones, and four to six large ones are also handy to have. Bar clamps in the 6, 18, and 24 in. sizes are great. If you can afford a pair of each size, try to obtain them. They can be pricey, however, so if you must compromise, a pair of 18 in. bar clamps should get you by. Large C-clamps can substitute for the 6 in. bar clamps. There is one expensive specialty clamp that is really nice to have, that is the perfect solution to an occasional situation. It is a deep-jawed locking clamp; mine is made by Vise-Grip®. It is possible to build a canoe without this clamp, so this tool is not a "must have" item.

Tool List

The following list is a summary of all the tools I used in making the canoe used to illustrate this book. The project is broken into its major stages, with a separate tool list for each stage. The main distinction between tools and supplies, for this purpose, is whether an item is used up or thrown away after a single use. Since I use disposable brushes, they are not listed under tools, but as supplies. And there were instances where nails and twine were used, but still in new condition when no longer needed, so they ended up in the tools list.

Milling Strips

Table saw with thin kerf blade
Push sticks
Clamps, as needed for holding long fence and infeed and outfeed tables in place
Thickness planer
Combination square
Router, mounted in router table
Bead and cove router bits (1/4 in.)
Finger boards, 4 each
Safety gear-earplugs, earmuffs, glasses, gloves, dust masks

Building the Mold

Table saw with standard combination blade
Jigsaw with plywood blades (6 TPI) and smooth scroll cutting blades (10 TPI)
Drywall T-square, 48 in.
Graphite pencil, 6B
Tape measure
Finishing nails
Seine twine
Drill, plus Phillips screwdriver tips, 1/8 in. drill bit, and 7/8 in. hole saw
Combination square
Long straightedge
Bar clamps, 6 in. grip, 4 each
Bar clamps, 18 in. grip, 1 or more
Permanent ink marker
Sawhorses, 2 or 3
Spring clamps, several medium and large size
Thumb tacks

Tracing wheel
Longboard, with 100-grit paper
Dual action sander, with 80-grit disk
Framing square
Compass
Air stapler with 7/8 in. staples
Drill press
Locking clamp, deep-jawed
Web clamp
Small angle grinder, with 24-grit disk
Spokeshave
Trimming plane
Medium-sized plane
Battens (scrap strips), 3 each

Stripping the Hull

C-clamps, 2-1/2 and 3 in., 16 each
Web clamps with plastic buckles (24 to 30 in. long), 10 each
Web clamps, 10 feet, 5 each
Spring clamps, medium-sized, 6 each
Spring clamps, small, 4 each
Bar clamps, various sizes, 6 each
Dozuki saw
Syringe
Block plane
Trimming plane
Utility knife
Sanding block
Finishing nails
Seine twine
Compass or dividers
Pencil

Builders planning to staple strips to the mold need a staple gun (equipped with staples suggested in Chapter 6). Those planning to nail the strips will need a hammer.

Preparing the Hull for Epoxy and Fiberglass

Spokeshave
Long (15 in.) plane
Trimming plane
Dual action sander, with 80-grit and 220-grit disks
Longboard, with 100-grit and 180-grit paper
Hand sanding pad
Scrapers, straight and curved edged
Vacuum cleaner
Chalk
Syringe
Sponge
Safety gear—dust masks, eye protection

Builders utilizing staples or nails to secure strips to the mold will need end-cutting nippers or a tack puller for removing the fasteners from the hull before sanding.

Addition of Outer Stem

Dozuki saw
Chisel, 1 in.
Trimming plane
Longboard, with 100-grit paper
Hammer
Drill, plus 1/16 in. drill bit
Web clamps, 4 each
Rubber tie-down straps, 2 each
Pliers
Side cutters
Scraper, with convex and concave cutting edges
Small, fine, flat file

Application of Epoxy and Fiberglass

Squeegees, 4 each
Syringe
Scrapers, convex and straight edged
Longboard, with 100-grit paper
Dual action sander, with 80-grit and 120-grit disks
Hand sanding pad
Bench brush
Awl or small nail
Toothbrush
Vacuum cleaner
Wire brush

Gunwales

Table saw plus thin kerf saw blade
Planer
Tape measure
Combination square
Miter saw
Pencil
Long rule
C-clamps and spring clamps (one clamp for every two spacer blocks)
Putty knife
Flat file
Round file
Dozuki saw
Angle grinder, with 24-grit disk
Router, with roundover bit
Wood rasp
Dual action sander, with 80-grit disk
Longboard, with 100-grit paper
Drill, plus adjustable combination countersinking drill bit
Center punch
Hammer
Screwdriver

Holes for Bow and Stern Lines

Drill, plus 1/8 in. drill bit
Hole saw, 7/8 in.
Tape measure
Long finishing nail
Syringe
Pencil

Thwart

Tracing wheel
Tacks
Jigsaw, with smooth scroll blade
Combination square
Tape measure or long rule
Pencil
Spokeshave
Longboard, with 100-grit paper
Bar clamps
Half round file
Hand sanding pad
Dozuki saw
Drill, with 5/16 in. drill bit and 5/8 in. Forstner bit
Box end wrench
C-clamps, 3 in., 4 each
    To save time, a router with a roundover bit could be used for shaping the thwart edges.

Seat Frame

Table saw
Combination square
Tape measure
Drill, plus 5/16 in. drill bit and countersink bit
Bar clamps, 18 in., 3 each
Bar clamps, 6 in., 2 each
Syringe
Hammer
Dozuki saw
Drill press, plus 1/4 in. drill bit
Long rule (at least 24 in.)
Spokeshave
Trimming plane
Longboard, with 100-grit paper
Angle grinder, with 24-grit disk
Dual action sander, with 120-grit and 220-grit disks
    A router with a roundover bit can be used to quickly shape the edges of the seat frame, saving much of the work I did with a spokeshave, plane, and longboard. (My router was not operational at the time I wanted to do this work, so I used hand tools.)

Seat Risers and Seat Installation

Table saw
Plane; a long one is preferable
Compass
Long level
Combination square
Pencil
Tape measure
Plumb bob
C-clamps, 3 in., 6 each
Scrap strip pieces, various short lengths
Drill, plus adjustable combination countersinking drill bit
Bar clamps, 6 in., 2 each
Screwdriver
China marker, also known as a grease pencil

Bulkheads and Decks

Dividers or compass
Felt tip marker
Long straightedge
Jigsaw, with fine-toothed scroll blade
Flat and round files
Dozuki saw
Combination square
Pencil
Utility knife
Trimming plane
Medium-sized plane
Sanding block
Dual action sander, with 80-, 120-, and 220-grit disks
Longboard, with 100-grit paper
Hand sanding pad
Drill plus 3/8 in. and 1/8 in. drill bits
Clamps, various sizes and types, as needed for clamping strips to plywood backing material while gluing. I used about a dozen bar clamps and large (6 in.) C-clamps.
Jig, for bending wood coaming and glue strip pieces
Headlamp
Syringe
Screwdrivers

The headlamp was used while filleting the joints between the upper edge of the bulkheads and the underside of the decks, with the canoe upside down on sawhorses.

Finishing

Scrapers, straight and curved edged
Longboard, with 180-grit paper
Dual action sander, with 120- and 220-grit disks
Sanding block, with 400-grit wet-or-dry paper
Hand sanding pad
Sponge

Safety

One of the attractions of building a boat is the pleasure and challenge of doing the construction work. Working with tools to create a tangible, useful item can be a source of great satisfaction. However, the tools, and also the raw materials, demand a certain measure of respect from the user. The wise crafts person will apply appropriate safety measures during all phases of the project. Building a strip canoe does not entail risking one's health, as long as certain common sense safety practices are faithfully followed.

A boat building project like this one has something in common with other woodworking projects in that there are a variety of both power and hand tools used, so all the same safety measures that are employed in other woodworking projects will also apply here. If you are not familiar with the use of woodworking tools, I recommend attending a class in woodworking at the local community college. That is an excellent way to learn to operate the tools and the safety devices that come with them, and to learn how to avoid potentially hazardous situations. Much of safety consciousness is recognizing hazards and eliminating them before problems develop. Such a class will inform you of how to manage a work area for maximum safety in terms of proper storage of flammable liquids and building materials, dust control, avoidance of exposure to vapors, and disposal of used or waste materials. Of additional benefit, of course, would be learning what routine practices give the best results. Examples of some of these practices are how to effectively use the tools, how to properly maintain equipment, and how to store equipment so that it stays in good working order.

For power tools in general:
1. Eliminate any distractions that will keep you from concentrating on what you are doing.
2. Operate the tool at an appropriate speed. The highest speed is not always the best.
3. Secure the piece being worked on with clamps or a vise rather than holding it with your free hand. It will be easier to make smooth cuts, drill at the desired angle, or grind off just the right amount if the object is secured to a solid support. This also reduces the risk of injury.
4. Ensure that extension cords for electric tools are of appropriate gauge and in good condition to support the current drawn by the tool in use.
5. Don't use electric tools in wet conditions.

Standard safety practices in the use of saws are:
1. Use a push stick when working anywhere near the blade of a running table saw.
2. Don't elevate the blade of a table saw any more than necessary to accomplish the task at hand.
3. Wear effective hearing protection and eye protection.
4. When using a jigsaw, be aware of where the blade of the saw is in relation to any nearby object or body part.

In the use of hand tools:
1. Keep cutting edges sharp. That way less pressure is required to make the cuts, results will be more uniform and precise, and there is less danger of slipping out of position and accidentally cutting something else.
2. Use good judgment when considering whether to use a tool for something it is not specifically designed to do. Some imagination and innovation are a good thing, but all tools have their limitations. Also, some tasks demand exactly the right tool, so substitution of another will produce less than great results.

Materials used in strip canoe construction include wood, fiberglass cloth, epoxy resin, adhesives, and varnish or paint. All of these are safe to use when handled properly.

Wood snaps if pressed beyond its limits of flexibility. It can produce slivers, and it will burn. The sanding of wood can generate a lot of airborne dust, which is best kept out of the lungs. Some of the hardwood dusts seem to have an astringent quality, and long term exposure to western red cedar dust is known to have adverse health effects. The use of dust collection equipment during sawing and sanding operations greatly reduces the amount of dust in the shop atmosphere. Whether or not your shop is outfitted with dust collection devices, wear a dust mask during all sanding steps. If you are already sensitive to wood dust, a respirator with replaceable cartridges would be more effective than a dust mask in filtering out dust.

Fiberglass cloth is almost completely risk free by itself, but frayed cloth that is impregnated with cured plastic resin often has a multitude of sharp, needle-like projections that can be hard on hands. Sanding fiberglass-reinforced epoxy produces a dust that irritates the lining of respiratory passages, especially if the resin has not fully cured. Fiberglass dust on the skin causes itching. Minimize exposure to these dusts by wearing a dust mask or respirator, and covering arms and legs with clothing or rinsing off after sanding.

Epoxy resin and hardeners in liquid form should be handled in such a way that they don't get on hands and other surfaces not intended for application. Except for being sticky and hard to get off, unmixed resin causes few problems, but the hardener, either by itself or mixed with resin, frequently causes some level of skin irritation. Some people develop a sensitivity to it as a result of repeated contact, and others are sensitive upon the first exposure. The best defense is to not allow it to contact skin. Wear clothes or barrier cream to prevent contact, and always wear gloves. Latex gloves are better than vinyl gloves, but vinyl is better than none. Barrier cream should not be worn under gloves because the cream dissolves the glove material. If you do get epoxy on your skin, do not try to remove it with a solvent. That would most likely have the extremely undesirable result of driving the material into the skin, causing greater exposure, rather than rinsing it off. Instead, use a waterless hand cleaner. Another way to minimize exposure to mixed epoxy is to discard brushes that have been used to apply epoxy. It is more trouble (and probably expense) to try to clean brushes than to throw them away, and results of cleaning are usually not good anyway, because it is very difficult to get all the epoxy out of a brush. Most solvents such as acetone actually present as great or greater risk for the user than the epoxy. Other epoxy coated items, such as squeegees, trays, and plastic cups can be dealt with by setting them aside and allowing the epoxy to cure on them. After that, plastic items can be flexed to crack the cured epoxy loose, and the epoxy may be disposed of, leaving the plastic surface clean. Trays can be re-used with hardened epoxy in the bottom. The only item I clean uncured epoxy from is a syringe. Even those can be treated as a disposable item if you prefer to completely eliminate the need for strong solvents in your shop. There is another alternative in the form of a concentrated epoxy cleaner available from System Three Resins, Inc., which I have not yet tried, but plan to. A fellow strip boat builder has told me it is very good, yet is a much safer solvent than acetone. This cleaner would have to be more effective than acetone to adequately clean brushes for re-use (maybe it is), but for cleaning up syringes and accidental spills it certainly sounds attractive compared to acetone. Cured epoxy is quite inert, and no further handling precautions are needed once the curing process is complete. For comprehensive information on precautions in the handling of epoxy resins and hardeners, consult your epoxy supplier, and in particular, request a Material Safety Data Sheet.

Shop ventilation may be a consideration. Mixed epoxy has a detectable odor, but produces hardly any fumes, and not to anywhere near the degree that polyester resin does. Use of epoxy doesn't usually call for extra ventilation in the shop, but if the builder has already become sensitized to epoxy, additional ventilation and/or a respirator equipped with cartridges designed to filter out organic vapors are advised. Varnishing produces fumes. In fact, the drying of the varnish depends on the evaporation of the volatile components of the varnish. The use of a thinner usually introduces more vapors due to spills and the characteristic of thinners to completely evaporate. Pay attention to how you feel during your finishing activities, and if you notice an effect, go out for fresh air. Either make provisions for better ventilation in the shop or use a respirator that will filter out organic vapors.[1]

The shop heating system, if it exists, may be a safety concern. A lot of backyard shops seem to have wood heat. If that is the case in your facility, check to make sure the stove and chimney system are in good shape, operate the stove according to the manufacturer's directions, and don't store combustible materials near it. Place a fire extinguisher of appropriate size and type in a strategic location. Actually, that is a good idea whether or not you have wood heat.

Attending to safety matters is a priority item that serves to preserve the builder's health and enjoyment of the project. It is something you do for yourself. And, after all, a motivating factor in taking on this construction project is to create a canoe that you will be able to use for years into the future. It makes sense to take responsibility for your own welfare so you can reap the rewards of your labor. Safety consciousness is better than the best insurance, and is less expensive besides. Make it a habit.

Chapter Three

Structural Materials

One of the aspects of strip canoe building that makes it a good project for home builders is that there is a range of different materials that can be used in producing an attractive and service-able canoe. Materials selected by the builder reflect local availability, price, weight, ease of application, harshness of anticipated use, aesthetics, and the builder's own priorities regarding these factors. A wood strip boat is, therefore, a very personal craft.

As an overview, materials customarily used are:
1. Softwoods, for their light weight, flexibility, and ease of workability, for the hull;
2. Hardwoods, for their strength and abrasion resistance, for the load-bearing and wear-prone parts such as gunwales and seats;
3. Fiberglass cloth, for its ease of application and repair, strength, and transparence, for the hull;
4. Epoxy resin, for its toughness and adherence to resinous softwoods like cedar, for application of fiberglass and some assembly work;
5. Brass, stainless steel, or silicon bronze hardware, for its corrosion resistance, for mechanical fastenings; and
6. Carpenter's wood glue, for its convenience of use and non-toxicity, for most assembly work.

Strip Stock

Wood for the hull is chosen primarily for its ability to wrap around a mold in compound curves without splitting, ease of cutting and sanding with hand tools, and relatively light weight. Wood color and grain are also worth considering. Rot resistance is not a large issue because the wood will be sealed away from moisture by a sheath of fiberglass reinforced plastic.[1] Wood strength requirements are not sufficiently high enough to warrant use of a hardwood, which would generally have major shortcomings in the areas of primary concern. The fiberglass cover-ing the interior and exterior of the hull is such an important component of hull strength that fairly weak woods will serve adequately as a core material. However, among softwoods there is con-siderable variation in strength. In fact, many softwoods are really quite strong, especially if the wood is of good quality. Wood quality can significantly influence the practical strength.

Boat building in general demands high quality wood, and strip canoe building is typical in that respect. For our purposes, the notion of quality encompasses three characteristics that can be evaluated in any species of wood. Straightness of grain is very important. The straighter the grain, the better. Uniformity of grain is also important, and this includes freedom from defects such as knots and pitch pockets, which alter wood strength. Fineness of grain is also of interest. I try to get as fine-grained wood as possible; the more grains (growth rings) to the inch, the better. I have mostly used western red cedar, and in that species I have found fine-grained wood to be softer and easier to work, more uniform in its properties, more flexible, and less likely to split. I must confess that I have occasionally found coarse-grained (with wide growth rings) strips that were unbelievably flexible, but those are the exception. I don't know if this is true for all species; it might be worth your while to do some research on this if you anticipate using another type of wood.

Condition of the wood must be taken into account. Evidence of decay is not something you want to find. If you obtain your wood in the form of new lumber, it needs to be dry (12 percent or less moisture content). Don't accept twisted lumber, since it will be difficult or impossible to saw well. Some lumber defects that you can live with, if they aren't very pronounced, are bends to one side, slight cupping (the edges tilt upwards), and checks, which are lengthwise cracks in the end of a board. Much of the cracked end may have to be discarded, so consider the length of the cracks in determining whether the board is long enough to meet your needs.

Obviously, you want boards with perfect grain, that are perfectly straight, and in perfect condition. Unfortunately, you may be much older by the time you find one. If you do find one, I suggest that instead of using it in your boat project, you sand it, varnish it, and hang it someplace highly visible as a trophy! (You can always use it later if you *really* need it.) If you want your wood in a reasonably short interval of time, you need to hunt around for the best wood you can find, recognizing that some compromises will be necessary, and also that this kind of lumber commands a fancy price. Call potential sources of wood to see if they stock what you need, and if they do, look it over yourself before deciding whether to buy. Hold out for mostly flat grain (more on this later in this chapter), fairly straight grain, small knots or other defects, clustering of defects rather than having them scattered so as to compromise the whole board, and at least eight growth rings to the inch. That figure is somewhat arbitrary, but in my experience wood that is more coarse-grained than that is tough to deal with when putting the hull together. Besides the lumber yards, check the classified ads not only for lumber, but independent sawmill operators willing to do custom orders.

If there are no local sources of suitable wood, an alternative is to buy the material, usually in the form of milled strips, from a specialty products supplier. These companies regularly adver-tise in magazines such as *WoodenBoat* and *Boatbuilder*, and sometimes paddle-sport magazines like *Canoe & Kayak*. (Some sources are listed in the Appendix.) The strips will cost more, but then buying them "ready made" saves you a lot of time spent doing that work yourself. I have not taken advantage of these sources, but other builders have indicated that the quality of the strips from the two companies listed is consistently high.

For those who are interested in an "economy option," try salvaging used lumber. This has become my usual practice lately. As good quality wood becomes scarcer and demand swells, prices for new lumber continue to climb. At times, suitable material is plain hard to find. With some nosing around, though, it is possible to uncover a bonanza of top-quality material available for little cash outlay. The cost may even be limited to that of transportation. (Get the owner's permission, of course!) I have obtained red cedar in the form of old fence posts (never used as such) and painted siding from a house that was usable for boat building. I once met a couple who discovered when tearing down an unwanted deck adjoining their house that the entire deck was of Alaskan yellow cedar. When I talked to them, they were about two-thirds done with a 16-foot canoe of this yellow cedar.

Using "non-new" material makes sense if you can accept the inevitable tradeoffs. It is usu-ally cheap to buy, if you have to buy it at all. The quality of the undamaged wood is often much better than what is presently being sold now, because chances are the salvaged material came from bigger, older, better trees, which were more plentiful a couple decades ago. This is one of the main reasons I go to the trouble of utilizing salvaged lumber. Some of the cedar I've ripped into strips had over fifty-six grains to the inch and was a joy to work with. Also, manufacturing a durable, useful item of material that would otherwise be burned or thrown away is an exercise in respectful use of limited resources, which is always a good thing. I encourage even those who have the means to buy new lumber to explore this alternative.

Using salvaged wood does have its disadvantages. The lumber is rarely of proper dimensions to cut into strips when you get it. First the wood must be re-sawn into suitable pieces, taking into account grain orientation and defects in the material. That means the wood has to be handled more times to produce usable strips. Also, salvaged material frequently has a lot of defects due to nail holes, decay, splits, and stains. Even worse than that, nails may still be lurking in those nail holes. Small nooks and crannies can harbor pebbles, dirt, wire, and other objects hazardous to precision cutting edges. Examine the wood carefully for foreign objects and debris before putting a good blade at risk. Because salvaged lumber is sometimes irregularly shaped, a bit of figuring is called for in determining how to best utilize the material. Generally, the idea is to make approximately one-inch thick, flat-grain boards from which to slice vertical-grain strips. Some of these one-inch-thick "boards" may only be wide enough to cut two strips out of, but that works. Another feature of salvaged material is that it is often shorter than the canoe you propose to build with it. However, in some localities, that is also true of the new lumber available. Short strips can be joined end to end to get the length needed. As a result of the necessary re-sawing of salvaged wood and discarding of unusable pieces, there is usually a considerable amount of waste wood and sawdust generated. Ripping strips from new lumber generates some waste, but not as much (mostly in the form of sawdust).

As can be deduced from the foregoing discussion, the advantages of using new lumber are that it is more convenient to use, is clean, is more quickly converted into strips, results in less waste accumulation, and is perhaps more readily available in full-length pieces. You, the builder, need to weigh the value of your time against your other values and liquid assets in deciding how to acquire your wood strips.

Cedar strip boats, whether of eastern or western cedar species, are strong, lightweight boats. For normal recreational use, cedar is plenty durable. Western red cedar and eastern white cedar are by far the most popular species used for wood strip hulls. Cedar is not as strong or as resistant to blows from sharp objects (like rocks) as other species, however. Where a canoe might be expected to receive more impacts, typically below the 4 in. waterline, the hull is frequently reinforced with an extra layer of fiberglass cloth. This provides more protection where it is needed without adding the weight of heavier cloth or more layers where it isn't needed. Another option would be to switch to another species of wood below the waterline.

Other softwood species that have been or could be used for stripping the hull are sitka (and possibly other species) spruce, Alaskan yellow cedar, Douglas fir, redwood, Port Orford cedar, and some species of pine. Pine is not a wood I've seen suggested in print, but I did see a canoe that contained a number of pine strips, so it evidently can be a viable option depending on the species used. As of this writing I don't know which to recommend, although I suspect what I saw was ponderosa pine, a.k.a. western yellow pine. Veteran boat builder "Mac" McCarthy indicates that cypress and juniper are also worth considering.[2] Nearly all of these woods are heavier than cedar (the cedar species vary also), but most offer more strength. Many, if not all of these woods are harder than cedar. For impact resistance, that is an excellent quality. For ease of sanding, it's not. Redwood reportedly has an unpleasant tendency to split, and sitka spruce can be somewhat unpredictable to work by hand with cutting tools like a spokeshave or plane. Different species have their own unique combinations of qualities.

Before going in search of lumber for strips, it is important to be able to recognize what you are after. As mentioned earlier, flat-grained wood is most suitable for manufacturing strips out of, although vertical-grained wood can be made to work.

Flat-grained boards. The two boards on the left are western red cedar. The board on the right is Oregon ash.

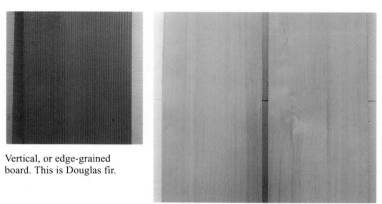

Vertical, or edge-grained board. This is Douglas fir.

Vertical-grained western red cedar. This is the kind of fine, straight grain pattern one likes to see in the wide sides of milled strips.

The grain pattern referred to is that showing on the widest face (or side) of the lumber.

When you get done milling the strips, they should have a vertical-grain pattern on the wide sides. They will be easier to sand and plane smooth, and less likely to split when bending and twisting than flat-grained strips.

The other thing to figure out before searching for strip material is how much lumber you need. First, calculate the number of strips required to complete the hull at the widest part of the canoe. Measure the distance (in inches) around the outer edge of the middle station, from sheer to sheer. (See the chapter on mold building.) Then, take that distance and divide it by the width of the strips to be used to give the number of strips needed. For example, 42 in. around the widest station divided by 3/4 in. strips equals 56 strips. If you plan to shape the strip edges so they

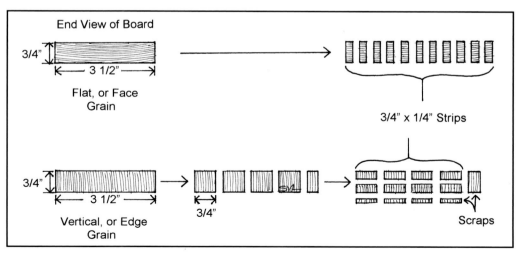

End View of Board

3/4" ← 3 1/2" →

Flat, or Face Grain

3/4" × 1/4" Strips

3/4" ← 3 1/2" → 3/4"

Vertical, or Edge Grain

Scraps

Milling vertical-grain strips from a flat-grained board like that shown on the upper row is just a matter of slicing strips from the edge of the board. However, the lower vertical- or edge-grain board must first be sawn into 3/4 in. to 1 in. wide pieces, then turned 90 degrees and re-sawn to get the desired vertical-grained strips. Unfortunately, this scenario requires more handling of the wood, takes more time, and yields fewer usable strips than an equal-size piece of flat-grained lumber. However, it is better to saw a vertical-grained board this way than to make flat-grained strips by sawing it as in the example at the top.

interlock with each other, add another 20 percent to the number of strips to give a revised total. Shaping narrows the width of the exposed face of the strip, so you need more strips.

Now that you have an idea what your needs are, figure out how you can cut the strips from the lumber available to you, with the saw blade you will be using. See how you can saw it to give the greatest number of strips. Take into account the prevalence of defects that will cause some pieces to be thrown away. With good quality lumber you should probably get 10 percent more than you think you have to have. If you are planning to use salvaged wood, get around twice as much as you estimate you need, because there will most likely be a lot of waste. Not all of the lumber needs to be full-length pieces that run all the way from one end of the mold to the other. In fact none of it does if you don't mind joints. If you want no joints in your strips, then about two thirds of the lumber needs to be as long as the finished canoe plus an extra foot. The rest of the lumber can be shorter; I suggest not more than 2 feet shorter than the long material.

Consider what other milling work you plan to do with the strips before you adjust the saw for strip thickness. I prefer to plane the strips on both sides for this type of project, because I can do a better job of fitting the strips together on the mold, and there is less sanding to do later since major irregularities in the strip surface have already been removed. If you have access to a planer, I suggest doing that additional step at the beginning of the project; it will pay off later. That means the strips need to be ripped a little thicker than you want the planed strips to measure.

The edges of the strips may be shaped to interlock with each other, or else left square. The matter of planing and whether to shape the strip edges before beginning to assemble the wooden hull is raised now because it figures into how thick to make the strips. Bead and cove (also called bead and flute) router bits for canoe strips are made to shape 1/4 in. edges. If the strips are not exactly 1/4 in. thick, the edges will be less than satisfactory. Thin strips usually end up with an offset to the shaped edge, while thick strips have a "step" in

one or both sides of the edge. Neither problem will render a strip completely useless, but it does require more attention on the builder's part to utilize such strips effectively.

The order of operations in milling the strips for the canoe I want to construct goes as follows:

1. Rip the strips to 5/16 in. thick.
2. Match the short strips for color and grain pattern and join them to make full-length strips.
3. Plane the strips to 1/4 in. thick.
4. Shape the interlocking bead and cove edges.

This canoe will be built of salvaged lumber plus some pieces leftover from earlier boat projects. If you have purchased new 1 x 6 or 1 x 8 in. flat-grained boards, you can skip ahead to where strips of proper thickness are sliced off the edge of the board. My description of converting salvaged wood into strips will illustrate the process for those who like that concept. The lumber

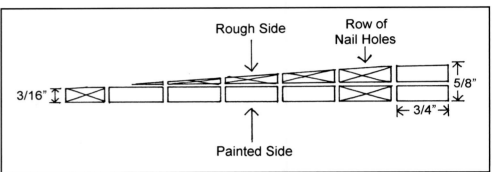

Converting used house siding to strips. The painted side was preferred for cutting into strips because it was square with the wide edge of the piece. The straightest edge was placed against the fence while the siding was cut into 3/4 in. pieces. That way the wide sides of the strips have the desired grain orientation: vertical. (If the siding had been of flat-grained lumber, the siding would not have been thick enough to saw 3/4 in. wide vertical-grained strips out of.) Usually, one of these 3/4 in. wide pieces was thrown away due to the presence of a row of nail holes. After sawing all the siding into 3/4 in. wide pieces, the saw was adjusted to cut 5/16 in. strips out of these pieces. Some of the pieces from the widest edge of the siding produced two usable strips. Most of the 3/4 in. wide pieces were run through the saw to trim off the excess wood even when there was no hope of getting two good strips, because it was more efficient to trim the strips to thickness with the saw than to plane away that much material. Each piece of siding typically yielded six good strips.

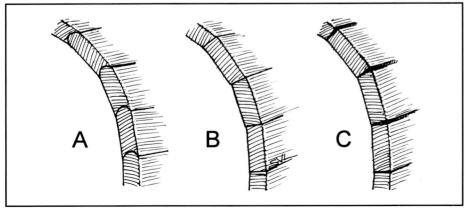

Treatment of strip edges. A. Both edges of each strip have been shaped with matching router bits. The rounded edge is the bead edge, and the grooved edge is the cove, or flute edge. Bead and cove edges interlock, making it easy to align strips and obtain tight joints. It takes some time to do this step at the beginning of the project, but it saves time during construction of the hull. B. One edge of the strip is hand beveled with a plane to match the edge of the previously placed strip. This method yields very good fits and doesn't require special power tools, but is quite time consuming. C. No shaping of strip edges is done after ripping. This method takes the least time, but results in the weakest joints—only the inside corners are in contact. For more discussion of these various methods of edge-joining the strips, see the chapter on stripping the hull.

I acquired is in the form of cedar siding which was torn off a house and replaced. The siding is actually in good shape, though twenty or so years old. The pieces range from 6 to 8 in. wide, and 5/8 in. thick at one edge tapering down to 3/16 in. at the narrow edge. All the pieces are vertical-grained. The siding does have some damaged places, and each piece has a row of nail holes, but the quality of the usable wood is good. The price was very agreeable; that is, free. The first step in the use of any salvaged wood is to examine it for presence of nails, wire, gravel, dirt, or any other blade ruining item and remove it. The next step is to plan for the best utilization of the material.

When you mill the strips yourself, you can make them whatever dimensions you want. The customary dimensions are 3/4 in. wide by 1/4 in. thick. This has much to do with the standard dimensions of lumber available for sawing strips out of, and also router bit size for edge shaping. Not only that, this size strip is easy to handle and just generally gives good results. However, a builder may decide to make strips as much as 1 in. wide, and strip thickness can range from 3/16 in. for a lightweight boat on up to 3/8 in. for a stronger hull. The thin strips do result in less weight, but be advised that such thin strips don't offer much margin for error in sanding after the hull is assembled. Regarding strip width, using wider strips allows the builder to put the hull together with fewer strips, and therefore fewer joints between strips. I would not advise making the strips more than 1 in. wide, however, because of the difficulties that are likely to arise when wrapping the strips around the tighter curves on the mold.

The space requirement for ripping strips is considerable. There must be room for the longest board to go completely through the saw; that means the full length of that board plus a few feet on both the infeed and outfeed ends of the saw.

Setup for ripping strips. The infeed and outfeed tables are of plywood shelving stock. Each table has a 2 x 4 screwed to the underside for support, and a single 2 x 4 leg at each end. This design allows the tables to be easily adjusted by moving the legs up or down as needed and clamped to a sawhorse. A piece of saw track is clamped to the fence that comes with the table saw. This serves as a longer "fence," and because it extends over the edges of the saw table, makes a good point of attachment for the infeed and outfeed tables. That way the surfaces of these tables are even with the surface of the saw table. The bar clamps used for fastening the in/outfeed tables are more visible in the next photo. Other straight, smooth, substantial shop items can be substituted for the saw track. Safety equipment recommended for ripping strips includes hearing protection, gloves, push sticks, dust masks, and glasses.

Hold the strip stock against the fence just ahead of the saw blade. Always use push sticks when working within a foot of the blade. A long, flexible stick was the perfect tool here. The plywood piece in the foreground is another tool used to push the trailing end of the strip stock through the saw. Home-made, expendable tools are standard for this operation at our shop. There is no stress associated with "modifying" a tool by accidentally sawing a corner off.

wood through the saw, and the other person holds the stock firmly against the fence at a point just ahead of the saw blade.

If you are using red cedar or another aromatic wood for the strips, the work area will be filled with the scent of the wood. I find the "game" of turning discarded material into quality strips rather fun. It certainly reduces the monotony of ripping. When using new lumber for the manufacture of strips, expect to spend a couple of hours on the ripping process. Since I was using sal-

I have ripped strips with and without infeed and outfeed tables, and it was well worth the effort to construct the tables for the substantial improvement in ability to handle the lumber and strips. They do not have to be very special or expensive, and you can use them later for ripping gunwale stock. They are also very handy as a long temporary workbench when connected to each other.

If possible, try to do all the ripping in one day, without changing settings on the saw once it's adjusted the way you want. That way the strips will be fairly consistent in thickness. If you do this operation in more than one session, you are apt to end up with strips of varying thickness (as I did in this project). That complicates life later on.

When milling the lumber, do your best to enlist the help of a capable friend. It is possible to do this job by yourself, but the work goes more than twice as fast with a helper and is a lot more fun. One person holds the strip stock as parallel to the saw fence as possible while pushing the

Close-up view of ripping in progress. For better saw cuts, adjust the blade so it extends 1/2 in. above the upper surface of the wood. That also enables the downward pull of the cutting edge of the blade to aid in holding the stock down against the saw deck. Note the flat grain pattern on the upper surface of the wood.

Cedar strips, many with paint still on one side. Several short strips are stacked on the near side of the pile. These are only about 5 ft. long, which is about the shortest I attempt to use. Pieces that are under 8 ft. long have to have exceptionally fine grain or color to get my attention.

vaged material, which requires visual examination and re-sawing, about five hours went into the cutting of strips. If you want to incorporate special feature strips into the hull of your canoe, this is the time to make them. (See Chapter 6 for more on that.) I wanted my canoe to have a single strip of Alaskan yellow cedar on each side, so I cut those now.

These are the unusable pieces that were trimmed from the siding.

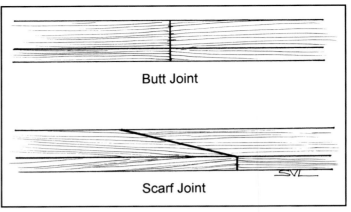

Two ways to join strip ends.

Since I prefer to scarf the strips together before using them, I incorporate that step into the process of milling the strips. It is more efficient to make long strips out of short ones before planing and shaping takes place. That way there are fewer pieces to handle during those operations.

Even using a thin kerf (1/16 in.) saw blade, the amount of wood converted to sawdust was considerable. There would probably be half as much sawdust had I used new, flat-grained lumber for strip stock instead of the salvaged siding.

Match short strips by color and grain pattern. Such variation is natural in western red cedar. Joints can be made nearly invisible if the joining strips match well.

I make fairly long scarf joints so there is more glue surface area for a stronger joint, and also to make the joint harder to see.

A 4-to-1 scarf. For each 4 in. of run lengthwise of the strip, the joint angles across 1 in. of width.

Short strips are quite usable for hull construction, but they require joining to provide the needed length. There are two kinds of joints that will work. When the square ends of two strips are joined together, that forms a butt joint. These joints are made while the strips are being put on the mold, and the joint is placed so that the strip ends are located over a station for support. The other type of joint is a scarf joint, where the strips are cut so that the joining faces come together at an angle or bevel. This joint can be made while putting the strips on the mold, but I much prefer to do it beforehand. The joint is strong enough that the long strip created by joining shorter strips can be treated like any other full-length strip. That means no joining is necessary while the process of stripping the hull is underway. (See Chapter 6 for more discussion of the two types of joints.)

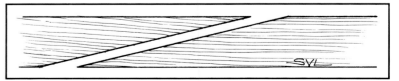

Jig for cutting scarfs with a table saw. The strip is pressed into the channel on the top of the jig.

The strips are clamped into place while glue dries. A gray layer of foam padding protects the strips. I use the brown-dyed carpenter's wood glue for darker wood, but on the really light-colored strips I used the regular cream-colored version. The glue was allowed to dry for twelve hours. Of about 30 scarf joints made this way, none broke. The only scarf joint that did break was one that had dried only eight hours before I tried to put the strip on the mold.

Bottom of scarf cutting jig. The block on the bottom slides in the groove in the saw table, keeping the jig in a straight line as the cut is made.

Next, the strips were planed to 1/4 in. thick and the edges were shaped with a router.

The strips were planed in two stages so we could exercise an option to plane both sides of the strips rather than just one. Here, strips with white paint on one side are getting the paint planed off. Frequently the strips are flipped over and planed again in order to remove marks left by the saw. The person in the photo is allergic to cedar dust; thus, the respirator. Dust masks are definitely recommended.

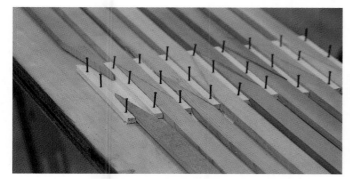

Scarf gluing jig. Matching strip ends are pushed together until they fit tightly for gluing. Small hardwood pieces with three holes drilled in them for nails are spaced just far enough apart for a strip to fit between. The channel in between is lined with tape to keep the strip ends from being glued to the jig.

On this home-built router table, the router body is screwed to a piece of 1/4 in. Plexiglas, which in turn is mounted on a pair of wooden rails. Infeed and outfeed tables are also attached to these rails. A fence is made up of two pieces of aluminum angle stock attached to a wooden bracket that goes around the opening for the router bit. The comb-like feather boards apply pressure to the strip to hold it in position as it is pushed through the apparatus. The router bit for making the bead edge is just visible in the center of the picture, behind the large C-clamp in the foreground. As a safety measure, the router bit should be covered by some type of guard, although not shown here.

A strip is pushed through the router. The rounded bead edge of a strip is much more resistant to breakage than the cove edge, so shape the bead edges first. Then, while the cove edges are being cut, the bead edges will stand up to the pressure from the feather boards. It took quite a bit of tinkering to make this setup work correctly. While this apparatus works satisfactorily, readers are encouraged to experiment with improvements or use a commercially built router table that offers greater precision in adjustment.

Framework Materials

The framework of a wood strip canoe consists of the stems, gunwales, the thwart(s), and decks. These parts are most often made of hardwood stock due to the demands placed on them when the canoe is in use. Other pieces that are normally made of hardwood are seat frames and keels. Neither of these are necessary to support the boat itself, but seat frames contribute a lot toward the paddler's comfort and certainly are load-bearing structures. All of these items are subject to at least moderate load stresses and/or abrasion while the canoe is in service. Hardwoods provide more substantial support and resist wear better than softwoods, generally speaking. There are species of hardwood that in reality are quite soft and make less than ideal stock for wear prone parts such as gunwales. In general, hardwoods hold mechanical fasteners such as screws better than softwoods, so that is a consideration in certain situations.

Woods favored among boat builders for framework items are ash, oak, cherry, and mahogany. My experience with ash thus far supports its reputation as being the best for parts that must be bent for use in construction, and for parts that may suffer quite a bit of abrasion or bumps against hard objects. Ash is suitable for all of the hardwood parts of a canoe, but it is especially popular for gunwales, stems, and keels. Oak will also serve well, except for one limitation. While oak accepts most glues as well as ash, oak does not bond well with epoxy. Epoxy is the adhesive of choice for many applications in boat building, so this lack of compatibility requires us to look at other alternatives. Resorcinol resin glue is waterproof and bonds well with oak, but is a dark purplish color. Rather than use an off-color glue, a more usual solution is to use metal fasteners, either with or without an epoxy adhesive, to attach oak pieces. Dowels may also be used to support joints, as in seat frames. Before I knew about the oak/epoxy "problem," I glued oak gunwales onto one of my canoes, without also using screws. All seemed well at first, but after about a year, the glue joints began to fail. In researching the problem, I learned that there is something in oak that disrupts the structure of the epoxy, so that those joints will not last. I put the gunwales back in place with screws. Now, I always use screws for attaching gunwales anyway, regardless of what wood the gunwales are made of, so my selection of ash or oak for those pieces doesn't really depend much on glue-ability with epoxy. Oak is a hard, durable wood that holds fasteners well and also bends surprisingly well. Oak is heavier than ash and not quite as tough, but is easier to finish with hand tools than ash, and is still an excellent choice for framework parts.

Mahogany has been used fairly extensively for gunwales, with good results. It is beautiful finished, and is lighter in weight than ash or oak. It is also softer and less wear-resistant. There are actually many species of wood that are marketed as mahogany, and species suitability and quality vary a lot. African and Honduran mahogany are preferable.[3] Cherry is a favorite among

builders who have access to it. It is becoming more difficult to find, especially in pieces that will run the full length of the canoe. Cherry is reported to finish the best of the four woods suggested, have a very attractive color, and is satisfactory in terms of strength and weight. It is not as hard as oak or ash, however.

Other hardwoods can be utilized with good results. Maple, butternut, and birch have been used and do work, but I do not know how they compare to ash or oak.[4] There may be hardwoods native to your locality that are worth considering. Characteristics to take into account are weight (usually given in pounds per cubic foot), availability of long pieces, flexibility, hardness, gluing ability, straightness of grain, and to some extent color and finishing characteristics. Most woods are an acceptable color, but there are some odd ones. It might be tempting to experiment with tropical hardwoods other than mahogany. Do some homework beforehand to find out how suitable these woods are. Several species are so heavy that they actually sink in water; others are not that heavy, but are still heavier than oak. That kind of weight doesn't make a positive contribution to the finished weight of the canoe.

For lightness of weight, softwoods such as spruce are sometimes substituted for hardwoods in making gunwales and decks. Spruce is a good choice if one must use softwood. I've tried Alaskan yellow cedar for gunwales and decks, and it is adequate. It looks pretty and is lighter than the better hardwoods available, but softwoods have a problem alluded to in their generic name: they are soft. The yellow cedar gunwales on my canoe are perennially dented and gouged from minor accidents during ordinary use. Even allowing the gunwale to strike my belt buckle as I pick up the canoe will leave marks. Unless you don't mind treating your canoe as if it were made of bone china, my observation is that one is better off using a durable hardwood for gunwale stock. If saving weight is a concern, then reduce the dimensions of the pieces, but use hardwood, at least for the outwales. The outwales seem to suffer more misfortunes than the inwales, so a builder could probably get away with using a softwood for inwales and not sacrifice too much resistance to wear. Decks don't seem to be a part of the canoe that receives a lot of abuse, so either hardwood or softwood stock is satisfactory there. I have been happy enough with the yellow cedar decks on my canoe.

Traditionally, inner stems have been made of hardwoods, which provide greater strength but are heavier and harder to shape than softwoods. Softwoods found favor with builders making canoes specifically intended to be light in weight, and their success has prompted the adoption of softwoods for all types of strip canoes. Softwood is lighter, easier to shape, and takes staples better than hardwood stock.[5] Hardwoods remain an option for those who prefer to use them, however. A hardwood well suited to this purpose is ash, thanks to its native flexibility. Flexible softwoods useful for stem laminations are spruce, white cedar, Douglas fir, Port Orford cedar, and probably certain pines. The quality of the wood affects its suitability. Straight, close, vertical grain in the individual pieces to be laminated is desirable. Some of these species, including ash and spruce, are not rot resistant, but can be used with success in this situation because the wood will be completely encased in epoxy by the time construction is finished. The organisms that cause wood to decay require both oxygen and moisture, which the epoxy seals out.

Flexibility of the wood is one of the most important factors to consider. Ash, spruce, and the other species previously listed as suitable for laminating up inside stems are flexible enough to bend into shape without requiring steaming or soaking. There may be other locally available woods worth trying, too. In my area, there is a type of wild cherry that fits into this category. Cutting the wood into thinner pieces expands the possibilities to include species that are not ordinarily known for their flexibility, so if you have some straight-grained wood around you could do a little experimenting with 3/4 in. wide by 1/8 in. thick strips. Clamp the end of the strip to the upper end of the stem form and bend the strip gradually around the perimeter of the stem form. If it doesn't break, and the other characteristics of the wood are up to your standards, go ahead and use it. One of the advantages of using four or more thin (1/8 in.) strips in laminating up the stem is that when the glue has cured, the resulting stem piece will retain its proper shape better than one made up of only three (thicker) strips. The more layers that a laminated piece is made up of, the less "spring back" there will be when the piece is released from its mold.

When shopping for material to use for framework pieces, pay attention to wood quality (as always). Straight grain, free of knots and other defects, is a high priority for gunwale stock. Grain orientation isn't a big issue. Or rather, equally good arguments can be made for using flat-grained, vertical-grained, or in-between-grained wood, so suit yourself. The lumber needs to be about a foot longer than the canoe is to be, to allow for the outward curve of the hull sides, and checks (splits), or other common defects in the ends of board.

How the gunwales are to be made influences how much stock you need, so see the chapter on gunwale installation before making your purchase. *Usually* the outwales are 3/4 in. thick by 3/4 in. wide. The inwales are the same thickness but width varies from 3/8 in. to 3/4 in. or more. Take saw kerfs into account when estimating your needs. A 1 in. x 6 in. board the length of the canoe plus one foot is usually sufficient for gunwale stock. If you find such a board and after cutting the pieces you need from it you have a long piece left over, save it for another special project rather than sawing it into little pieces for things like seat frames. Wood of the length required for seat frames, decks, and thwarts is readily found at lesser cost than the premium quality stock needed for gunwales.

If lumber long enough for gunwales is unavailable, two shorter pieces can be joined to get the desired length. Gunwales are important structural members in a canoe, so the joint must be up to the job; the joint needs to be as strong as the solid gunwale stock. A long scarf joint will provide the necessary strength. Instead of the 4-to-1 bevel used for joining strips, an 8-to-1 or 7-to-1 bevel is called for.[6] The strength of the joint comes from a large glue-surface area. That means that if the gunwale stock is not square, the bevel should be cut on the widest side. The scarf cutting jig shown for use with strips can be modified to cut longer scarfs in individual gunwale pieces. Thickened epoxy (discussed in the section on installing gunwales) is the adhesive of choice for these high-strength joints. When the gunwale pieces are installed on the boat, it is good practice to stagger the position of the joints in the inwales and outwales. If you join two lengths of oak to make gunwale material, remember to use screws in the installation of gunwale pieces so that the epoxy joints are mechanically fastened together.

The amount of lumber needed for the decks, thwarts, and seats depends on the size and how many of them are needed to fit out your canoe. As mentioned previously, these items can be manufactured from pieces 3 ft. or less in length. That can translate into an outstanding array of quality woods to select from, at affordable prices. Decks are often made of fancy woods, which can be a gorgeous touch in the finished craft. All these parts can be made from 3/4 in. thick material.

Fiberglass Cloth

Fiberglass cloth bonded with resin to the inner and outer surfaces of the wood hull greatly improves the strength of the hull, so that the boat may be used and enjoyed under normal conditions. There actually are a variety of fiber types available, but fiberglass cloth provides the best combination of strength, ease of application, transparence, and price for the purpose of home-building a strip canoe.[7]

The woven cloth is sold by the yard or by the roll, and comes in a range of fiber coarseness. The coarseness, or weight of the cloth is given as ounces per yard. The two most common weights used in canoe building are 4 oz. and 6 oz. cloth. The lighter cloth is mostly reserved for models that are specifically intended to be light weight. These are usually under 14 ft. long and

often carry only one paddler. The small size of the canoe and the relatively light loads the craft is expected to carry permit a less-sturdily built hull to serve its purpose. The heavier 6 oz. cloth is the standard weight for strip canoe building. It offers a good balance of strength for its weight, and is suitable for use on canoes of all sizes. Where extra strength or abrasion resistance are needed, two or more layers of the cloth can be put on the hull. A double layer is seldom needed over the entire hull, but it is not unusual to have two layers on the bottom up to the waterline. (See Chapter 8 for an example.) Ask yourself how the canoe is to be used and where it is to be used; a tandem canoe does not have to have a double layer of cloth on the bottom, and if it is not needed it only adds weight and cost to the boat.

The amount of cloth needed for the project will be twice the length of the hull, plus 1/2 yard for "insurance" and scraps to cut special pieces out of. If you plan to put two layers of cloth on the bottom, add one more hull length to the total yardage needed. The cloth is measured and sold by the yard unless you buy a whole roll, so an 18 ft. canoe would require 2 x 18 ft. x 1 yd./3 ft. = 12 yds. of cloth (single layer, inside and out), plus 1/2 yd. for a total of 12-1/2 yds. Cloth is available in at least three widths; 60 in., 50 in., and 38 in. wide. A tandem canoe usually requires 60 in. wide cloth. To find out for certain what you need, measure around the perimeter of the widest station on the mold, from sheer to sheer. You may find out that you can get by with 50 in. wide cloth, which would be less expensive. If the widest station is over 60 in. around, don't panic. Two lengths of cloth can be laid side by side over the hull, with the edges overlapping along the keel line. Of course, the yardage would have to be doubled, but narrower cloth could be used. Another option would be to cover as much of the hull with 60 in. wide cloth as possible, and then use scraps to fill in the gaps. There are always fair-sized scraps left over from the sides near the ends of the hull.

Fiberglass cloth is treated with a sizing agent to make it easier to handle and to keep it from absorbing moisture. The sizing used affects its compatibility with resins. Make sure that the cloth you buy is made for use with epoxy resin. The safest bet is to buy the cloth from the same supplier you get your resin from.

If you have the opportunity to do so, look at the glass cloth before you buy. See if the woven fibers are of uniform size and the weave of the fabric is regular. Do the fibers look as if they have been snagged or distorted somehow? Are there loops or curlicues in fibers that should run straight? Uniform cloth gives uniform performance. Lest the reader be alarmed at the prospect of having to order cloth sight unseen, it should be mentioned that the differences in quality are usually small. If cloth is ordered from one of the better known suppliers, the cloth will most always be satisfactory.

Once you have the cloth in your possession, take care of it. Avoid handling the cloth unnecessarily, and keep it clean. Try not to crease it, because that stresses the fibers and it may be hard to get the crease out later. Keep the cloth loosely rolled in a dry place until you need it.

Epoxy Resin

Plastic resins such as epoxy are used in boat construction because they are more or less waterproof, they bond the parts of the hull together into a single unit, they form a durable coating that protects the wooden hull, and some kinds (including epoxy) form strong joints when used as an adhesive. The incorporation of fiberglass cloth within a coating of resin greatly improves the tensile strength of the resin, and the cloth/resin matrix becomes a major structural component of the hull. This matrix is referred to as fiberglass-reinforced plastic. There are several types of plastic resins on the market. Epoxy is by far the most popular resin with strip canoe builders. It is tougher, more waterproof, and more adherent than polyester resins. That makes for a superior hull covering. Epoxy is also safer and more pleasant to use than polyester, because it does not give off the powerful fumes typical of polyester resins. Epoxy is easier to mix for consistent results, and is compatible with plastic materials that are dissolved by the styrene in polyester resins. Epoxy is often used for bonding structural parts of the canoe together. Enough reputable builders have switched from polyester to epoxy resin—based on their own experiences with both—that I have followed their advice and never used a resin other than epoxy.[8]

Epoxy is mixed of two parts: the resin, which makes up the larger share of the mix, and hardener. There are quite a few different formulations of epoxy. Some formulations are good for a wide range of uses, but others are not. The first specification to look for is suitability for marine use. You want an epoxy system (a term used to refer to the resin and hardener combination) that is made especially for boat construction.

Magazines geared for a boat building audience regularly contain advertisements from epoxy suppliers. Do a little shopping and get literature from suppliers that serve your area. Resin characteristics to look for are clarity, ability to cure within a reasonable amount of time at temperatures you will be working in (it should be possible to sand it 48 hours after it is applied), and good penetrating ability when applied to cloth or mixed with adhesive fillers (thickening agents such as wood flour). Often there is a range of hardeners that alter curing times, viscosity, and sometimes clarity of the coating. Use the information provided by the epoxy distributors to select the system best suited to your situation. Pay special attention to temperature and humidity conditions in your boat shop. If you buy a hardener that requires a minimum of 65°F to effect a cure, and your shop never gets above 60°F, any resin you mix with that hardener will not cure. Names of some well-established sources of epoxy for boat building are listed in the appendix. These sources tend to be toward the high end in price, but they are top-quality brands. Interviews with other experienced boat builders in your area may turn up additional possible brands of epoxy resins.

Most people who build strip boats like to put a clear finish on them, so the beauty of the wood shows through. In order to show off the wood to maximum advantage, the epoxy/fiberglass matrix must be as colorless and transparent as possible. This is affected not only by the visual characteristics of the resin itself, but also by its ability to wet out the cloth, and how the resin and cloth are handled. If the resin is able to completely penetrate the fibers of the cloth, and air bubbles trapped between layers of cloth are driven out, then the fiberglass will turn fully transparent, leaving no observable hint of its presence. Overworking the resin with a brush or squeegee causes air bubbles in the form of a cloudy froth to be trapped in the resin, which will appear as a slightly opaque spot on the hull if left to cure. Therefore, you do not want to have to work the resin very much to get it to saturate the cloth. You need resin that is "thin" enough to soak in on its own. Also, you need it to stay thin long enough to soak in completely. Here is where you can get into trouble using a low temperature hardener during hot weather. If the epoxy begins to set up too quickly, it will never completely penetrate the cloth fibers, and the woven fibers will be somewhat visible in the finished work.

I have adopted use of a combination of two different resin formulations for the application of fiberglass to wood strip boat parts, because no single type of resin will do everything I want it to. (See Chapter 8 for more specifics.) An extra thin, extra clear resin is best for saturating fiberglass cloth. But for building up a substantial layer of plastic over the cloth after that has been wet out, a more standard viscosity resin is appropriate, mainly because it is less quick to run off the hull. Also, it requires fewer applications to build to the desired thickness. This heavier resin is better suited to use in joining parts together as well, providing additional incentive to use the two different types of epoxy resin in the construction of the boat. There is some discussion of the merits of thinning standard resins with a solvent like acetone to reduce viscosity, so the resin soaks into wood and fiberglass more readily. Epoxy suppliers discourage this practice for boat building, because it may weaken the cured resin, and also leave the plastic coating more permeable to water vapor.[9] System Three Resins, Inc. flatly states to never add solvents to their epoxy for fiberglassing or gluing. It is best to use resins that have the properties needed without tampering with them.

Epoxies must be mixed in the correct proportions or they will not cure. This requires us to measure what we're mixing. There are a couple ways to do this. One is to use disposable graduated paper cups. Measuring with these cups is easy and convenient, and offers more flexibility in mixing batch sizes, because quantities can be more finely adjusted. The drawback is that there is more potential for a spill when pouring from a quart or gallon jug into a cup. Another way to measure resin and hardener is to use pre-calibrated pumps for dispensing from your containers. With the pumps, you count the number of squirts into a mixing container, making sure that the number of pumps of resin to hardener are in the correct ratio. Many builders find this way of measuring even easier and more convenient, and it reduces the possibility of spilling materials. If you decide to purchase the pumps, make sure you understand how the pumps are calibrated. The pumps may be designed to deliver the same quantity of either resin or hardener. In that case, to get the right mixing ratio, you would count five pumps of resin for each one pump of hardener, using a 5:1 mixing ratio as an example. Alternatively, the pumps may be calibrated specifically for resin and hardener, so that one pump of resin and one pump of hardener will give the proper proportions of each; not necessarily a 1:1 mix. For example, the resin pump may be designed to deliver twice as much as the hardener pump, so that one squirt of resin and one squirt of hardener yield a 2:1 mix.

The major resin suppliers sell all the equipment you need for handling epoxy, so get their catalogs. Another thing to get is the technical manual for the use of their products. These booklets are a virtual gold mine of information on how to get the best results with these products. The manuals are complete and easy to read. (At least this is true of the material from WEST SYSTEM Brand and System Three Resins, Inc.; I have not yet perused the others.) When I have called my resin supplier for technical advice, I have almost always found later that the information was in the technical manual, only I overlooked it. Assuming I am a fairly typical builder in my ability to miss information that was already available, it is no surprise that most resin suppliers don't have a toll-free number for technical support. They are very knowledgeable and helpful in the event you think you have to call them, though. By all means, obtain and read the manual offered by your epoxy distributor. Manuals are the best source of information on the specific materials you will be using.

How much resin do you need to buy? This is a perfectly reasonable question and if you are familiar with the price of epoxy resin, it is an important one. This is one of the most expensive materials needed for the project, so you probably don't want to end up with a sizable surplus, which will have cost you a pretty penny. If you are lucky, the designer of the plans you buy will be able to tell you how much resin it takes to build that particular model. Sometimes this information is not available, so a little figuring is needed before placing that resin order.

Factors that bear on the resin requirement are the surface area of the hull; the weight of the fiberglass cloth used; the number of layers of fabric that are used; the number of coats of resin applied; and the number and size of the other canoe parts that are coated, assembled, or installed with epoxy. The heavier the fiberglass cloth and the more layers there are, the more resin is required to apply the cloth. If you make bulkheads and strip decks for the canoe, more resin will be needed to assemble the pieces, fiberglass them, and install them in the canoe. One thing that probably does not make much difference is the choice of low-viscosity resin or general-purpose resin. To get a certain level of build, it takes about the same amount of epoxy, but more coats of the low-viscosity type because the film thickness per coating is less. The low-vis epoxy penetrates wood more deeply, and more applications of thinner coatings means more brushes discarded with some epoxy in them, but I doubt the difference in the amount of resin required is significant.

After you have made your decisions on the weight of fiberglass cloth you think is appropriate and number of layers you want to apply, you are about two-thirds prepared to estimate the volume of resin needed. The remaining variable is the surface area of the canoe. How do you calculate the surface area, accounting for the curves and planes whose boundaries are indistinct, to say the least? In the absence of a more direct method for determining surface area, I offer an indirect means of arriving at a workable figure.

After the wood strip hull has been assembled, sanded smooth, and dusted off, lay out a rectangular length of cloth (perhaps the fiberglass cloth to be used in the epoxy layup) over the hull, so that the entire length of the hull and sides are covered. Then, measure the length of cloth required to do this. Smooth the fabric down along the sides of the hull so it conforms fairly well. Now, look at the excess cloth and figure out how much of it is hanging loose below the hull. By measuring the amount of extra cloth that is surplus, calculating its surface area in square feet and subtracting it from the surface area of the entire rectangular piece (of known length and width), you can come up with the surface area of the hull itself. Remember that this figure must be doubled, because both the inside *and* outside of the hull are to be covered with fiberglass.

Doing these calculations for your own canoe will give a more accurate picture of what you need for your specific project. This exercise may be impractical for some folks, so here is a table of figures I've calculated based on my experience with my own canoes. The total hull surface area is the area of the outside and inside, added together. If an extra layer of cloth is placed on the hull for added protection below the waterline, that cloth will take one "saturation coat" quantity of resin. The area of that extra layer is usually about half the surface area of the exterior of the hull. Since it takes more resin to saturate the cloth than to fill the weave with subsequent coats, additional layers of cloth definitely increase the total amount of resin needed for the layup.

Canoe Size	Total Hull Surface Area, in Sq. Ft.	Surface Area of Extra Layer of Cloth, to 4 in. Waterline, in Sq.Ft.
11 ft. 3 in. L x 29 in. beam	65.3	16.3
13 ft. 3 in. L x 31 in. beam	87	21.7
15 ft. L x 34 in. beam	118.5	29.7
16 ft. L x 34 in. beam	126	31.5
17 ft. 6 in. L x 34 in. beam	138	34.5
18 ft. L x 35 in. beam	159	39.7

Due to differences among designs that are of similar length and beam, surface area can easily vary by 10 percent. For example, the 17-1/2 ft. canoe in the table is only 11 in. deep in the middle. If it was only 1 in. deeper, the hull surface area would have been about 144 sq. ft., a difference of 4 percent.

To arrive at the amount of resin needed to cover the hull, multiply the total surface area of the canoe (in square feet) by .021 gal. epoxy/square foot, if you are using 4 oz. fiberglass cloth, or .022 gal. epoxy/square foot if using 6 oz. cloth. This gives a quantity of epoxy measured in gallons, including both resin and hardener. These conversion factors are derived from actual usage records, including a normal amount of waste. The coverage estimates in manufacturers' technical manuals are sometimes inaccurate for this type of project. I suspect that differences in the species of wood used as a substrate for the fiberglass, techniques of resin application, and probably other factors are responsible for the large difference I've observed between actual use and estimated use based on their coverage figures.

For the Wee Lassie II:

87 sq. ft. x .021 gal./sq. ft. = 1.81 gal. of epoxy

If additional layers of 4 oz. cloth are being applied to the hull bottom (not counting bias cloth strips), add the area of the additional layer times .0045 gal. epoxy/square foot to the original estimate. This figure is derived from my records of resin needed to saturate cloth over sealed wood. (The resin required to seal the hull is part of the first estimate.) So, if I planned to add an extra layer of 4 oz. cloth on the hull up to the waterline, I would add 21.7 sq. ft. x .0045 gal./sq.

ft. = .098 gal. of epoxy to the earlier estimate of 1.81 gal. I have not calculated the conversion factor for 6 oz. fiberglass, but it would be a higher number, perhaps .0055 gal./square foot.

The use of epoxy for other things besides hull construction can significantly increase consumption. For the assembly of strip decks and bulkheads, and installation of gunwales, decks, bulkheads, seat risers, and other parts, I used an additional 30 oz. of epoxy (.23 gal). (Most of that went into decks and bulkheads.)

The total quantity of epoxy I used to build the Wee Lassie II was 2.04 gal. (1.81 gal. + .23 gal.) Two thirds of that was Clear Coat™ resin, and the remaining third was System Three's general purpose resin. One thing you may find as you look at your resin supplier's catalog is that epoxy is sold in incremental quantities that might not add up to your exact estimated need. In that case, buy more than you think is required. There is hardly anything worse than running out of resin partway through a project! Besides, leftover epoxy is nice to have if you want to make paddles or need to repair the canoe later on. If, in order to come up with the right total quantity of resin, you want to vary the proportions of low-viscosity resin and general purpose resin, you can do that. The main thing is to have enough of the "thin" resin for sealing the bare wood hull and applying the first coat of resin to the cloth. It is nice to have enough to apply another coat or two, but you could substitute the regular resin for all subsequent coatings.

The following table shows *approximate* quantities of resin needed for canoes of different sizes. For the most accurate estimates, builders should calculate expected usage for their own particular projects.

Length of Canoe	Quantity of Epoxy
11 ft.	1-1/3 gal.
13 ft.	2 gal.
15 ft.	2-1/2 gal.
17 ft.	3 gal.

Fasteners

One of the attractions of wood strip canoe building is that relatively few mechanical fasteners are required. There are usually four bolts or screws for each seat, two to four bolts or screws for each thwart, and screws on about 6 in. intervals along the gunwales. There may be other features such as coamings, stem bands, or deck plates fastened with screws. This is a minuscule amount of hardware compared with that required for traditional wooden boat construction.

The metal fasteners in any boat need to be of a type that resists corrosion in a wet environment. Ordinary steel screws are poorly suited for boat building due to degradation of the fastener by rusting and the resulting stains on the boat. Galvanized fasteners are better than un-plated ones. In areas where a screw will be put in and then varnished over (for instance, on gunwales) they will work well enough. In places where part of the fastener will be exposed to moisture, you are better off using something besides a galvanized fastener. Brass, silicon bronze, stainless steel, and monel screws and bolts are all more corrosion resistant, though to varying degrees.

Brass has a long tradition of use in boat building and works well in construction of strip canoes. Brass is widely available in a good range of sizes, is moderately priced, and has a pleasing appearance where the heads of the fasteners are visible. The main drawbacks of brass are that the quality varies and the metal is soft. Look at the screw heads and note whether the heads are symmetrical, and if using slot-head screws, see if the slots go across the middle of the head. The threads should have sharp edges rather than blunt ones. I always buy extra screws, because given any number of screws to drive, the slot in the head of at least one of them gets messed up during installation. This is partly due to the softness of the metal, and can be largely alleviated by using a new screwdriver and rubbing wax or soap on the threads of the screw before driving it.

Silicon bronze fasteners are stronger than brass, more corrosion resistant than brass, and are an attractive coppery brown color. They are also more expensive than brass and harder to find. If a builder can get the desired fasteners at an agreeable price, though, silicon bronze is an excellent choice.

Stainless steel is actually a generic term for a fairly wide range of alloys. All of the ones I'm aware of are more corrosion resistant than steel. They have an advantage over galvanized fasteners in that there is no corrosion resistant coating to peel off. Stainless steel fasteners are some degree of silvery gray. If that color is not appealing, consider that varnish over the top of it will impart a honey color to the metal. Finding galvanized carriage bolts too susceptible to rusting where the threads are exposed, I have turned to stainless bolts. Stainless steel is somewhat more costly than the galvanized version of the same item, but is still a better value where parts of the fastener are exposed to the elements. Stainless is stronger and harder than brass, so it would be a sensible substitute for brass fasteners if color is not a concern.

Monel is acknowledged to be the strongest, most corrosion resistant alloy around. So far I don't know of monel fasteners in the sizes and types used for strip canoe construction, but they may be available now or in the future. At any rate, price will be a consideration, as monel is quite expensive. Brass, silicon bronze, and stainless steel fasteners are adequate for building canoes, and use of monel fasteners would not yield much improvement in the practical use of this type of boat.

Adhesives

It did not take much experimentation for me to settle on just two adhesives for strip canoe construction. All my gluing needs are served by wood glue and epoxy with thickening agents added.

Carpenter's wood glue has a good combination of characteristics for use in gluing the strips together during hull construction. It requires no mixing, is water soluble for easy clean up, is sufficiently strong, is non-toxic, and doesn't set so fast that you can't get the pieces together before it hardens. Once the glue has dried, it is water resistant (not waterproof). If excess glue is wiped up with a damp rag before it dries, the glue presents no problems during sanding. And, in the event that stray drips do harden in place, water will soften the glue enough to allow you to scrape it off, given a little time to work. I built one canoe hull using hot melt glue and was not satisfied with the results. My main complaint is that the beads of glue I drew out on the strip edges began to harden immediately, at times making it impossible to fit the strips together very tightly. The finished canoe shows daylight between the strips when I lift it overhead. The other problem I had was that I nearly branded myself by accident with the glue gun several times, thanks to the cord catching on things while I was handling the strips. I switched to wood glue for my next canoe and have been so pleased that I stopped experimenting with alternatives.

Thickened epoxy is mixed epoxy resin with a filler added to it. The type and amount of filler added depends on what characteristics the builder needs in the mix, either before it hardens, after it hardens, or both. Fillers are added to epoxy to ensure that most of the resin stays in the joint instead of wicking away into the wood or running out. Thickened epoxy is also used to fill gaps, to reinforce existing joints, and to reshape the joint surfaces by puttying inside corners. Fillers available for use as thickening agents include silica; cotton, linen, and plastic minifibers; wood flour; phenolic microballoons and quartz microspheres; graphite powder; aluminum powder; milled glass fibers; and chopped glass strand. Each of these has properties that make them especially suited to particular applications.[10] Fortunately, we only need two fillers: silica and wood flour. Furthermore, you can make all the wood flour you need during the process of sanding the hull. That means you will need to buy a small package of silica thickener, which is also known as colloidal silica. This material weighs almost nothing, so don't be surprised if the container seems to be full of air when you heft it. You can also buy wood flour if you prefer; System Three offers a 1 lb. bag at small cost. Otherwise, collect the dust generated by sanding wood. One cup of fine dust should be plenty, but you can save more if you think you might want it. You can always discard the excess.

Epoxy, when used as an adhesive, is usually applied in two steps. If one or more of the joining surfaces is bare wood, the wood is coated with mixed resin (without filler), to encourage good penetration of the epoxy into the wood. Then, the filler is mixed into the resin to give the desired consistency (ketchup is the usual comparison) and the mixture is applied to one surface. Then, the joining pieces are clamped together with enough pressure to hold them in position, but not so much that all the resin squeezes out. Scrape up the resin that does squeeze out with a putty knife before it cures.

Not all fillers are suitable for use with epoxy resin as a structural adhesive. Colloidal silica and wood flour are. These fillers are dense enough and are added in small enough quantities to the resin that the strength of the cured resin is not compromised.

List of Materials

Here is a list of materials that were used in the construction of the canoe in the photo illustrations for this book. These are items that were used up or permanently attached to the boat in the building process. This list is included to provide a basis for estimating the needs for such a project, but of course, the exact amounts will vary depending on the size of the boat being built, the strength of construction, and the builder's standards of quality. Larger canoes require more materials. A canoe that is intended for rigorous use, and therefore built using extra layers of fiberglass, with more thwarts, and maybe painted instead of varnished, will need more and in some cases different materials. And, for those who are interested in a really fine finish that takes lots of sandpaper. So this list is best used as a guide, and adjustments will be needed to suit individual projects.

Mold

Two sheets 15/32 in. A/C plywood, for strongback and stations
Two dry 1 x 4s, 16 ft., for sides of strongback and interior bracing of strongback
12-1/2 ft. of 1-1/2 in. x 1-1/2 in. wood for cleats (short pieces OK)
3/4 lb. of 1-1/4 in. dry wall screws, for assembling strongback
Thirty 2-1/4 in. dry wall screws, for attaching cleats to strongback
3/4 in. staples or finishing nails, for securing clamping cleats to station edges
Carpenter's wood glue, for gluing clamping cleats to stations
One roll wide masking tape or plastic packaging tape for edges of stations and stem forms
One 24-grit disk for angle grinder, for shaping station edges
One 80-grit disk for DA sander, for shaping station edges
Two 100-grit paper strips for longboard, for shaping station edges
One sheet carbon paper, for tracing station outlines onto plywood
Two or three Phillips screwdriver bits, for drill

Hull (Wood Part)

Sixty-seven wood strips, 12 to 14-1/2 ft. long, with bead and cove edges
Six spruce strips, 1/8 in. thick x 5/8 in. wide x 30 in. long, for inside stems

Carpenter's wood glue
One box 9/16 in. long, 3/16 in. or 1/2 in. crown staples, if needed, for fastening strips to mold
One box 1/4 in. long, 3/16 in. or 1/2 in. crown staples, if needed, for fastening strip edges to each other
17 x 7/8 in. steel wire nails, if used, for fastening strips to mold
Twenty-four small wooden pads (1/8 in. thick x 3/4 in. square) for clamp pads; if using nails to fasten strips to mold, then 1 pad is needed for each nail

Smoothing Outer Hull (Preparation for Fiberglass and Epoxy)

Eight 80-grit disks for DA sander
Three 100-grit paper strips for longboard
Four 180-grit paper strips for longboard
Six 220-grit disks for DA sander and hand sanding pad
Dust mask(s)
Filler, for cracks between strips

Adding Outer Stem

Four ash strips, 1/8 in. thick x 1/2 in. wide x 32 in. long, for outer stems
Carpenter's wood glue (or thickened epoxy) for laminating strips
Twenty-eight small finishing nails, for holding laminates in place while glue sets
Twenty-eight wooden nailing pads
One 100-grit paper strip for longboard, for shaping outer stem after installation
Twenty-eight round toothpicks, for filling nail holes in laminates

Applying Fiberglass and Epoxy, Exterior and Interior of Hull

Ten yards 4 oz. fiberglass, 50 in. wide
1 gal. 48 oz. Clear Coat™ epoxy resin
63 oz. regular System Three epoxy resin
Ten 6 oz. graduated mixing cups
Seven 3 oz. graduated mixing cups
Three metal pie pans, for mixed epoxy
Six pairs of latex gloves (some were worn twice)
Nine natural bristle brushes, 1-1/2 in. to 3 in. wide, for applying resin
One foam brush, for eliminating bubbles from epoxy surface
Seven 80-grit disks for DA sander, for sanding before last coat of resin on exterior of hull
Five 120-grit disks for DA sander, for sanding before and after last coat of resin on exterior of hull
Seven 100-grit paper strips for longboard, for sanding after last coat of resin on exterior of hull
One medium coarse Scotch-Brite™ pad for cleaning hull surface
Dust rag
Three dust masks

Smoothing Inner Hull (Preparation for Fiberglass and Epoxy)

Seventeen 80-grit disks for DA sander and hand sanding, before the first coat and between coats of resin
Six 120-grit disks for DA sander and hand sanding, before the first coat and between coats of resin
Four 220-grit disks for hand sanding before the first coat of resin

Filler, for cracks between strips
Plastic bag, for loading filler into syringe
Medium steel wool
Three dust masks
Five pairs latex gloves

Gunwales

Four ash strips, 3/8 in. thick x 3/4 in. wide x 14 ft. long
Forty-two ash blocks, 3/8 in. thick x 3/4 in. wide x 3 in. long
4-3/4 oz. regular System Three epoxy resin
Colloidal silica and wood flour, for thickening epoxy
Five 3 oz. graduated cups
Stir sticks
Four acid brushes, for applying thickened epoxy
Three pairs latex gloves (some were worn twice)
One plastic cup, for dipping epoxy out of
Plastic sheets for protecting work surface from epoxy
One roll plastic tape, like filament tape, for positioning spacer blocks on inwales for gluing
Thirty-four brass wood screws, #6 x 1-1/4 in., for inwales
Eight brass wood screws, #6 x 3/4 in., for ends of inwales
Wax or soap, for lubricating threads of screws
Four 100-grit paper strips for longboard, for smoothing and shaping gunwales
Four 80-grit disks for DA sander and hand sanding, for smoothing and shaping gunwales
Coarse and fine sandpaper for hand sanding gunwales smooth, in preparation for finish

Through Holes for Ropes

8 in. of 3/4 in. schedule 40 PVC pipe
3/4 oz. System Three epoxy resin, thickened with colloidal silica and wood dust
Stir stick
One 3 oz. graduated cup
One pair latex gloves
One piece medium coarse sandpaper

Strip Bulkheads and Decks

Two pieces cardboard or heavy paper, for bulkhead patterns
1/2 sheet 3 mm 3-ply plywood, for bulkhead and deck backing material
Five dozen short strips, assorted leftover pieces
Carpenter's wood glue
4 oz. fiberglass cloth scraps, enough to cover all the bulkhead and deck pieces
13-1/2 oz. Clear Coat epoxy resin
6-3/4 oz. regular System Three epoxy resin
Colloidal silica and wood flour fillers, for thickening the epoxy resin
Six pair latex gloves
Ten 3 oz. graduated cups
Stir sticks
Four 1-1/2 in. natural bristle brushes
One acid brush
Plastic sheet for covering workbench

Masking tape, for controlling width of fillets

Coarse sandpaper, for shaping plywood backing pieces to fit

Medium sandpaper, for shaping strip edges

80-grit, 120-grit, and 220-grit sanding disks, for sanding the strip faces of the bulkheads and decks in preparation for fiberglass; and also between coats of epoxy

100-grit longboard paper, for sanding bulkhead and deck pieces flat

Two pieces of ash stock, 3/8 in. x 1/4 in. x 16 in., for glue strips under curved (inboard) edges of the decks

Four wood screws, #4 x 1 in., for fastening the ends of the glue strips to the inwales

Two deck plates, 6 in. size, for bulkheads

One small tube silicone sealant, for sealing the joints between deck plates and bulkheads

Twelve small brass wood screws, to fit holes in deck plates

Coamings

Two pieces ash stock, 1-1/8 in. wide x 1/4 in. thick x 16 in. long, for coamings

3/4 oz. regular System Three epoxy resin, for bonding coamings in place

Colloidal silica and wood flour fillers, for thickening the epoxy resin

One acid brush

Plastic sheet, for protecting the inside of the hull

Thwart

One piece ash stock, 3-1/2 in. wide x 3/4 in. thick x 32 in. long

One sheet carbon paper

One 24-grit disk, for angle grinder, for shaping thwart

One 100-grit paper strip for longboard, for smoothing and shaping thwart

120-grit and 220-grit disks for DA sander and hand sanding pad

Two stainless carriage bolts, 1/4 in. x 2 in. long

Two stainless washers, 1/4 in.

Two stainless nuts, 1/4 in.

Seat

Two pieces ash stock, 1-1/2 in. wide x 3/4 in. thick x 28 in. long

Two pieces ash stock, 1-1/2 in. wide x 3/4 in. thick x 9 in. long

Eight hardwood dowels, 5/16 in. diameter x 2-1/2 in. long

3/4 oz. regular System Three epoxy resin (actually need less than this, but can't mix in any smaller batch), for assembly work

Colloidal silica filler, for thickening the epoxy resin

One 3 oz. graduated cup

Stir stick

One pair latex gloves

One acid brush

Plastic sheet, to protect work surface

Six 100-grit longboard paper strips, for shaping and smoothing the seat frame; this much paper was used because the longboard was used extensively as a substitute for a router in rounding over frame corners

Two 120-grit disks for DA sander and hand sanding pad

Two 220-grit disks for hand sanding pad

Two brass wood screws, #10 x 1-1/2 in., for installing seat

Seat Risers

Two cedar blocks, 1 in. wide x 1-1/2 in. high x 19 in. long

3/4 oz. Clear Coat resin, for sealing the wood

3/4 oz. regular System Three epoxy resin, for bonding risers to the hull

Wood flour and colloidal silica fillers, for thickening the epoxy resin

One 3 oz. graduated cup

One pair latex gloves

Stir stick

Masking tape, for controlling spread of epoxy around bases of seat risers

Finishing

1-1/2 qt. marine gloss varnish

1 pt. mineral spirits/paint thinner

Four to six plastic cups, for straining varnish into

Twelve paint strainers

Four stir sticks

6 ft. of cheese cloth, used in 1 ft. pieces

Two rolls masking tape

Six foam Poly-Brushes, 3 in. wide, for hull

Six foam Poly-Brushes, 1 in. wide, for seat frame, thwart, gunwales, decks, and coamings

Three 180-grit longboard paper strips, for finish sanding epoxy hull surface

Eight 220-grit disks, for finish sanding epoxy and between coats of varnish

One Scotch-Brite pad, for cleaning residues off the hull and raising tooth on smooth spots, so varnish will stick

400-grit wet-or-dry sandpaper, for sanding between coats of varnish on exterior of hull; 1-1/2 sheets used each time the hull was sanded

One container of sanding lubricant, such as Behlen's Wool Lube™

Chapter Four

Choosing Plans

The first order of business in choosing plans is to determine what kind of canoe you need. As with other vehicles, there are tradeoffs in hull design features and resulting performance. As a boat is designed with more specialized features that suit it to a particular use, it becomes correspondingly less suited for other activities that demand the opposite design features. Two extremes in canoe design are flat water racing canoes and solo whitewater "playboats." The flat water racing canoe is long and narrow, with a flat keel line, and not very deep. On the other hand, the whitewater canoe is shorter, wider (relative to the length of the boat), and deeper, with blunt, upswept ends. To try to switch the roles of these two canoes would invite frustration at the least, if not serious trouble.

Appropriate questions to ask in your search for a suitable set of plans would be:

1. How many paddlers will usually be in the canoe at a given time?
2. What is/are the paddlers' skill level? (And what level would the paddler like to attain?)
3. How much other cargo is likely to be aboard?
4. Will the canoe be used mostly on ponds, large lakes, or rivers? If on rivers, what is the highest difficulty class rating expected to be navigated?
5. How heavy a canoe can the paddler(s) comfortably carry?
6. Are windy conditions and rough water likely to occur during use?
7. How fast do you want to be able to go on flat water?
8. How important is maneuverability?
9. What is your personal taste in hull shape; what is visually pleasing to you?

Canoe hulls can be long or short; wide or narrow; deep or shallow; flat-bottomed, V-bottomed, or round-bottomed; with a flat keel line or with rocker; with high or low-profile stems; with plumb stems or recurved stems; with or without keels; with outward, vertical, or inward-curving sides; decked or not; and so forth. All of these variables influence some aspect of performance of the boat, so you need to determine how you want the boat to perform and select a plan that incorporates the features you need to get that performance. This is a topic that is widely discussed in boat-building and canoeing literature. If you are not already familiar with the concepts of hull design, some research at this point will help you choose a plan that will yield a canoe suitable to your needs.[1]

Notice that the last question on the list addresses aesthetics. As logical beings, we are likely to announce for the public record that this question is barely relevant; that choice of hull shape should be based on intended function, not appearance. We might as well admit that at least one of the reasons we are attracted to strip canoes is their physical beauty, so why feel guilty about taking our tastes into account? If you aren't a professional boat builder, you will not be motivated to finish a canoe that you dislike because you think it's ugly. Just be aware that the features you like will affect the way the canoe handles one way or another, and prepare to live with it if you sacrifice practicality for looks. I've never heard of a builder being accused of being superficial based on his or her choice of designs. (Of course, the builders I know are able to extol the virtues of their favorite design based entirely on the perfect relationship between form and function, to demonstrate that any other rational person would certainly have arrived at the same choice!)

Once you have established the size and shape of the canoe you want to build, it is time to shop for plans.

General example of a study plan.

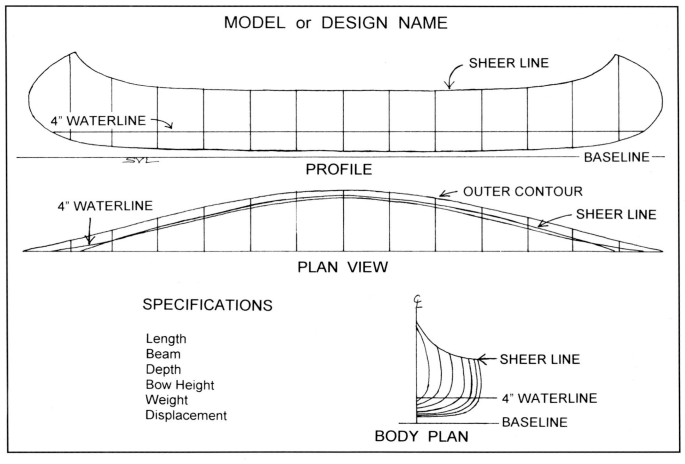

Plans are available from a variety of sources. Some authors provide full-size or reduced-scale plans for canoes in their books.[2] Other authors show study plans for various canoes in their books, and sell the detailed plans separately.[3] The purpose of the study plans is to show enough pertinent information about the hull shape to permit the potential builder to make a decision as to whether this is the boat he or she wants to build. Study plans show a profile of the boat from the side, a view looking down at the top (called the plan view), the shape of the hull at the waterline, and sometimes end-on views (called the body plan) of the boat. An illustration of the body plan is standard for sailboats and power boats, but not always for canoes.

The vertical lines marked off on the profile and plan view are at specific, uniform intervals, which would be identified on the study plan. The body plan shows those same lines, but compressed together as if they were drawn on the outside of the boat and then viewed from the end of the canoe. The 4 in. waterline is drawn on the plans because that is how deeply a canoe settles in the water with an "average" (not maximum) load. The shape of the hull at the 4 in. waterline is of interest because hydrodynamics there will have a significant impact on how well the canoe tracks, turns, and glides through the water. The length is the total distance from extreme end to end. The beam is the width of the craft, and may be measured at the widest point and/or at the gunwales. The depth is measured in the middle of the canoe where the sheer dips the lowest. At that point, depth is from the sheer line down to the keel line. The bow height is the difference between the highest point of the stem and the keel line at its lowest point. The estimated weight of the boat is often offered, but keep in mind that the weight depends on the materials (and how much of them) the builder uses. The displacement is sometimes given as a measure of weight carrying capacity. The maximum safe load is generally accepted to be the amount of weight it takes to make the canoe settle in the water to where there are 6 inches of clearance (freeboard) between the gunwales and the water surface. The displacement is the weight of the water displaced by a canoe so loaded, and corresponds to the weight of the canoe plus its load. Maximum load capacity is also sometimes simply given in pounds, not including the weight of the canoe. Other specifications are often listed in the study plans; these are among the most commonly given.

A number of independent designers and builders advertise and sell their own plans, or sell plans through a distributor who does the advertising. Some of these people will draw up custom plans. A reliable place to find ads is in magazines that cater to builders such as *WoodenBoat*, *Boatbuilder*, and *Messing About in Boats*. (These magazines also have ads for materials and hardware you may have trouble finding locally.) Some magazines geared toward the sport of canoeing also have advertisements for plans, although the bulk of advertising in these publications is directed to people who want to buy and use the equipment, not build it. Designers will send study plans and sometimes color photos of their boats if you contact them requesting information. There is often a small charge to offset the cost of printing and mailing the materials. People and businesses are known to move on occasion, so for up-to-date addresses, look in periodicals of recent issue.[4]

Another source of "plans" is to lift the lines off an existing canoe that you especially like. Sometimes manufacturers cease to produce older models of canoes in favor of newer designs, so unless you build your own, it may be nigh impossible to come up with a copy of that old design. Or maybe your friend has a nifty canoe made of Kevlar® that you think paddles like a dream, but you feel it would look much better made of cedar strips, so you set out to build one. (Ironically, the prototype for that Kevlar canoe was probably made of wood strips.) The process involves carefully tracing cross-sections of the canoe, taken at regular intervals along the length of the boat, onto cardboard or light plywood. Those tracings are translated into a set of forms, which are then anchored to a strongback at the same spacing intervals as the tracings were taken from the source canoe. The boat is built in the same manner as one from any other set of plans. The tracings of the canoe cross-sections can be made from either the interior or exterior of the hull. If you think you would like to try this, I suggest reading about both methods before deciding which suits your situation best.[5]

The remaining source of plans is your active imagination. If you are a beginning canoe builder, as this book is intended for, I advise that you take advantage of existing plans rather than attempting to draw up an entirely new design. Results are often disappointing if you don't really know what you're doing. Minor modifications to existing plans are often successful, however. Changing the shape of the stems somewhat, or lengthening or shortening the canoe by a few inches (as long as you don't delete stations to accomplish it) are not particularly risky. If you want to change something more than a little, depending on what it is, you should probably be looking for a different set of plans, or perhaps contact a designer about having custom plans drawn up.

The craft chosen as a subject for the illustration of building techniques for this book was selected because I wanted a solo canoe for use on quiet waters, designed for a paddler of over 200 pounds. I have built another canoe from plans by this designer and have been pleased with that boat, so I had confidence that other designs from the same source would be equally good. The model illustrated here is called the Wee Lassie II, from Feather Canoes, Inc. Each builder must evaluate his or her own needs and desires in choosing a set of plans. I made this choice based on what I wanted in terms of performance. I leave it to the designers of plans to make recommendations as to the suitability of their craft; don't be shy about asking the questions you need to ask in order to choose the right plans for you.

Chapter Five

Building the Mold

After familiarizing yourself with the plans and instructions (if there are any), the next step in the creation of your boat is to make the mold, or jig. This is the framework that holds the strips in position until the outside of the wooden hull is locked into shape with epoxy and fiberglass.

Obviously, the mold has everything to do with the final shape of the canoe. The two critical elements of the mold that yield a specific hull shape are station (also called form) shape and station spacing. The two elements are equally important. When you look at a set of plans, you will see a series of curved outlines representing the outer edges of the stations, and somewhere there will also be notations indicating the spacing of those stations.

As indicated in the pictures, the mold itself is made up of two parts. One part is the full set of stations, which are cut out according to the patterns in the plans. The other part is the strongback. It serves to hold the stations firmly in place until it's time to remove the hull from the mold. The strongback must be straight and rigid. Since any twists or bends that develop in the mold will be transmitted right into the canoe built over it, you need to do everything you can to eliminate that possibility, and that means starting with a solid strongback.

Examples of molds. These two molds are each made up of a series of stations, which are cut out in the shape of the inside of a canoe at specified points along its length. The stations are attached to a platform called a strongback, which holds the stations firmly in position while wood strips are assembled (over the mold) into a hull. The vertical pieces that project out to the ends of the mold are the stem forms. One of the molds has stem forms set up to accommodate the use of structural pieces called inside stems, which are shown clamped to the stem forms. As strips are added to the hull, they are also glued to the inside stems, and when the hull is eventually removed from the mold, the inside stems go with the hull.

The Strongback

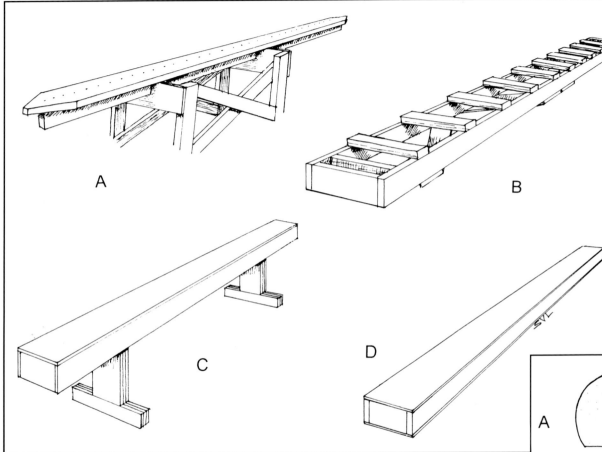

A

B

C

D

Four commonly used types of strongbacks. A. The T-beam strongback requires a purpose-built stand or modified sawhorses for support. B. The open-frame strongback can be set on ordinary sawhorses. C. The box-beam strongback rests on legs that fit up into the box from underneath, or can be placed on sawhorses. D. The closed box strongback is supported by regular sawhorses.

There are at least four types of strongbacks commonly used for building strip canoes. All of the ones illustrated work well for this purpose. The top two are generally built of solid lumber, while the bottom two are made of plywood, sometimes also including lumber.

For my own use, the closed box strongback is my favorite. It is compact, can be set on just about anything wide enough to support it, and offers a wide, flat surface on top to make marks and set things on. Also, I think it is more resistant to twisting, bending, and racking than the others. I hauled a partly stripped canoe hull on its mold, which had this type of strongback, around in the back of a pickup truck a few times with no ill effects to the canoe. By my standards, any strongback that will support an unfinished canoe hull that well under those conditions deserves top honors. (I should mention that that strongback was built of 7/8 in. nine-ply flooring grade plywood, with all joints glued as well as screwed together. I got a good deal on the plywood.) Most of the other types of strongbacks would have suffered some twisting and bending just getting them into the truck and tied down, let alone being transported at freeway speeds to another location and unloaded.

Since I feel the closed box strongback is the best, that is the one I will be making for use in constructing the canoe for this book. You can get good results with the other types of strongbacks however, and instructions for their construction are available.[1]

One of the first decisions you will have to make will be what size to make the strongback. The length of the strongback needed for a certain length canoe can vary some-

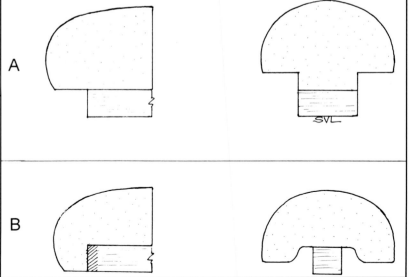

A

B

Stem form (side view) and station form (oriented crosswise of hull). A. Form and station mounted on top of the strongback. B. Form and station with the strongback recessed into the underside. The shaded part represents a beveled-off corner on a box-beam strongback.

what, and how the stations fit to the strongback can be a determining factor. There are a couple of ways the stations and strongback can go together.

One is for the stations to stand above the strongback, so the hull (when built) ends up completely above the strongback. In this case, the strongback *can* be about any length (longer or shorter than the canoe), as long as it's not more than about a foot shorter than the overall length of the canoe. (You don't want the strongback to be so short that the stem forms, which extend lengthwise of the strongback, are poorly supported, allowing them to wobble.) An optimum length for the strongback is somewhat shorter than the canoe (usually 6 in. at each end), rather than the same length or longer. Working near the ends of a canoe, I find that I occasionally need to get my tools or fingers up under the lower edge of the strips, and having the strongback in the way makes that more difficult. Using a strongback longer than the canoe also complicates working at the extreme ends of the boat. The advantage of variable size is raised to show that a separate strongback does not have to be purpose-built for this and all other models of canoes you decide to build. You could use a strongback of intermediate length to build a number of canoes of differing lengths.

The second way for the stations and strongback to fit together is for the strongback to be recessed up into the lower edges of the stations, so that the hull is built with the strongback up inside the boat. In that case, the strongback *must* be shorter than the boat. Also, the strongback might need to have tapered ends like the T-beam version illustrated earlier. (You would need to check to see that the corners of the strongback didn't hold the strips out away from the stations during assembly of the hull.) The actual length of the strongback is more critical in this case because the stem forms fit down snugly over the ends of the strongback. When the stem forms rest on top of the strongback, they can easily be adjusted fore and aft until the length is right, but when they fit down over the ends of the strongback, it's a little less convenient to make those adjustments, and still make sure the stem forms are well supported.[2]

The main drawback to having the strongback recessed up into the mold in this way is that if a time comes that you have to unfasten the stations from the strongback to get the hull off the mold, the attachments between station and strongback may be hard to get at and impossible to see. If the boat you build has plumb stems and vertical sides, that should not be a problem. The hull should slip right off the mold. Many of the classic designs have recurved stems and tumblehome in the sides, though, and the individual stations will have to be disconnected from the strongback in order to twist them out of the hull. Dealing with inaccessible fasteners is a challenge I prefer not to take on, and so I have avoided setting up my molds this way. This situation could be remedied by fastening the cleats holding the stations to the strongback with carriage bolts and wing nuts. If you receive plans that show the strongback recessed into the stations, and you don't want to do it that way, it is a simple matter to alter the patterns so that the hull will be constructed above the strongback rather than around it. (Jump ahead to the section on stations and stem forms for instructions.)

Returning to the subject of strongback dimensions, strongback width is also variable. The main consideration is that the bearing surfaces between the strongback and stations be wide enough to prevent the stations from tipping or turning during the construction of the hull. A secondary factor is the stability of the whole mold: if the strongback is simply set on sawhorses for support, you don't want the whole works to tip over sideways. Using a closed-box strongback for a small solo canoe, a 10 in. wide strongback is adequate. For a 14 to 16 ft. canoe, a 12 in. wide strongback would probably be better, and for a longer canoe you might want to bump up to a 14 in. wide strongback. These guidelines are very general, and you can suit yourself to a large degree. You could no doubt build an 18 ft. canoe on a 10 in. wide strongback, but you would probably need to clamp the strongback to the sawhorses to keep the thing from tipping during some sanding operations, when you lean into the work.

Closed Box Strongback Construction

Pull out the plans for your canoe and figure out how long the mold (not just the strongback) is actually going to be. To do this, add all the spaces between stations together, plus the length of the two stem forms which extend out to the ends of the canoe. The thickness of the material you cut the stations out of is not added in. The spacing indicated in the plans is actually between planes, whose locations will be marked by the stations. That way stations can be cut out of stock that is anywhere from 1/2 in. thick to 1 in. thick, so you can use what you like and not have to refigure the station spacing. Some designers intend for their stem forms to stand completely apart from the other stations, while others have the stem forms attached to the last crosswise station in a "T" configuration (looking down on it).

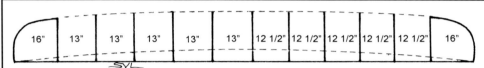

Figuring the length of the mold. These are the station spacings for the boat I am building, plus the length of the stem forms. The sum is 159-1/2 inches.

Now that you know the length of the mold you can make an informed choice on the size of the strongback you need. It is easier to work on the ends of the canoe if the stem forms extend out past the ends of the strongback. Ordinarily, for a boat this short, I would make the strongback a foot less than the length of the mold (so the stem forms extend 6 in. out at either end). However, I would like to use this strongback to build a 14 ft. boat sometime, so I decided to compromise and make the strongback 13 ft. long (156 in.), which is only 3-1/2 in. shorter than this mold will be, when it's assembled. Since the mold I'm building is for a fairly small boat, the width of the strongback will be adequate at 10 in.

The simplest way to build this strongback is to make the top and bottom pieces of plywood and use 1 x 4 lumber for the sides, ends, and interior bracing. You could use plywood for all the pieces, if you have a way to make your cuts really straight.[3] The plywood needs to be at least 1/2 in. thick (the more stout, the better) A/ C plywood. Assemble the pieces so the "A" quality side is outside, and you will have a nice smooth surface to make all your pencil markings on. The 1 x 4 lumber should be dry and straight. If you buy the "pond-dried" kind, it will cost less (by quite a bit, probably), but be-

Plywood with cutting lines marked out for the top and bottom of strongback. (See illustration for detail.) Remember to allow for the saw kerf so all the pieces turn out the same width. All the lengthwise cuts were made on a table saw, with assistance from a helper. The crosswise cut was made with a saber saw. If you have to do this by yourself, you would be better off using a hand-held circular saw for all the cutting.

ware; it may assume some un-desirable shape in the process of drying out. I have experimented with wet lumber for this and the wood wanted to twist as it dried, even though it had screws along both edges, supposedly holding it in place.

Cutting lines on ply-wood. (Not to scale)

Clamp the matching plywood pieces together, so you can drill holes through both at the same time. Mark a line 3/8 in. (half the thick-ness of the 1 x 4 side pieces) in from the edge of the plywood by locking the rule on the combination square to that mark and then sliding it along the edge of the plywood, holding a pencil against the end of the rule to mark the plywood as shown. Then mark off screw hole locations along the lines at about 8 in. intervals. I use screws to put the strongback together because they hold better than nails and I don't knock things out of position when driving screws. Note the 16 ft. 1 x 4s to the left, to be cut into sections for the strongback sides, ends, and bracing.

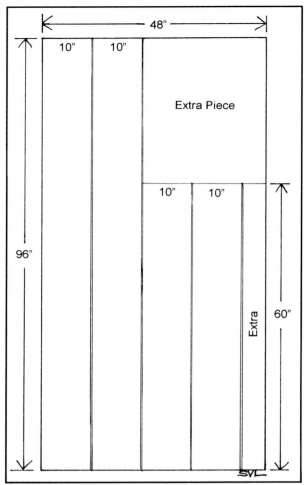

Screw the sides of the strongback to the ends. Cut the 1 x 4s to length for the sides, and then cut pieces for the ends and interior cross bracing. (Cut enough bracing pieces to have one every two or three feet inside the strongback.) Clamp the side pieces to the end piece so the corners are square, and drive one long drywall screw into each side. I use a drill with a screwdriver tip for this and nearly all operations calling for screws. There is no need to pre-drill the holes in these 1 x 4 pieces as the wood is soft and will not split. (You may want to evaluate your lumber for "split-ability" and drill holes if you need to.) Be careful not to "over-drive" the screws; it's easy to strip the screw holes in softwood lumber. Put both ends of the box together, but leave the bracing pieces for later.

Fasten the top (or bottom) of the strongback to the sides. With all the corners squared up where the sides and ends meet, lay the plywood pieces on top of the box and clamp them in place. Drive the shorter drywall screws into the holes along the edges of the plywood. If you accidentally strip one of the holes, substitute a longer screw. Note that the top of the strongback is of two pieces of plywood. Either before or after (I did it after) attaching the top pieces to the sides, join the two plywood pieces together (matching the factory-cut ends, if your cuts weren't as straight) by screwing them to a piece of scrap wood overlapping the joint underneath. (See next photo.)

The strongback is ready for closing up. The bracing inside the box is in place, and the scrap wood joining the two pieces of plywood on the strongback top is visible next to one of the 1 x 4 braces. The braces are fastened with one screw at each end, in the strongback sides. (More screws will be added later.) The main thing at this point is to get the bracing in so that it is exactly perpendicular to the 1 x 4 sides and the one plywood side, and located so that it doesn't interfere with the scrap wood blocks at the plywood joints. The joints in the plywood are staggered so that they won't lie in the same place on the top and bottom of the strongback.

Mark the location of the inside bracing. Using the combination square as shown, mark a line through the centers of the screws to the edges of the plywood.

Establish the centerline. All of the stations and stem forms will be located relative to the centerline, so it has to be straight! Chalklines are not foolproof, so instead I've driven a nail in the middle of each end of the top of the strongback and stretched a string in between.

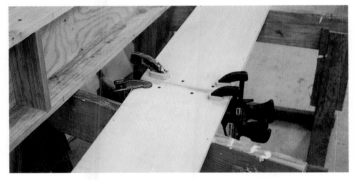

To join the factory cut ends of the plywood pieces for the bottom of the strongback, clamp a scrap wood piece (cut the right length to fit inside the strongback!) to the underside of the plywood joint. Drill through the plywood first, then drive drywall screws through the plywood into the block underneath. Fit the bottom onto the strongback, and fasten in place.

Anchor the plywood faces to the cross bracing. Using a straightedge, draw a line across the top (and bottom) of the strongback connecting the markings on the sides of the strongback. If you were successful in fitting the bracing in square with everything, the lines now drawn on the plywood should go right down the middle of the 1 x 4 pieces inside. Drill holes through the plywood and drive drywall screws into the bracing. Do the same thing at the ends of the strongback.

Use a fine pointed pencil to carefully mark the location of the string at frequent intervals. Then lay a long straightedge along the markings and draw a dark line to connect them. An alternative method is to slide the string down the nails until the string touches the strongback, and then spray paint a line along the string, straight down on it. Then when you remove the string, an unpainted line will be left.

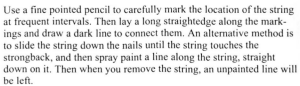

Stations and Stem Forms

Like the strongback, the stations and stem forms are reusable. The local scout troop could build a whole fleet of identical canoes from the same mold, or you could even trade it to another builder when you're done with it. For the mold to have value, though, you have to be able to build a decent canoe over it, and to be able to build a decent canoe on it, you must have applied a little attention toward making nice station forms. Besides, you want your first canoe to be a winner, right? This is one of the parts of this project that it's really important to do to the best of your ability. Shortcuts here will probably cause you grief later. Fortunately, making the mold is not difficult. But it will require some time.

The stations and stem forms can be cut out of plywood, particle board, or even pieces of solid lumber. Plywood or particle board would be preferable for ease of handling and better dimensional stability (less likelihood of warping and so forth), and lower cost as well, unless you have the lumber lying around already. Plywood is lighter weight than particle board of the same thickness. However, particle board has a more uniform structure, making it somewhat easier to cut rounded shapes out of. You can take your pick. If you decide to go with particle board, the kind made of hardwood is a better choice than the softwood type, *especially* if you plan to staple strips to the stations. Softwood particle board will not hold these fasteners. The mold needs to be sturdy, so make the stations and stem forms out of 1/2 in. to 3/4 in. material.

Examples of clamping cleats. One of the molds has cleats cut out of scrap 1/4 in. plywood. The other has cleats made from short pieces of wood about 1 in. wide. As it turned out, the 1/4 in. wide material provided all the gripping surface needed. There is no real benefit to making the clamping cleats deeper than that, and deeper cleats require more beveling along their corners to keep them from interfering with the lay of the strips.

A factor to consider in your choice of station material thickness is how you plan to hold the strips in place while the glue between strips dries. You can either staple the strips to the edges of the forms, or you can clamp them. If you staple the strips, the hull construction will be easier and go faster, but it does leave rows of tiny holes in the hull, which are visible in the finished product (if you put a clear finish on the canoe). Of course, if you plan to paint the canoe, this is of no consequence. If you clamp the strips in place, it is more work to put the clamps on, and the building process will go slower because you'll have to wait until the glue dries before you can remove the clamps and put the next strip on, but you can end up with a flawless hull. To clamp the strips to the stations, you have to have something on the stations to hook the clamps to. In stapling the strips to the mold, the staples go right into the edges of the stations, so nothing extra is required, and 1/2 in. material will serve nicely.

If your choice is to clamp the strips on, you have two options for providing suitable gripping places for clamps. You can add clamping cleats onto the stations, in which case you can use 1/2 in. material to make the stations out of. Clamping cleats are fashioned of some handy pieces of scrap wood and are fastened onto one face of each station, along the edges.

The other option is to rout a 1/4 in. deep by 3/8 in. wide groove along a line drawn 1-1/4 in. in from the station edge so a lip is left for clamps to grip.[4]

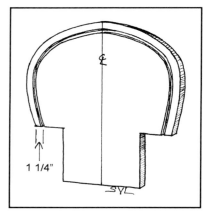

Station with a groove routed into one face to provide a purchase for clamps.

In this case, you would need at least 5/8 in. thick stock to cut the stations out of, so the routed groove doesn't compromise the strength of the outer edges of the stations.

An item that affects the amount of material required for forms is how the inside of the stems of the canoe are constructed, as far fetched as that may seem. The two alternatives are either with, or without a curved wood stem piece incorporated into the ends of the canoe during the stripping of the hull.

With an inside stem, the strips at the extreme ends of the hull are supported by, and glued to, a structural member that stays with the canoe when it is removed from the mold. In this situation, the stem forms are cut from a single thickness of plywood or particle board.

The inside stem is clamped to the stem form while the hull is assembled over the mold.

Without an inside stem piece, the strips at the ends of the canoe rest directly against the stem forms, as they rest against the station forms everywhere else on the mold. Strips from the two sides of the canoe come together at a very tight angle at the stems, and the stem forms need to be thick enough to permit beveling of the edges in order to provide sufficient support for the strips. That means making the stem forms of a double thickness of plywood or particle board, so the stem forms require twice as much material as when going the alternate route using an inner stem piece.

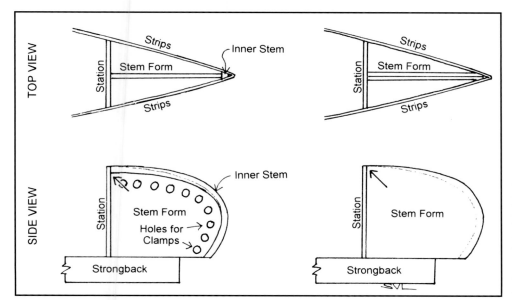

TOP VIEW — Strips, Station, Stem Form, Inner Stem, Strips / Strips, Station, Stem Form, Strips

SIDE VIEW — Station, Inner Stem, Stem Form, Holes for Clamps, Strongback / Station, Stem Form, Strongback, SWL

Comparison of molds with and without an inside stem. Left: Mold with inner stem piece. Right: Mold without inner stem. These two examples show molds that have a station attached to the inboard end of the stem form. Note that in the example on the left, the station stands higher than the stem form. The difference in height is to allow for the thickness of the inner stem, which serves as part of the stem form until it's time to take the canoe off the mold. In the example on the right, the top of the stem form and the adjacent station are flush with each other.

Someplace in the plans you have acquired there should be an indication of how the ends of the canoe are to be put together. If the plans call for inside stems, it will also specify how thick these pieces need to be. Instructions on how to make them follow later in this chapter.

It is natural to wonder why there are two different ways of constructing the stems of a strip canoe, and which is best. The use of the inner stem goes back to the days before fiberglass and modern adhesives, when wooden boats had to have stems as part of the framework holding the craft in shape and to provide surfaces for fastening the planking to. In modern wood strip canoes, the fiberglass/epoxy sheath holds the strips in place, but the inside stem still renders necessary support and lends a traditional touch that is often associated with good craftsmanship. How, then, are some builders able to get away without using built-in stems? The answer is that once the "stem-less" hull is off the mold, a structural putty is forced into the joint previously occupied by the stem form. This material cures hard and is quite permanently bonded to the strips. The joint is finished off by placing a strip of fiberglass cloth over it and epoxying it in place, so that the cloth bridges the filled joint that now forms the "inside stem," and laps an inch or more onto the sides of the hull on either side of the putty filler. This results in a composite "stem" that offers excellent support for the ends of the canoe.

Which is best? In terms of strength, at this point I am not really convinced that one is better than the other. Both methods are good. I have tried both and each was satisfactory. Other builders and I have subjected our canoes built without wooden stems to rigorous use (or punishment) that might have been expected to cause the ends of a canoe to split or cave in, but that hasn't occurred except in the worst cases, usually where other parts of the canoe failed first. I haven't "abuse-tested" a canoe built with wooden stems in this way, but there is no reason to think they wouldn't hold up as well.

The main questions influencing your choice are, is your preference to work with wood, or epoxy putty; do you intend to build the hull without using staples or nails; and do you want the canoe to have a traditional look? Laminating up wood stems prior to hull construction represents adding another step at the front end of the project, just when you may be getting impatient to start gluing strips together in a boat shape. On the other hand, some people much prefer to work with wood rather than epoxy, especially those who have little experience with epoxy. Joints filled with a structural putty can look very good, however, and instructions for making a strong, nicely finished joint are in a later chapter of this book. If speed of construction is a consideration for you, then filling the stem joints with epoxy putty is the way to go, because it takes less time to do that than to build wooden inside stem pieces.

One definite advantage a wooden stem offers is more gluing surface at the ends of the boat where strips from both sides come together (under considerable stress in places). If you are inclined to do this project without relying on staples or nails to hold the strips in place, your chances of success are much better if you have lots of glue surface at the stems. And without a doubt, wood stems look good. Some builders will want to put bulkheads in the ends of their boats for additional hull strength and flotation, or dry storage space, or all of the foregoing. In that case, no one will know what the stems look like, because they will be hidden by the bulkheads, so visual effect is not an issue.

Both ways of doing the stems will be presented in this book. If you look at your plans and find that the plans call for one method and you really want to do it the other way, just add or subtract the thickness of the inside stem from the outside edge of the stem forms to get what you want. If the plans specify that an inner stem is to be used, look for the note saying how thick the stem is to be made, and that is how much you will add to the outer edge of the stem form if you'd rather not make a wooden stem. If your plans don't call for an inner stem, but you want that feature, you will have to figure out how thick to make the stem and subtract that thickness from the outer edge of the stem form. See the section in this chapter on making the stem pieces for more details.

Other modifications may be in order if you don't like the way the stations are supposed to fit to the strongback. If the plans for the canoe you have decided to build indicate a mold that has the strongback set up into the forms, and you prefer to build the hull above the strongback rather than around it, you need to convert the station patterns to suit your preferences. It is a simple operation, as shown in the following illustration.

Raising the forms. On the stem form pattern (left), measure the pattern as it is printed to find out what "y" is. Extend a line down from the straight end of the pattern by distance "y." Extend the lower edge of the form to meet the new line just drawn. On the other station patterns (right), extend the centerline of the pattern down by distance "y," and use a square lined up with the centerline to draw a new base for the pattern that is exactly perpendicular to the centerline. The width of the new pattern base is not critical but should be at least as wide as the top of the strongback.

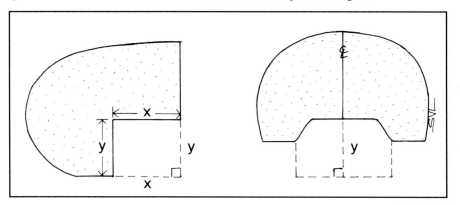

Cutting Out Stations and Stem Forms

The amount of plywood or particle board needed for stations varies with the size of the canoe to be built; or more specifically, the size of the stations and how many of them there are. For a very small canoe (10 to 12 ft.) all the stations can usually be cut out of a single 4 x 8 ft. sheet of material. Stations for larger canoes will require some or all of another sheet.

Tracing the shapes onto the stock material and cutting them out is easier if you cut the material into sections first. Measure the height of the tallest station (the one in the middle of the boat-to-be) and use that as a guide in determining the minimum width of the sections you cut. The stations will be laid out in a row on each section of plywood (or whatever you're using). It is worth your while to figure out if you get the best utilization of the sheet material by cutting it into sections lengthwise, or crosswise. Measure the widths of the station patterns and play with different arrangements on paper to see if you can get more pieces cut out of a sheet with the patterns laid out one way rather than the other.

Items used for transferring station outlines from plans to plywood. There are lots of ways to accomplish this task; the way shown here is simple, expedient, and keeps the sheet of plans intact. The drywall square is especially handy for this job, but a smaller square and a long straightedge could be substituted. The brown-handled tool is a tracing wheel, obtainable at sewing shops. The pencil has soft (6B) lead for making dark lines. The plywood is 15/32 in. thick. I wanted 1/2 in. plywood but it wasn't available.

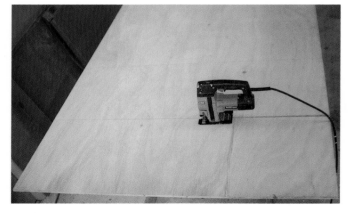

Cut the plywood into sections. The tallest station will be just under 17 in. high, so the plywood is marked for cutting into 17 in. wide sections. The saber saw being used here is outfitted with a plywood cutting blade having 6 teeth per inch.

Prepare to trace the largest station pattern onto the plywood. To ensure that you don't end up with a shortage of plywood for the larger stations, trace them first. The smaller stations can be fit around the larger ones. When you determine where this station will be placed on the plywood, make a mark on the plywood where the centerline should be. Then, using a square, draw a dark vertical line representing the centerline there on the plywood. Fold the plans

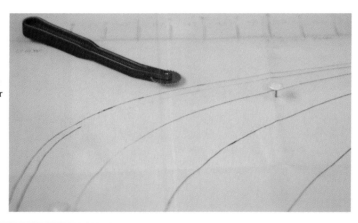

exactly on the centerline, and line up the centerline of the plans with the centerline on the plywood. The pencil in the photo points to the centerline fold in the plans, placed over the centerline drawn on the plywood. Then adjust the plans up or down so that the base of the station rests right on the lower edge of the plywood. Tack the pattern in place.

Slip a piece of carbon paper under the plans and then run the tracing wheel along the outline for that particular station. The tracing wheel leaves a line of carbon dots on the plywood.

To trace the opposite half of the station, turn the plans so the printed side faces down on the plywood, line up the centerline fold with the centerline on the plywood, match the base of the station in the plans to the lower edge of the plywood, and tack in place as before. When you traced the first half of the station, the tracing wheel left a line of tiny perforations along the outline of the station, so now all you need to do is slip the carbon paper under the plans and re-trace the same outline with the tracing wheel. For this photo, the outline of the first half of the station has been drawn with a dark pencil over the carbon dot line on the plywood.

With a dark pencil or other marker, go over the carbon tracings so you will be able to easily follow them with a saber saw. Label the station with its number, and it's a good idea to note the name of the design, too.

To get all stations laid out on plywood, look over your plans carefully to determine how many of each form you need. Some designers number their stations starting at one end of the boat and going to the other, so you need only one of each station. In other instances, the middle station will be numbered either "1" or "0", with the remaining stations numbered sequentially fore and aft of the middle, so you need two of each of the other stations. There are other station-numbering schemes, too. Sometimes the bow and stern stem forms aren't exactly the same, so check that also.

Make as smooth a cut as possible on the outside edge of the station outline you've drawn. It's better to cut the station out a little "fat" than to wander inside the line. For this operation, a smooth scroll cutting blade with 10 teeth per inch is recommended.

A longboard with 100-grit paper is ideal for smoothing up irregularities in the edges of the stations. Avoid sanding away the station outline markings. The DA sander to the right, with 80-grit paper, is only used for the worst places. It is very easy to create additional problems with the DA sander here, so pay attention to which direction the disk is turning where it actually contacts the wood and use it sparingly.

Since I want to build this boat without using staples or nails through the strips, I need to put clamping cleats on the stations. These could have been made from 1/4 in. material, but 15/32 in. plywood is what's handy so that's what I'm using. (Actually, I found it easier to cut these narrow pieces from 15/32 in. plywood.) As done here, the station is placed on the plywood, a dark pencil line traced around the outer edge of the station, and then a compass set to 1/2 in. width used to mark the inner edge of the cleat. The number of the station is noted on each piece, at or near the centerline. Most of the cleats are made in two halves due to limited material. If you have elected to use thicker station stock and rout a groove in one face of each station for hooking clamps into, now is the time to the routing. It is best to rout the groove into the side of the station having the centerline on it. The reason for this will be apparent later.

Cut the cleats out, and glue them to the appropriate stations. Attach the cleats to the side of the station that has the centerline marked on it. The carpenter's wood glue used here probably would have been sufficient to hold the cleats in place during hull construction; the small staples were driven in as a convenience for holding the cleats in position while the glue dries. If the mold you are building has the first crosswise stations at the ends of the mold attached to the stem forms, leave a gap at the centerline for the stem forms (and inside stems, if you'll be using them) between the clamping cleats. Jump ahead ten photos for an illustration of this.

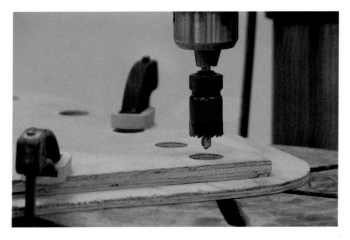

If you will be making laminated wood stems in the construction of your canoe, you need to make holes to hook clamps into. Use a compass or some other means to mark a line 1-1/2 to 2 inches in from the curved edge of the stem form. Then make marks at about 4 inch intervals along this line for the centers of the holes. The holes can be anywhere from 7/8 to 2 in. in diameter, and should be sized to suit the C-clamps you will be using. I used a 7/8 in. hole saw chucked into a drill press for this, but the job can be accomplished using a hand-held drill. If both of the stem forms for your mold are identical, you may be able to save time by clamping them together and cutting holes in both at the same time. Smoothing up the edges of the holes with sandpaper will spare you slivers in fingers later.

If you have elected to build your boat without laminated wooden stems inside, then your double-thickness stem forms should be glued together now. Regular wood glue plus a few screws or nails will do; just remember not to drive any hardware in near the curved edges, which will be beveled soon.

Mounting Stations on the Strongback

This is the part of mold building that revs up your enthusiasm for the rest of the project. With the mold all together as a unit, you can really begin to visualize your boat, *built,* by sighting down the mold and mentally filling the spaces between stations. Few things sharpen anticipation more than the sight of the mold, ready to hang strips on!

The first order of business is to mark the locations of the stations on the strongback. I like to start in the center and work toward the ends. When I start at the ends and go towards the center, one

Mark a line across the middle of the strongback to serve as a reference point for the rest of the station locations.

of Murphy's laws always comes into play, and adjustments have to be made. So, find the middle of the strongback and draw a pencil line at that location, perpendicular to the centerline.

If your canoe is to be symmetrical (bow and stern halves identical), then the line you have just drawn is where the station in the middle of the canoe will be placed. Measure fore and aft along the centerline, marking locations of the other stations according to the spacing in the plans. Remember, at this point station thickness need not be considered; just mark the strongback according to the prescribed spacing.

If your canoe is to be asymmetrical (long and narrow in the bow, blunter in the stern), then the widest station will be aft of the middle of the boat. That means you will *not* be placing that station in the middle of the strongback; it will be offset from the middle by a few inches. Look over the station spacing in the plans and figure out where that station needs to be and mark it on the strongback. Then go ahead and mark the other station locations referenced from the widest one. (Don't get the bow end station spacing mixed up with the stern; they may be different!)

There are different ways of mounting the stations on the strongback, which all work. The way I do it is presented here, with some alternatives offered in a later section for your consideration. You can make up your own mind. The convention I follow is to place my stations so that they are centered over the locations marked on the strongback, which completely obscures those markings. That makes it necessary to mark lines on the strongback where one face of each plywood station will lie, to line the stations up with.

Station locations marked on strongback. The lines going all the way across the strongback are on the spacing intervals indicated in the plans. The shorter lines parallel to these are half the thickness of the station plywood away, and will be used for lining the faces of the stations up with. I drew these lines on the side opposite of where the cross cleats will be attached, so the cross cleats won't obscure the lines.

The widest station, in the middle of the mold, clamped to a cross cleat and positioned so this face lines up with the appropriate marking on the strongback.

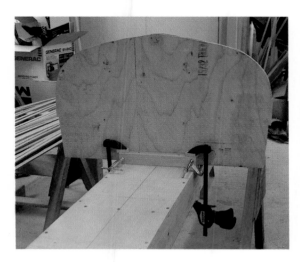

The widest station, clamped to a cross cleat and the strongback as in previous photo, viewed from the back. Check the cross cleat with a combination square to make sure that the sides that will be against the station and strongback are perpendicular to each other. The cross cleats are made of some dry fir 2 x 4s, cut down to 1-1/2 in. square.

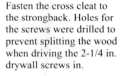

Fasten the cross cleat to the strongback. Holes for the screws were drilled to prevent splitting the wood when driving the 2-1/4 in. drywall screws in.

Square up the centerlines before attaching the station to the cross cleat.

Fasten the station to the cross cleat with 1-1/4 in. dry wall screws. Drill holes for the screws first.

Repeat this operation with the other stations, working toward the ends from the middle. This way it is easy to see the centerlines without having other stations obstructing the view, and without the cross cleats covering the point where the centerlines of the strongback and stations intersect. That's also why I have the stations set up with the sanded sides bearing the centerlines facing the ends of the mold, and the cross cleats on the unsanded, unmarked sides of the stations.

In order to locate cross cleat pieces for the last crosswise station, it would seem more sensible to simply run screws through the centerline of the crosswise station into the inboard edge of the stem form and then screw them both down, but that plan has not worked for me. I find it best to deal with the two pieces independently and then attach them to each other. Notice that Station 6 is being put on backwards of the way the other stations were mounted, except that the clamping cleats along the edges are still on the side toward the nearest end of the canoe. I did this so I could line up the combination square with the centerline of the station and strongback without the stem form being in the way. If your station corresponding to this one has the centerline and clamping cleats on the same side (the same way you made all the others), you can mount it on the strongback the same way you did the rest of them. The key items here are that the clamping cleats on the station be toward the stem, and that the centerline on the strongback be visible where it meets the centerline on the station. Since I mounted this station on the strongback independently of, and before the stem form, it ultimately didn't matter whether the stem form would have hidden the centerline on the station or not.

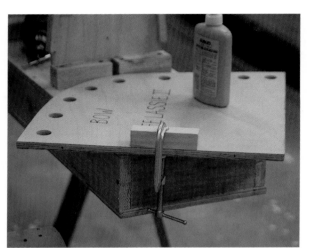

Glue a cleat onto the aft edge of the bow stem form. It needs to be square and lined up evenly with the edge of the form. This cleat will be used in fastening the stem form to Station 6. Gluing keeps the parts from scooting around while I'm trying to screw the pieces together. (See next photo.)

Screw the lengthwise cleat to the strongback.

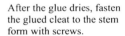

After the glue dries, fasten the glued cleat to the stem form with screws.

The stem form is snugged up to Station 6 in preparation for fastening to the lengthwise cleat on the strongback. The black strap is a piece of nylon webbing with an adjustable plastic buckle clip.

Locate a lengthwise cleat for the stem form. The vertical cleat (which was just glued and screwed to the stem form) is not attached to Station 6 yet. At this point I am only concerned with lining up the stem form with the centerline on the strongback.

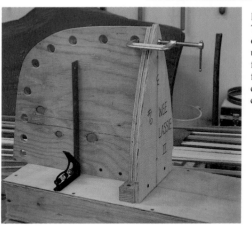

Prepare to fasten the stem form to Station 6. The stem form has been screwed to the cleat on the strongback. The last variable to bring under control is the angle at which the stem form meets the strongback. With the stem form perpendicular to the strongback and clamped in that position to Station 6, holes can be drilled for screws. (See next photo.)

Fasten stem form and Station 6 together. One screw was driven into the vertical cleat (just below the "W") and an additional screw was driven through the upper end of Station 6 into the edge of the stem form. The vacant screw holes on the centerline of Station 6 are from an earlier attempt to screw into the edge of the stem form. When the screws went into the edge of the plywood, they tended to drift due to the laminations in the plywood, forcing the stem form out of plumb. The use of the vertical cleat remedied that problem.

of the hull. Beveling can be done with hand tools or a small angle grinder if you are already proficient with it. (This is not the time to practice, if you're not.) Take care to leave the basic outline of the station intact; just remove the interfering corners.

With the clamping cleats and station edges beveled off, the batten now lies flat against the station edges. The tools used are shown here. The spokeshave and trimming plane were the most effective of the hand tools, with the larger plane, Surform rasp, and large file providing some additional benefit. The presence of the clamping cleats on my stations made this a larger job than it would have been without them, and I resorted to use of the angle grinder with a 24-grit disc to expedite the work. The wisdom of placing the clamping cleats on this side of the stations may seem questionable here. The clamping cleats are placed this way to take advantage of the fact that the clamps will naturally bend the strips around in the direction you want them to go, which is toward the ends of the mold.

If the mold you are putting together has the stem forms standing separately from the last crosswise stations, you will need to devise a way to hold the stem forms firmly in position. One option would be to make a triangular plywood brace similar to Station 6 in this photo series, but with the edges well out of the way of the path of the strips that will bridge the gap between stem form and the last actual crosswise station.

Now that you have the mold assembled, stand back and have a look at your handiwork. Seeing the three-dimensional form of the boat, full-size, always gives me a little rush at this point. This usually marks the beginning of many episodes of daydreaming about how fast the canoe will cut through the water; what wildlife I will slip up on, undetected; and what sunset skies I will observe from the middle of the lake. (At some point in the future I intend to build a river canoe; that project will be fueled by daydreams of a less tranquil nature, you can bet.)

When you are done with your musings and perhaps a good night's sleep, it is time to put the finishing touches on the mold. The refinements you make now are generally minor, but necessary. There are always little flaws that have crept in despite your best efforts, and this is the time to correct them.

First, bevel off the station edges that will dig into the wood strips. It is unnecessary and not particularly enjoyable to sand out dents that were left by the stations inside

Next, check to see that the centerlines of all the stations match up to the keel line defined by the two stem forms. You will likely discover that several small adjustments need to be made. Just remove one of the screws holding any deviant stations to their cross cleats and tip the stations so they line up with the tautline correctly. Then drill a new hole and secure the station to the cross cleat again.

A batten clamped to the mold shows sharp corners on stations. Use a scrap strip for a batten to determine how much beveling is necessary to allow the strips to rest against the stations without denting. Note that the clamping cleat on Station 5 in this picture actually holds the batten out away from the station edge, effectively altering the shape of the station. The clamping cleat must be pared down so the batten rests against the station edge.

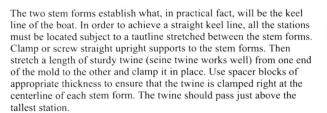

The two stem forms establish what, in practical fact, will be the keel line of the boat. In order to achieve a straight keel line, all the stations must be located subject to a tautline stretched between the stem forms. Clamp or screw straight upright supports to the stem forms. Then stretch a length of sturdy twine (seine twine works well) from one end of the mold to the other and clamp it in place. Use spacer blocks of appropriate thickness to ensure that the twine is clamped right at the centerline of each stem form. The twine should pass just above the tallest station.

Tautline setup viewed from the side.

Battens are clamped along the keel line, the sheer, and at the turn of the bilge, the same way the strips will run.

Adjusting a station to bring the centerline of the station into agreement with the tautline. After identifying a station that is out of alignment, remove one of the screws holding it to its cross cleat and tip the station until it lines up correctly. Drill a new hole and redrive the screw.

Sight down the batten at the turn of the bilge. Most canoes only have convex curves, but this one will also have concave curves, as seen in the foreground.

Now, with the edges of the stations all in good order, put tape on them. Use either masking tape or plastic packaging tape to completely cover the station edges. This will prevent the canoe hull from being bonded (perhaps permanently) to the mold later on. If you are going to make inside stem pieces for the canoe, put tape over the stem forms also, so the stems don't end up glued to the forms during the lamination process. If you will not be making stem pieces, skip the tape on the stem forms for now, because some beveling there is still required.

Tape the edges of the mold.

Now, check the mold for fairness by clamping or tacking battens onto the mold and sighting down them, looking for irregularities in the way they lie against the mold. By looking critically at the stations under a batten placed along the keel line, you may see that an entire station may need to be raised or lowered (not just one side) to give the keel line the shape it is intended to have. Before making that adjustment, check to see if that station seems to be right at the sheer and other points between the sheer and the keel line. If the station looks good every place else, then the adjustment should be made by trimming off the extra height at the top of the station or adding a thin piece of wood there to bring it up to height.

On the sides of the mold, clamp or tack the batten along the lines you expect the strips to follow. Check at least three places at even intervals between the sheer and keel line. Look carefully for flat spots and sharp, irregular curves. Reshape stations with a plane, spokeshave, rasp, or grinder to make the battens lie along the nice, smooth, curving lines you want. Be conservative, and only remove what is necessary. If you find that you have reshaped with a little too much gusto, glue a thin slice of wood onto the station edge and try again.

The canoe mold assembled, faired up, and with all the edges taped.

Alternative Ways to Mount the Stations

Methods of mounting stations on the strongback can vary in several respects. What follows are a few different possibilities you may want to entertain as you prepare to put all the pieces of the mold together.

Placement of the cross cleats in relation to the stations is a matter of the builder's preference. Some builders have all the cleats on the side of the stations toward the bow (or stern). Others maintain that the cleats must be placed on the side closest to the nearest end of the canoe. This would be opposite the way I've shown it in the photo series. I have tried a couple of different ways, and have not been able to discern any advantage in terms of the final product of one placement pattern over another. As long as the cleats serve the purpose of anchoring the stations solidly in place, the cross cleat being fore or aft of the station matters little.

Placement of the stations themselves in relation to the marked station intervals on the strongback is also subject to builder preference. Instead of placing the stations squarely on top of these lines as I have done, you can put one face of each station against the line specified in the plans for that station. In that case, always put the face that has the markings on it (including the station outline) against the line on the strongback. I suggest putting the rough side toward the nearest end of the mold. Then, when you bevel the station edge, you can do it without removing the outline drawn on the station, thus reducing the risk of altering the shape of the station by accident. Note that if you are planning to put clamping cleats or routed grooves at the edges of the stations, those should be put on the backs of the stations rather than the sanded faces (opposite of how I did it in the photo series).

Another thing that can be done differently is to combine the use of the tautline and strongback centerline to position the stations for attachment to the cross cleats the first (and only) time. First, fasten all the cross cleats to the strongback. Then, set up the two stem forms. Stretch a tautline between the stem forms. Position the stations so that the centerline on the strongback meets the centerline at the base of the stations, and the centerline at the top of the stations passes directly under the tautline. Clamp the stations in place and fasten them with screws to the cross cleats. This eliminates the need to correct the alignment of the stations later, but you have to work around more stuff initially.

Making Inside Stems

The inside stems used in the construction of strip canoes are made of thin pieces of wood glued together in layers. The strength of these laminated structural members is due only partly to the strength of the wood used. A good measure of the strength is actually from the glue joints themselves. Laminated stems retain their shape well and are less apt to be compromised by undetected defects that can affect a single, solid piece of wood stock.[5]

Species of wood vary significantly in strength, weight, gluing properties, and flexibility. These factors are to be considered in the choice of lamination stock. Some of these properties can be influenced by how the wood is handled. For example, cutting wood into thinner pieces, and treating it with steam or water will improve flexibility. I prefer to use woods that will give satisfactory performance with a minimum of fuss. (More information on the choice species appears in the Chapter 3 section on framework materials.) Sometimes these species are hard to find, however, so it is good to be familiar with techniques for coaxing uncooperative wood species into submission.

Gluing properties of the wood can be a concern. Softwoods and most hardwoods can be laminated with wood glue, but epoxy produces even stronger bonds. If you are going to use a hardwood (presumably for strength), it makes sense to glue up the laminate with epoxy. Recall that most species of oak do not bond well with epoxy. So if you want to use oak, use resorcinol glue or carpenter's glue instead.

If you would like to utilize one of the harder, stiffer wood species in making the inside stems, steaming or soaking the pieces to make them flexible may be a necessity. Such treatment will also improve the ease of bending the more flexible woods of course, and there are benefits to performing this additional step. For one thing, you can use thicker pieces of stock, which means you don't waste as much material making sawdust while you saw thin pieces in sufficient number to glue up a laminate of the thickness you need. You will use less glue if fewer laminations are needed to make the piece. Also, there is less risk of accidentally snapping one of the pieces if you bend them wet. Additionally, laminates bent into shape when wet are less prone to misbehave by springing out of shape when dry. For instructions on soaking and steaming wood for bending, please see the section on coamings in Chapter 10.[6]

Before starting on the inside stems, get out the plans again and see if the designer says how thick these pieces are to be. Or, note what the difference in height is between the stem form and the station attached to it, if they are attached. If you are altering the plans to allow for use of inside stems, plan on making the stems 3/4 in. thick for full size models (over 14 ft. long) and 1/2 in. thick for small, lightweight models (14 ft. or less).

If you plan to steam or soak the pieces before bending, you can make the individual laminate pieces up to 1/4 in. thick, so you would need three of them for a 3/4 in. thick inner stem. If you plan to bend the pieces into shape dry, use more pieces, cut thinner. The thinnest you would want to go from a practical standpoint is 1/8 in., and you will probably have to plane them to get to that size.

Regarding laminate width, 3/4 in. is fairly standard. Small, lightweight canoe models that feature sharp ends often have 5/8 in. wide stems. To find the length that individual pieces must be, measure the outer perimeter of the stem form, keeping in mind that the pieces on the far outside of the curve will need to be longer.

Stem form taped and clamps assembled for laminating inner stem piece.

Use the stem forms as jigs for bending the laminates over. If the pieces are soaked or steamed first, then bend the whole stack of laminates for one stem at the same time, and leave it clamped to the stem form until the wood pieces are all dry. Then, separate the laminates, spread thickened epoxy on the joining surfaces, and clamp the pieces back together. Scrape excess epoxy off before it hardens. The photo series shows how to bend and glue laminates without soaking or steaming the wood.

For this lightweight model canoe, the stems are being made of 1/8 in. thick by 5/8 in. wide by about 30 in. long spruce strips. The strips are being bent over the form dry. For ease of construction and better shape retention, a laminate of four thin strips (instead of three thicker ones) is being made. Spread glue (in this case wood glue) on the surfaces to be bonded, line up the ends of the strips at the upper end of the stem form, and put the first clamp there. Bend the strips down over the form and place successive clamps one by one, working forward and down over the leading edge of the mold. It's a good idea to do this exercise once without the glue prior to this operation to see if the individual strips will take a bend without breaking.

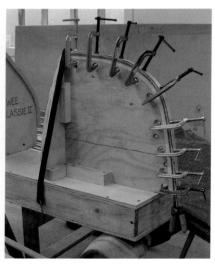

When the inside stem lamination is clamped in place, allow the glue to dry completely before removing the clamps.

Wood strip canoes can also be fitted with outer stems. These are external structures that are located so they actually form the leading and trailing edges of the boat. They are optional, and the merits of adding these parts are discussed later on, in Chapter 7. Outer stems are laminated in the same manner as the inner stems. That means the laminates can be bent dry and glued in place at the time of installation, or else they can be steamed or soaked, bent, and glued ahead of the time of installation. In the latter case, the outer stems are usually intended to seat against the inside stems. (See the illustration on page 55, the example at right, for a depiction of this type of fit.) If you'd like to make this kind of outer stem, then you need to bend the outer stem laminates at the same time you bend the inside stem laminates in order to get a good fit between the inner and outer stems. Steam or soak the whole stack of laminates for the required time, arrange the pieces in the proper order, bend them over the stem form, and allow them to dry as described before. Then, before you glue the pieces together, place a piece of tape or plastic between the group of inner stem laminates and the outer stem group. That way, when the laminates are being glued, the outer and inner stems don't end up bonded together before you're ready for them to be.

Since the outer stems are designed to provide strength and impact resistance at the ends of the boat, they are almost always made of a hardwood. The outer stem laminates are cut the same thickness as the inside stem laminates, but a little wider (7/8 in. wide), and long enough to reach from the inboard end of the stem to the sheer at the very end of the hull.

Once the glue joints in the inside stems have dried, you may want to shape the inboard ends by rounding over the corner of the laminate that is at the top of the stem form, against the stem form. This will be exposed in the finished canoe (if not hidden behind a bulkhead) and will have to be shaped sometime. It can be done later, but probably would be easier now, particularly if the stems are of a hardwood.

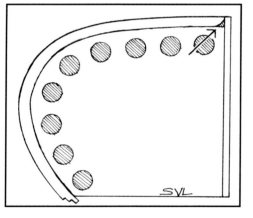

The inboard end of stem piece after shaping.

Beveling Stem Forms or Inside Stems

Whether your canoe is to be built with inside stems or not, the ends of the mold, where the strips forming the two sides of the hull come together, must be beveled. This is to provide a solid bearing surface for the strips while the hull is assembled. The proper angle of the bevel is indicated by the angle at which a batten laid against the mold crosses the stem form or inner stem piece. This angle changes as you slide the batten up or down along the stem. Likewise, as strips are glued together to form the hull, the successive strips will meet the stems at changing angles. The easiest way to get the bevel right is to trial fit a batten against the inner stem (or stem form) and work the stem down by removing the excess wood until the fit is good.

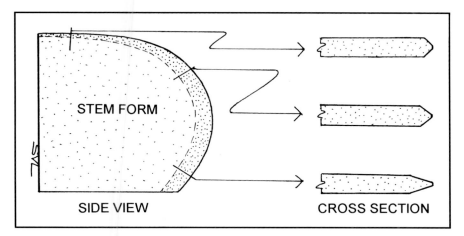

STEM FORM

SIDE VIEW   CROSS SECTION

Imperfect fit of batten against inside stem. The midline drawn on the stem piece is visible here. Allow a 1/8 in. wide flat to remain on the outer edge of the stem; 1/16 in. on each side of the midline.

Changing bevel (also known as rolling bevel) at the stem. This is illustrated on a stem form with no inside stem attached. If an inside stem is used, the bevel is exactly the same, but the inside stem would be beveled, not the stem form. The strips come together at a sharp angle along the leading edge of the stem, where the hull is designed for cutting through the water. Moving up along the stem to what starts to become the bottom of the canoe, the strips meet at increasingly wider angles, giving the hull more breadth for increased bouyancy.

Beveling the inside stem or stem form. The work to be done here is the same whether the object to be beveled is the stem form itself, or a laminated inside stem, as in this photo. If you are using an inner stem, get it clamped squarely on the stem form. The next step is to draw a line down the middle of what you're going to bevel. (This is not necessary if you already have a glue joint between two pieces of plywood to go by.) This is a reference point for keeping your work straight and even on both sides. The pencil line I drew on the stem piece does not show in this photo; see next photo for the enhanced version in ink. See how the batten is clamped onto the mold so it mimics the lay of the strip that will go here. Note that for the inside stem piece, multiple C-clamps are needed to keep the laminate from wiggling out of position while being worked. Start at the lower end, where the sheer meets the stem, and work short sections at a time. The tools used for this are mainly the spokeshave and trimming plane, with the angle grinder (24-grit disk) called upon where wood is to be removed in quantity. As suggested by this photo, both sides of a section of the stem should be done before moving on to another section.

Proper fit of batten against inside stem.

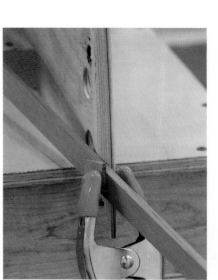

The other side beveled to match. For this canoe, the strips will meet the stem at such an acute angle at the sheer that the plywood of the stem form also needed to be beveled off to keep it from interfering with the lay of the strips.

Working farther up along the stem. Note that small pads of softwood are used under the clamps where the leading edge of the stem is finished. For even better protection of this edge, wooden blocks with V-notches cut in one side that match the shape of the inside stem could be used in place of the softwood pads.[7]

The beveling of this stem is completed. Notice that this canoe will still have a pronounced "V" to the bottom where the stem meets Station 6 (the first crosswise station next to the stem form). This is fairly unusual. Most canoes will exhibit more roundness here, so the uppermost section to be beveled will generally be much flatter than this.

Upon close inspection, the midline drawn on the stem seems to disappear near the upper end. That is because the stem stood a bit higher than Station 6, and the trimming plane was used to reduce the height of the stem piece to match that of the station. (The 1/8 in. wide flat at the midline was retained.)

You will find that having shaped one of the stems, the second one will go faster since you know what to expect. Sharpen tools as often as needed. This operation can be hard on tool edges, and dull tools make it really tough to get good results.

When both ends of the mold are done, rummage up the masking or packaging tape again. If you plan to staple the strip planking directly to the stem forms, cover the beveled edges of the stem forms with tape, as was done with the station edges. If the strips are to be glued to inside stems, check to see that the tape between the stem forms and the inside stems is intact. If not, cover the gaps with fresh tape.

You have just reached a major milestone in your canoe construction project, and a celebration is warranted. (An additional cause for celebration is the promise that the next phase of the project will be a lot more fun.) In case you have come to view mold building as a test of your mettle, you can take some consolation in my assurance that even the most committed, habitual boat builders dislike building molds. Now that it is done, however, and you look at the mold, the canoe just begs to be built. You should also feel a deserved sense of confidence that all the care you put into making a good mold will be rewarded with a quality product in the end.

Chapter Six

Stripping the Hull

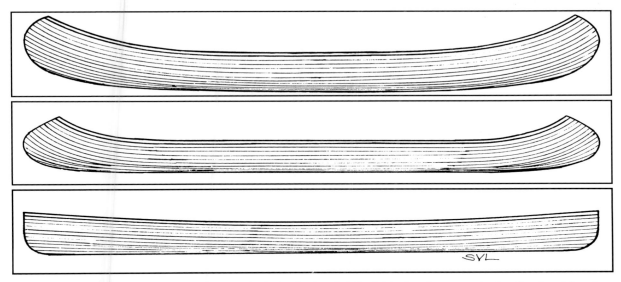

An advantage to placing the strips parallel to the sheer line is that the sheer is defined right from the start, so the sheer line doesn't have to be marked and cut out after the stripping is completed. A disadvantage is that it usually is necessary to use specially fitted short strips near the bottom of the stems (with the canoe upright) to get subsequent strips to lie flat on the mold, and these special strips are extra work to make and fit. Also, depending on how much curve there is in the sheer, it can be somewhat difficult to get the strips to lie flat on the sides of the canoe; additional nailing or stapling may be required to get the strips to assume a pronounced curve without also twisting. (Not drawn to scale.)

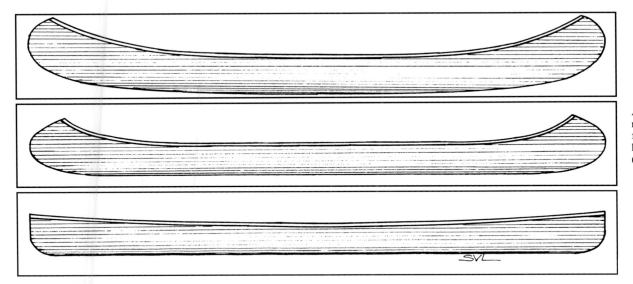

Now comes the part of the project you've been waiting for; assembling a recognizable wooden hull. Not only is it satisfying in terms of producing tangible boat-like results, this is also an opportunity to exercise your "creative bone" by customizing your canoe with a distinctive pattern of wood strips. One's practical side and artistic side get to work together here. Your personal canoe can simply be a serviceable, fun craft, or a statement in three-dimensional art, or anywhere in between. There are all kinds of ways to personalize your canoe at the stripping stage.

Stripping Patterns

Almost every established professional wood strip canoe builder seems to have a signature pattern of stripping hulls that is at least somewhat unique. This tells us that there are several ways to produce a satisfactory wooden hull, which means you can let personal taste be your guide to a significant extent. Most of the professional builders have settled on a particular pattern for reasons of efficiency and good results, and these considerations will be of interest to you as well.

The illustrations here show a variety of alternatives that are in fairly common use. Notice that a particular strip pattern can look quite different on different types of canoes. What may look terrific on one model may appear awkward on another, depending on your perception of beauty. And to present more possibilities, there are at least four variations on the manner in which the bottom of the craft can be closed in.

Advantages in laying the strips level is that there is less likelihood of needing special short strips during hull assembly, and the strips tend to lie flatter against the mold. A disadvantage is that after the outside of the hull has been fiberglassed, the sheer line has to be marked and cut out. (Not drawn to scale.)

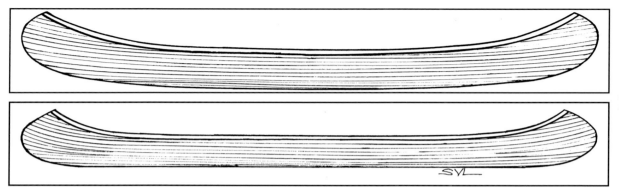

Here, strips are laid mostly parallel to the sheer, but with less upsweep at the ends. The first strip on each side is laid parallel to the sheer in the middle of the mold, but at the ends the strip is allowed to droop naturally. Less force is needed to get the strips to lie quietly in place than when strips are forced to follow the sheer line. This produces a graceful upward sweep in the strips toward the ends of the finished canoe and is, perhaps, the most aesthetically pleasing. However, this pattern requires cutting of the sheer after hull construction, and often demands the use of specially fitted strips. (Not drawn to scale.)

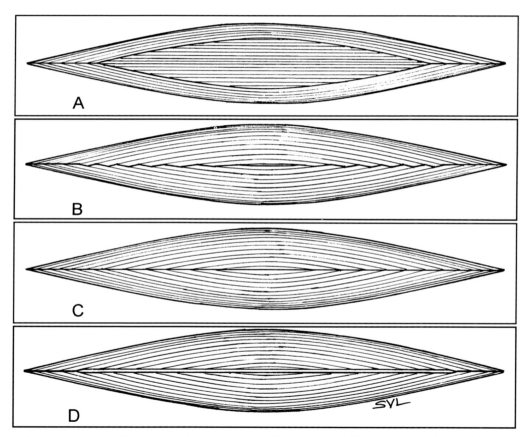

Bottom strip patterns. A. The bottom (below the waterline) of the canoe is filled in with strips running parallel to the centerline of the canoe. B. The flatter part of the bottom is filled in by placing strips on the hull on alternating sides so that the ends fit up against the edge of the previous strip. C. The ends of the strips meet along the centerline of the hull. D. Where the bottom of the canoe changes from a V-shape to a more rounded shape, a strip is placed along the centerline of the canoe and fit into the V-shaped notches formed by the strips coming together on both sides at the stems. Then, the bottom is filled in by adding strips to each side of the keel line. (Not drawn to scale.)

The stripping pattern of the bottom is somewhat a matter of taste, but there are practical considerations also. Each of these methods have their good points. Most of them also have some limitations, which can be worked around. I have first-hand experience with two of these patterns; the information on the others is from other builders.

The pattern shown in A divides the process of stripping the hull into two phases. Either the sides may de done first, and then the bottom filled in, or else the bottom may be done first and sides done afterward. I recommend that the sides be done first. I have talked to a couple of builders who did it the other way around and ran into problems. They found that by starting with the bottom, and then applying strips around the ellipse and working down the sides to the sheer, any irregularities in the way the strips fit on the hull bottom were carried right down to the sheer. These were really noticeable with the gunwales on the finished canoe, as the viewer's eye naturally observes the relationship between the sweep of the sheer and lay of the strips. This situation can be avoided by starting at or near the sheer instead and doing the sides first. Place a strip on each side of the mold, taking care to adjust the lay of each strip so it's the way you want it. Then, the subsequent strips will be oriented parallel to the first two reference strips, giving a nice even pattern on the sides of the canoe (which are highly visible in the finished product). When enough strips are placed on the sides of the mold that the ends of the strips meet at a shallow arched part of the bottom, stop. Next, fill in the bottom with strips running straight fore and aft. The most foolproof way to ensure the strips run in the right direction is to fit a lengthwise strip in at the keel line first, and then add strips alongside of that, placing subsequent strips from the midline out to the sides of the boat. If you are using strips with bead and cove edges, you would want to plane the upper shaped edge off of the last strips on the two sides of the open bottom to make it easier to fit the straight strips.

I have not tried this hull stripping pattern myself, but there would seem to be a certain efficiency in putting the strips on the bottom straight lengthwise; the strips would be easy to place, and stay where you want them with little pressure needed. Also, the bottom strips probably lie smoothly over the mold, reducing the possibility of unintentionally building unfairness into the bottom of the canoe. A good thing to keep in mind about this way of stripping the bottom is that you can switch to this pattern at any time after you work your way up to the bottom of the boat. Builders using stiffer species of wood for strip stock may find that the strips will not bend as tightly as they need to in order to fit into the opening near the center of the hull bottom, with the strips following the curve of the hull sides. The required bend is simply too tight. Instead of fighting a losing battle trying to force stubborn strips to conform, the best alternative is to change to this strip pattern, which lets the strips run straight.

The only disadvantage I know of is the one mentioned earlier, when the bottom area is stripped first. It is significant to note that in situations where the sheer strip must be exactly straight and level, David Hazen, the main proponent of this pattern, recommends starting with the sides.[1]

The stripping pattern shown in B on page 50 shows a zigzag pattern on the bottom of the canoe. Stripping begins at or near the sheer. Where the bottom has a V-shape to it, the ends of the strips are cut so they meet in a straight line along the midline of the boat. As the bottom makes the transition to a more rounded shape, the ends of the strips are mated to the upper edge of the strip just previously applied. The strips are placed on alternating sides, producing the zigzag pattern along the keel line of the boat. Usually the last couple of strips (in the center of the hull bottom) have to be fit at the same time.[2]

An advantage to working the hull bottom this way is that the strip ends are cut off at about a 45° angle, which I find easier to cut and fit than long, narrowly tapered ends. As you add successive strips toward the middle of the canoe, the strips already on the mold help hold the newly applied strips in position. Newly placed strips tend to want to spring out straight, but the adjacent strips prevent that from happening.

A limitation associated with this bottom strip pattern is that it is best used on round- or flat-bottomed boats, not V-shaped hulls. If it were used on a V-bottomed boat, there would be a risk of sanding off a corner of the end of each strip, leaving a small hole through the hull where that happened, in the process of sanding the hull into its final shape. (That is also the reason the characteristic zigzag pattern of fitting the ends to edges of the strips isn't initiated until the hull bottom changes from V-shaped to round.) Another consideration is that when strips with cove and bead edges are used, some special fitting would be required to make the sawn-off strip ends mate against shaped strip edges. As long as the bead edge is the one exposed, it would probably be easiest to deal with this by whittling away a short section of the shaped edge, creating a flat spot for the end of the next strip to seat against. A third potential drawback to this pattern is that the builder needs to pay special attention to the shape of the hull bottom as the strips are fit together; carelessness can lead to unwanted hollows and humps that may not be entirely remedied by sanding.

With these cautions out of the way, I'd like to state now that this is still my favorite way to strip a canoe hull bottom, primarily because I like how it looks. I've gotten excellent results putting canoe hulls together this way. Instructions on how to do it are included in this book, along with the instructions for the next pattern, which was adopted for the V-bottomed boat in the photo series.

The stripping pattern in C has a clean, straight joint running the length of the hull bottom, along the keel line. Stripping starts at or near the sheer, and progresses up toward the bottom. Strips are put on alternating sides until the sides are done. Then one side of the bottom is filled in with strips long enough that the ends cross the centerline of the mold. A tautline is used to locate the centerline on the hull bottom, and that line is marked across the strips. The excess wood is cut off, with the last part of that operation being done with a small plane to ensure that the finished edge is straight. Then the other side of the bottom is filled in, moving from the outside toward the middle. Each strip is individually fit. The last two strips usually have to be placed at the same time.[3]

One of the advantages of doing the hull bottom this way is efficiency. By trimming the ends of the strips for the first side all at one time, and leaving only the strips for the second side to be fit individually, the process is streamlined considerably. Also, this pattern is suitable for canoes of any hull shape.

It is important to make sure that the half of the hull bottom finished first is fastened to the mold (with nails or staples) while cutting the centerline, and also while fitting strips for the second half of the bottom. Otherwise, the first side springs up away from the mold. This seems to be more pronounced in the areas where the bottom has a deep "V" shape and less so where the bottom is fairly flat. One other thing

to note about this stripping pattern is that the strips for the second half of the bottom are all individually fit, and ends of the strips generally have long, tapering cuts at the ends. This is not a problem, but demands a bit more time and care on the part of the builder.

The stripping pattern in D features a single strip running along the midline of the hull bottom. Again, the stripping operation starts at the sheer and continues up the sides toward the bottom. Once the builder reaches the flatter part of the bottom, a "keel strip" is trimmed so that its ends will fit into the V-notch formed by the joint of the side strips near the ends of the mold. This strip needs to have plain, square edges, because the ends of the remaining strips will be cut to fit against the edges of the keel strip. This strip is nailed or stapled to the mold. The rest of the strips are added on alternating sides of the hull, and individually fit at the ends, with the short strips in the middle being the last ones placed.[4]

One of the selling points for this stripping pattern is that the center strip establishes a smoothly curving keel line for the hull (viewing the hull in profile). It serves as a guide in keeping the ends of the other strips in position, helping to avoid accidentally building unfairness into the bottom. Also, the keel strip helps hold the other bottom strips in position during fitting and gluing, providing resistance against the ends of the strips while they want to spring out of shape.

Allowances to make for the use of a keel strip include providing a flat spot on the molds for the strip to sit on. For round- and flat-bottomed hulls, this is a minor detail easily taken care of. For V-bottomed hulls, this fact requires more planning. Simply sanding a flat at the top of each station may cause unwanted changes in the shape of the keel line. Stations near the ends of the mold, having a sharper point at the top (on the centerline) will require a greater reduction in height to create a flat than the stations in the middle of the mold, which are broader at the top. An additional complication is that the stem forms are at an established height, which should not be changed without careful consideration. So, if you want to strip a V-bottomed canoe this way, and plans don't already show flat spots at the tops of the stations for a keel strip, you will want to broaden out the tops of the stations a bit and make a flat spot the width of a strip, without altering the height of the stations. The key to making this work is planning for it ahead of time. If you do modify plans for this reason, be extra sure to check the mold for fairness (as described in the previous chapter) before beginning hull construction.

The observations on making long, narrowly angled cuts at the ends of the strips for the previously discussed pattern apply in this case also.

Strip Color Selection and Feature Strips

How you put the strips on the mold is only one of the decisions affecting the appearance of your canoe. Another matter of cosmetic interest is choice of strip color or grain pattern. Possibilities here are practically unlimited, especially if you use different species of wood in stripping the hull. One of several reasons western red cedar has been so popular with strip canoe builders is its naturally wide variation in wood color.

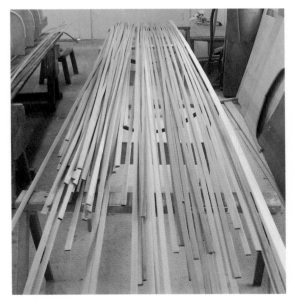

Cedar strips being sorted by length and color. The pale strips on the right are Alaskan yellow cedar; all the others are western red cedar.

A builder can produce a fine-looking canoe by either deliberately selecting strips according to color or by letting random strip selection generate its own unique pattern. One can even go so far as to select strips in pairs by color, putting one on each side of the boat so both sides are the same. I try to make the two sides of the hull match down to about the waterline, and from there I usually go with a more random pattern, except that I try not to put two strips exactly the same color next to each other. I like to make the last four pairs of strips in the middle of the bottom match.

Some really eye-grabbing patterns can be created using different species of wood. I like to use a light-colored wood that will contrast with the dark cedar for a feature strip. One word of caution, however. If you want to use different kinds of wood, keep in mind that most other species of wood are harder to sand than cedar. I have found that it can be a bit of a challenge to sand the hull fair where I have used different woods, and that unless I pay special attention here, the harder wood will end up standing a little proud of the softer red cedar next to it. When you select your wood, you definitely will not want to put something that sands like marble next to cedar or another very soft wood.

Feature strips make nice accents on a wood strip boat. A feature strip can range from a simple plain strip of a contrasting color to a laminated series of contrasting wood pieces, which are added to the hull as a single unit. You creative craftsmen can display your talents by concocting your own unique design in wood and putting it in a prominently located place on your canoe.

There are all kinds of ways to vary this basic theme by using different numbers, widths, and colors of strips. One can even include blocks of alternating colors in a row. There are other ways to make more or less elaborate patterns in a strip, too, so be as creative as you like.[5] As a general guideline, the feature strip should not be over 1-1/2 in. wide due to the difficulty of bending it if the strips are to have any amount of upward sweep at the ends of the canoe. Wider strips resist bending more than narrow ones. So, if you are stripping the hull in such a way that the strips have to accept a fairly sharp bend, a narrow feature strip would be the best choice, as a wide one would refuse to bend that sharply. However, if you are putting strips on the mold so they run straight, you might meet with success using feature strips even wider than 1-1/2 in.

The feature strip is most always put on the mold three or four strips from the sheer. The placement is driven by the builder's idea of what looks good. (Otherwise, why put on a feature strip at all?) The things to keep in mind with respect to placement are that the gunwale and feature strip complement each other, and the lower limit of the picture is the 4-inch waterline.

Placing the First Strip

The first strip on each side of the mold will serve as a guide for the way all the rest of the strips will lie. The process of getting the first strip onto the mold is about the same regardless of how much or little curve the strips are to have in the way of upward sweep towards the ends of the righted boat.

First, pick out a pair of strips that will run the full length of the mold. If the strips are to run straight (level) on the mold, choose strips that are straight (as they all should be but frequently aren't). If the strips are to be bent into a curve, eyeball your candidates for uniform flexibility, because a nice, smooth, even arc that will be the same at both ends of the canoe is what you're after. Hold the strip by the end or the middle with the wide side of the strip vertical, and observe how the strip bends toward the free end(s). If the strip seems stiff in one place but droopy elsewhere, try another strip. Another thing to keep in mind is that if you plan to bend the strips to run parallel to the sheer, don't use your most beautiful strips for the first ones on the mold, because they will be completely covered by the gunwales by the time the canoe is done. Dark strips tend to show

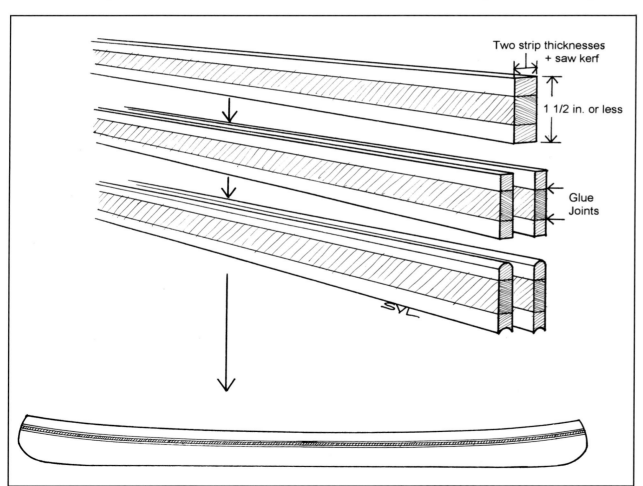

Two strip thicknesses + saw kerf

1 1/2 in. or less

Glue Joints

SVL

Laminated feature strips. Here is an example of a simple lamination that can be sawn into two pieces to use as feature strips. First, glue layers of wood together into a laminate that is no more than 1-1/2 in. "high," and is at least two strip thicknesses plus a saw kerf "wide." Then, saw the laminate into two strips. If you are using bead and cove strips, shape the edges of these matching feature strips so they will fit together with the regular strips used on the rest of the hull.

nail and staple holes less than light-colored ones, so if that is important to you and the first strip will *not* be completely hidden by the gunwales (i.e. does not follow the sheer) on your canoe, take note.

Once you have your first pair of strips picked out, take one of the strips and tack (with a small nail) or clamp it to the middle station at the sheer. Get into the habit of putting small wooden pads (cedar scraps are perfect) between clamps and strips, to save having to sand out dents later. If you are using bead and cove strips, put the bead edge up. Next, tack or clamp the strip into its tentative position

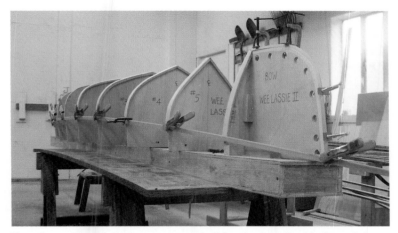

The strips on this particular boat are to run parallel to the sheer. Here the first strip is placed so the lower edge is even with the markings indicating the sheer line on the stations. Bead-and-cove-edged strips will be used for this canoe hull, and the bead edge is placed up because it will withstand more handling and clamping pressure than the cove edge will. I selected the two sheer strips before shaping the strip edges, and only shaped the bead edges of these two strips. The lower edges of the sheer strips were left square. With the sheer strip clamped or tacked onto the mold, sight down the strip, looking for irregular bends in the strip. Adjust the position of the strip a little up or down where necessary to obtain a smooth, sweeping bend.

moving from the middle of the mold toward the ends. Here is where the differences in stripping patterns must be taken into account.

If the strips are to run level on your boat, tack the first strip with its lower edge at the sheer line on the middle station, and bring the ends of the strip straight out to the ends of the mold. Use a level held along the edge of the strip to check the run of the strip. (Make sure the mold itself is level first, of course.) Sight down the strip and adjust it wherever necessary to make it straight. Since this strip will have other strips fitted up against it both above and below, the strip edges should be shaped the same as all the others.

For those wanting the strips to follow the sheer except at the ends, where the strips are to sweep upward in a gentler arc than the sheer line, start out clamping or tacking the first strip along the sheer as in the photos. When you reach a point along the sheer where the strip resists bending that sharply, let it droop in a more natural arc and clamp it at the stem. Sight along the strip, making any adjustments needed to yield a smooth curve in the strip, and tack the strip in place. Take care to make the bow and stern ends match; measure to find out if the two ends cross the stems at the same place. Here again, this first strip will have other strips added above and below it, so the edges should be the same as the other strips. Once the first strips have been placed on both sides of the mold, it's a good idea to see if the curves in the two strips match by placing a level crosswise of the mold, spanning the strips. If the strips accurately mirror each other, the level will indicate that.

When nailing strips to the mold, it may become apparent that more persuasion is required to make the strips lay flat against the stations. A solution to that problem is to drive the nail through a small piece of cedar and then through the strip, and drive the nail down flush with the top of the cedar piece. The scrap piece helps hold the strip in place without denting it, and when it's time to remove the nail, the cedar scrap can be broken away to expose the shank of the nail for pulling.

Wooden pads used with nails for securing strips.

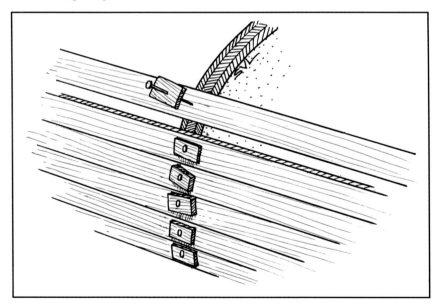

When you are satisfied that the sheer strip is the way you want it, use small nails (I used panel nails) to nail the strip in place at each station. If your canoe mold does *not* include inside stems, nail the strip to the stem forms also. If your mold *does* have inside stems, just clamp the strip there for now. Don't drive the nails down flush with the surface of the strip, because those nails have to come out later. Drive them just far enough to hold the strip in place. Visually check the curve of the strip again. If you don't like it, adjust it. When you do like it, give the nails another rap so they stay put. With the strip nailed securely in position, glue the sheer strips to the inside stems. (Carpenter's wood glue is fine for this.) Staple the strip ends in place, if you are not using clamps to hold the strips while the glue dries.

Use a Dozuki saw to cut the excess strip length off. Make the cut at the angle that the opposite sheer strip will intersect this strip. The beveled side on the other side of the stem form or inside stem, whichever is the case, serves as a guide in establishing the proper angle.

The first sheer strip cut to mate with the opposing sheer strip.

At the opposite end of the mold, again, use the inside stem/stem form as a guide to the proper cutting angle. I find it easy to make these angled cuts a little short. If I think I am erring on the long side, it usually turns out to be the right length.

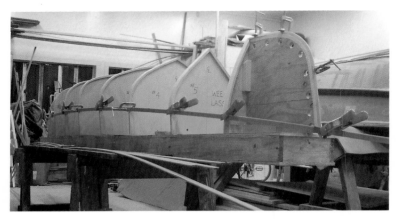

Second sheer strip being located on mold. Repeat the process used for the first strip. The ends of this strip should pass by the trimmed ends of the first strip.

Second sheer strip fastened in place.

Glue joint between opposing sheer strips and the inside stem. Here, the strips are glued to each other as well as to the inside stem. Where there is no inside stem, the strips are glued to each other, but only stapled to the stem form.

Trimming the end off the second sheer strip. Cut straight across the second strip, along the outer edge of the joint between the two strips.

Sheer strips glued and trimmed at the end of the mold.

If you are building your hull with inside stems, there is an alternative may to trim the ends of the strips. You can cut the strips on both sides of the mold off even with the leading edge of the inside stem. That will produce a wide flat at the end of the mold. This flat surface will provide the base for an outside stem, which is installed later.[6] If you have steamed and laminated outer stems that are designed to seat against the inside stems, then this is the way the strip ends should be cut off. If you do cut the strips off this way, adding the outside stem will be *necessary* in order to gain the sharp leading edge that makes the hull cut

Two different ways to trim strip ends.

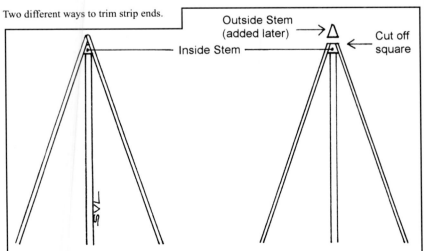

easily through the water. In contrast, if the strips are cut as shown in the photo series, addition of an outside stem is *optional*. Also, the outer stem can be made narrower if you do decide to add it. More information on outer stems is presented in the next chapter.

Stripping the Sides

Stripping the sides of the canoe is a straightforward operation. With the first two strips on the mold to control the run of subsequent strips, positioning the other strips is just a matter of making sure they fit snugly together. The strips are added on alternating sides of the mold, with one to three strips put on one side before switching to the other side. The routine I use now is to put a strip on one side, next to the first strip, then put two strips on the opposite side, and continue putting strips on two per side after that.

The means used for holding strips in place while the glue dries has a big impact on how fast stripping proceeds. So does the amount of fitting needed to meet your standards of quality. The fastest way to construct the hull is to use square-edged or bead-and-cove-edged strips, and staple them to the stations and to each other. That way, stripping can continue while glue is still drying between strips that have already been fastened in place. The second fastest way to put the hull together is to use nails to hold the strips at the stations, and staples to hold strips together between stations. The slowest way to build the hull is to hand bevel the edges of the strips to achieve tight fits, and clamp the strips together while the glue dries. The clamps can't be removed until the glue is dry, and are in the way of where the next strip needs to go, so drying time for the glue influences speed of construction. It also takes some time to position the clamps. Hand beveling the strip edges can take a surprising amount of time when you get into areas of the hull where the bevel changes significantly between the middle and the ends of the boat. The strips usually have to be trial fit at least twice before they are ready to be glued. With persistence, however, strips can be fit extremely well, yielding very classy results. The way I will be assembling the strips for my canoe is to clamp the strips while glue dries, but bead-and-cove edged strips will give tight fits without hand beveling.

Beveling a strip edge. Here, a strip is held vertical by setting it in a groove cut in a 2 x 4 with a table saw. The groove is a little wider than the strip is thick, and deep enough so that only the top 1/4 or 3/8 in. of the strip is exposed. Ideally, this jig would be as long as the longest strip, but a shorter one will work. The small upright piece of wood in the background is a wedge that keeps the strip from sliding in the groove. The plane is used to cut one corner of the strip edge down as needed to make it mate with the strip below it on the mold. Actually, I have a 15 in. plane I like better than this one; the cutting edge is at a better angle. Only one edge of the strip is beveled. It ends up being the lower edge when the strip is placed on the mold. When working on strips that have changing bevels along the edge, it is helpful to make marks (with chalk) on the strip that will line up with corresponding marks on the strip below. This helps in positioning the strip during the process of trial fitting and eventually gluing into place. (See photos showing how to make stealer strips for examples of these marks.)

Wood glue loaded in a syringe. The tip of the syringe is cut off to dispense the glue at an appropriate rate. This is a good way to get the glue just where you want it, and in the right amount. Remember to get the excess glue out of the syringe and draw water into it between uses though, because even partially hardened glue will cause the syringe to work poorly.

I put the glue directly on the upper edge of the strip being glued to. (The next strip goes on top of this one.) The bead of glue shown here is about 1/8 in. wide and is sufficient to do the job. You want some glue to squeeze out of the joint when the strips are forced together; then you know there is ample glue to fill the joint. Wipe off the excess glue with a damp rag. The glue is much easier to get rid of at this stage than it will be if you allow drips to dry on the hull.

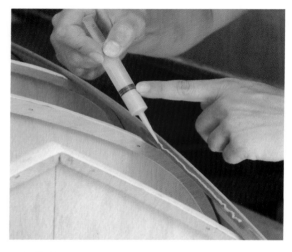

Stripping goes the fastest on the sides, where the ends and the middle of the hull are both more or less vertical. Whether the strip edges are square, beveled, or bead-and-coved, the strips go into place quite readily and fit together well. It gradually becomes more challenging as you round the turn of the bilge, and the strips must submit to considerable twisting to conform to the mold. Here is where the advantages of bead and cove edges become most evident. No additional hand shaping is required to get tight joints between strips, and the interlocking edges of the strips help hold them in position. Square- and beveled-edged strips require more encouragement to stay in place. Also, square-edged strips gap most in this area, resulting not just in a less pleasing appearance, but more importantly a poorer glue joint. The strips only touch at the inner edge, which is a very limited gluing surface. Once you reach the bottom of the boat (the top, when it's on the mold), where it is no longer necessary to twist the strips to make them conform to the shape you want, the strips are easier to manage, though not quite as easy as on the sides.

Stapling the strips is the most popular way to fasten them while the glue dries. It renders a large savings in time for the construction of the hull, and is also simply easier. If the builder is in a hurry to get a boat out on the water, stapling or a combination of nailing and stapling is the way to go. There are two drawbacks to this method. One is that all the staples and nails must be pulled, and in the case of nail holes, filled, before fiberglassing the hull. The other is that the holes are visible on a bright finished boat. Many people find these things easy to live with, or at least offset by the advantage of speedy construction. If you prefer to use staples, use a staple gun equipped with 9/16 in. staples for fastening the strips to the mold, and 1/4 in. staples for fastening the strips to each other between stations. The width of the staple crown can vary; 3/16 to 1/2 in. wide works well, but some builders like to use staples only 1/4 in. wide. The reasons shorter staples are used between stations are that long staple points protruding from the inside of the hull are a real hazard to the fingers, and the extra length beyond the thickness of the strips provides no additional holding power. You want the top of the staple to not touch the wood surface when driven, so practice with the stapler and make adjustments necessary to leave a slight gap under the crown of the staple. This provides a convenient grip when it's time to pull the staples, and frees you from having to sand out dents left by the staple crowns later.

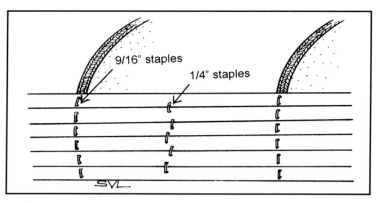

Stapling pattern. The 9/16 in. long staples are driven through a single strip and into the supporting stations. The rows of staple holes marking the station locations will be less distracting if care is used in positioning staples so they line up with each other. The 1/4 in. long staples are used between stations to hold two adjacent strips together snugly, and are placed according to need. They usually don't line up, and they may not be placed between every station for every strip. If a staple is not required to hold neighboring strips together, then don't use one. There will be fewer staples to pull later and fewer holes to mark the hull.

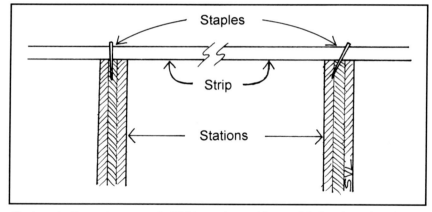

Staple angle. For most purposes, the 9/16 in. staples are driven straight into the station edge. Sometimes additional holding power is needed, or a strip may need some coaxing to lie in a desired curve. In that case, try driving the staple tilted to one side. If a staple driven at an angle still doesn't have the desired effect, try using a small nail driven through a wooden pad as illustrated earlier.

The second most popular way to fasten strips to the mold is to nail them. Steel wire nails, size 17 x 7/8 in., are recommended for this. Staples are used for holding strips together between stations. The most effective way to secure the strips is to drive the nails through small wooden pads and then through, or between strips. Driving the nails between strips leaves less obvious holes when the nails are pulled. The wooden pads need to be covered with tape on one side however, because the glue in the joint will latch onto the pads as well as the strips. It is easier to nail through the strips than between them, but the resulting holes are more visible.

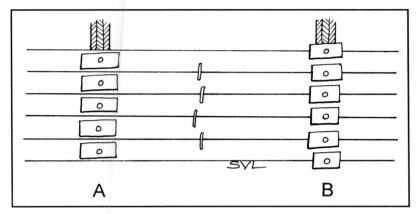

Having decided to go ahead and use this strip, I remove the clamps from one end of the strip to the middle. Starting in the middle, I apply a bead of glue to the upper edge of the lower strip and reclamp the new strip, working toward the end of the mold.

Two nailing schemes. A. The nails are driven through small wood scraps and then through the strips into the stations. The wooden nailing pads are broken away later to facilitate the pulling of the nails. Quarter inch long staples are used to tie strips together between stations. B. The nails are driven through wooden pads and through the joint between strips into the stations. The nailing pads need to be covered with tape on the bottom to avoid an unwanted glue bond. If you try this method and the pads split before you want them to, use 1 in. square pads cut of 1/8 or 1/4 in. plywood instead (with tape on the bottom side).[7] Or dull the nail tips before driving the nails through the wooden pads.

The least common way of controlling the strips as glue dries is to clamp them to the mold and to each other. The one reason for doing this is to get a wood strip hull that is free of the marks left by nails and staples. (Plus, you don't have any nails or staples to pull out of the hull.) The reasons most builders don't do this is that it takes much longer to put the hull together, it takes a lot of clamps, and it is not as easy as stapling or nailing. Some good news on the clamps is that about half the clamps needed are very inexpensive and can be made at home. It sometimes tests the builder's imagination to devise a system of clamps that will hold a balky strip in a compound curve, but that is the challenge that makes it interesting. Besides, a well-placed nail can always be employed as a last resort. I clamp strips because I like my varnished boats to look as good as I can make them. I also try to improve my craftsmanship with each boat I make, and a blemish-free hull on a bright finished canoe is an indicator of craftsmanship. Somewhere along the way I acquired a measure of reverence for wood that is of boat building quality, and I feel I owe it my best effort. It seems disrespectful to poke holes in good cedar if I don't really need to.

As strips are added to the hull of the canoe pictured in the photo series, the strips are shown clamped in place. If you decide to fasten strips one of the other ways, you can substitute your method for mine without having to change other aspects of the stripping operation.

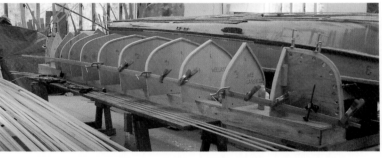

To glue the other end of the strip, I remove the clamps from the far end to where the glued part starts, close to the middle. Beginning there, I apply glue and clamps moving toward the opposite end of the mold.

The strip is glued in place. The damp rag on top of station four is used for wiping off excess glue.

Dry fitting a strip. A strip has been selected and clamped into place to see if it is as good a choice as it appeared to be. This strip will show in the finished boat (as will all the rest of the strips from here on), so it needs to be free of defects that can't be easily sanded out. If there is a minor flaw which can be sanded out, I usually put it on the exterior of the hull because it is easier to sand the outside of the hull than the inside. Dry fitting enables me to verify that the strip is indeed long enough, and that the fit between the upper and lower strip is good. I check to make sure that if there are joints in the strips, that they are staggered so that one doesn't end up right above the other.

The second strip on the opposite side is glued in place. The joints at the stems were done just the same as for the first sheer strips. After adding this strip, I put another on this side before switching to the other side again. From then on, I added two strips before changing sides. With the bead and cove strips, at the stems sometimes a cove edge will angle over a bead edge. I deal with this by dragging the Dozuki saw over the bead edge at the correct angle to make a small groove for the cove edge to fit into. Sometimes some additional work with a knife or round file is needed to get the strips to fit tightly at the stems. The main thing to watch is how well the cove edges seat against the bead edges of the strips below. Those joints need to be as tight as you can make them.

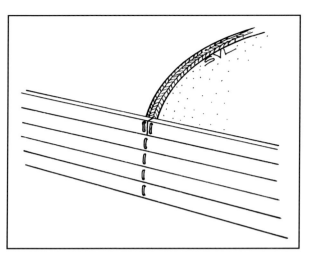

Butt joint. Two square-cut ends are glued and stapled at a station.

The reason I don't use butt joints is that when I am putting strips on the mold, I don't like to have to join strips during that operation. Also, I prefer not to use staples or nails. One situation that might make joining strips on the mold the best choice is if a long (18 ft. or more) canoe is being built by a lone builder, full-length strips might be too floppy to manage. Joining strips on the mold would permit the builder to use shorter, more tractable strips. (Short strips also require less storage space.)

The sides of the canoe are quite easy to strip and progress along at a good pace. The strips aren't required to assume complex bends in this area, and stack up vertically edge to edge with little fuss.

Balancing stresses on the mold. In the construction of this canoe, the strips were run level from one end to the other on the mold. The designer of this model recommended putting six strips on one side, then matching those with six strips on the opposite side, and that is what is being done here. [8] I did not experience any problems with this, but to be conservative, I would not put more than three or four strips on a side before changing sides now, at least this early in the project where there were no strips to help balance the tension on one side of the mold. The stations are not supposed to flex or be pushed to one side, but there is some potential for that. It is so easy to head off this possibility by alternating sides frequently when adding strips, why not do it?

The hull sides have been stripped up to the turn of the bilge. The web clamps with plastic buckles between stations hold the strip edges snugly together while conforming to the hull shape. The bead edge of the top strip is not damaged by the webbing, and fastening the buckles on the outside of the hull tips the upper edge into the position you want rather than allowing it to roll inward.

As strips long enough to run the full length of a canoe become more scarce and expensive, builders find themselves joining short strips together make long ones. Either scarf joints, which are covered in the chapter on materials, or butt joints may be used. With scarf joints, the best results are obtained by joining the pieces before the strip is added to the hull. Scarf joints can be glued on the canoe mold in a pinch, but it is harder to get a tight, smooth joint. Butt joints are routinely made on the mold. Two square-ended strips are pushed together end-to-end with the joint at the middle of a station, and both strip ends are stapled to the station. If care is exercised in matching the grain pattern and color of the adjoining strips, the joint can be hard to detect visually.

Strips twisting to conform at the turn of the bilge. If the edges of the strips were being hand beveled, the section of strip at the middle of the mold would need considerable beveling because the strip edges meet at an angle to one another. At the stems of the mold, the strips are still stacked vertically, so the edges would need little or no beveling there. There is beginning to be a pronounced twist in the strips as they run from the middle toward the ends of the mold.

If you are placing strips level on a hull that has a curve to the sheer, at some point you will want to start filling in the part of the hull below the first strip. This is an excellent way to use up short strips. Short strips seem to increase in population surprisingly quickly as the project goes along, and in the end there is usually a surplus of them. Conversely, good long strips are usually in short supply, so you probably won't want to cut up long strips for this.

Filling in ends of the hull below the first strip. On this canoe, the first strip does not follow the sheer. Short strips are added to fill in the sides between the first strip and the sheer line. Keep a batten handy to hold up against the mold to see where the sheer goes between stations. When choosing strips to add, make sure they will cross both the stem and sheer line. Were I building this canoe now, I would wait until I had stripped up the sides and bottom before I did this part. Stripping the bottom usually produces a number of short strips in the form of trimmed ends, and those can be used for covering the area between the first strip and sheer.

When the stripping has progressed as far as the turn of the bilge, the strips begin to resist the contortions they are asked to assume. The bends and twists become increasingly interesting to behold and also challenging to achieve. It is common to discover at some point that the strips simply won't bend as sharply as you need them to. Clever builders before us have conquered this problem with a handy innovation known as the stealer strip, or cheater strip. These tapered strips start at full width where they attach to the stem, and taper down to a point 18 in. or more in from the stem. Stealers serve to relieve sharp bends in the run of subsequent strips. There are other reasons a builder may decide to use stealer strips. Any time a builder needs to change the direction the strips run, these specialized strips may be employed.

Here is a situation where using a stealer (or cheater) strip is optional. The strips do not bend downward toward the stem so sharply that I couldn't continue stripping as usual. However, by eyeballing the relationship between the run of the strips and the top of the inner stem (and measuring for verification), I can see that the last strip needed to cover Station 6 (attached to the stem form) will probably lie right along the inner stem for 8 or 10 inches. That is not completely unacceptable, but in my experience places like that require quite a bit of fiddling to get things to fit. The end of the strip would have a long tapering point, with some twist and maybe some bend in it. The potential for breakage is fairly high. I can change the angle at which that strip meets the inside stem by adding a stealer strip. The next question is when to add it. It could be put in almost any time from this point on. I decided to do it now because where the inside stem is almost plumb, the fits at the stem are still easy to make. Also, there isn't much twist in the strips between Station 6 and the inside stem yet, which makes fitting easier.

Mark the length of the stealer strip. The cutting line at the stem, and the end of the tapered tip are marked in yellow chalk. There is no rule on how long to make these strips. The best guide is to look for the place where the last strip on the mold makes its sharpest bend downward, and put the end of the stealer strip in that bend. The trickiest part of fitting this strip is feathering the tip down thin enough to allow the next full length strip to pass over the end of the stealer strip with no gaps. This is easiest to accomplish in a place where there is a curve in the supporting strip below the stealer.

With the bead-and-cove-edged strip, a choice has to be made as to which edge to sacrifice. It is easy enough to make the bead edge by hand (not true of the coved edge), so I will preserve the cove edge. I place a straightedge so that it connects the upper edge of the strip at the stem with the lower edge of what will be the inboard end, and mark the cutting line.

The upper edge has been beveled with the trimming plane, and sandpaper will be used to further round over the edge to resemble the original bead. Check to make sure the edge is right by trial fitting against the cove edge of another strip.

The extra length has been sawn off one end; the other end serves as a handle. The stealer strip is clamped to another piece of scrap strip to support and protect the fragile coved edge while removing wood from the bead edge.

Checking the tapered end for fit. Look for a gap at the end of the stealer strip. Sand the end of the strip as thin as you dare to get a gap-free joint with the strip that will be above.

I start cutting pieces away from the upper edge at the narrow end and gradually work toward the wide end of the strip. A utility knife works well for this because it affords good control, and the thin blade cuts the cedar easily.

After whittling the strip down to this point, stop. A plane is used to make the edge straight and also for beveling off the corners of what will be the new bead edge.

To eliminate any remaining small gaps at this stage, set the end of the stealer strip slightly down into the strip below. With the utility knife, cut down 1/32 in. or less at the yellow marking, and then whittle a small recess back to it, no more than 1/4 in. long. This recess is present in the photo.

When you are satisfied with the fit, apply glue and clamps. Notice that the delicate end of the stealer strip is protected by a scrap strip placed above it during clamping.

The next full-length strip is placed above the stealer strip and the fit is tight all the way to the stem. Sometimes in the process of fitting subsequent strips over stealer strips, a little more touching up of the bead edge is needed, and is easily accomplished with sandpaper or a trimming plane.

ticular areas the strips tended to spring away from the stations slightly, even after the glue was dry, and a few staples, maybe at every third strip, probably would have eliminated that. Another place an occasional staple would have helped was near the keel line, when I was fitting strip ends up against the half of the hull bottom that was already complete (to be discussed shortly). The pressure of strips pushing against the opposite side caused the facing sides of the hull bottom to spring up a bit where quarters were too tight to use clamps to hold everything in place. This was partly a function of how I stripped the hull bottom; on previous boats where I filled in the bottom by adding strips on alternating sides I did not experience this. The net result of the localized "springing out" was a hull closely resembling but not exactly like what the designer had in mind.

Creative clamping becomes necessary at the stems when the clamping cleats are no longer accessible. Instead, the strip is gripped between two cedar scraps that overlap the strip below. The free end of the inside stem must be held in place while the strip is clamped to it. One of the clamp holes in the stem form provided a convenient solution; one end of the web clamp is threaded through the hole and down the inside of the hull and back up the outside, so when the clamp is fastened, it snugs the strip and inside stem against each other. The long web clamp wrapped around the strongback holds the strip down against the one below.

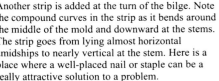

About this point in the stripping of the hull comes the recognition of an additional value of nails and staples. Not only do they hold strips in place while they are glued, they hold the hull to the mold as stripping continues. I did not rely on staples or nails in the construction of this canoe, but noted two specific situations where their benefits might have offset the negative effect of "holing" the hull (my opinion). This canoe is unusual in that it has concave curves in areas of the outer hull; most canoes have only convex or flat surfaces. In these par-

Another strip is added at the turn of the bilge. Note the compound curves in the strip as it bends around the middle of the mold and downward at the stems. The strip goes from lying almost horizontal amidships to nearly vertical at the stem. Here is a place where a well-placed nail or staple can be a really attractive solution to a problem.

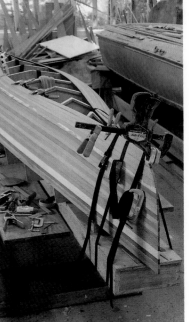

More creative clamping. This is the same clamping arrangement with more clamps added. A bar clamp is gripped onto the end of the strip to serve as a wrench. The size and placement of the spring clamp on the bar is adjusted to effect the right amount of twist on the strip. A makeshift clamp for holding the end of the strip down is devised of the end of the long web clamp and a C-clamp. The hull does indeed have a strip with paint on it, for those who wonder. I don't recommend it to others, but I took a chance by using this strip cut from house siding. The strip was slightly under thickness so that planing did not remove all the paint, but evaluation of the other side of the strip indicated that the grain and condition of the wood was excellent.

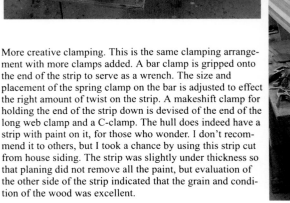

Beveled strip end. Fitting strip ends becomes more complex at the transition from leading edge to the bottom of the hull. I first cut the end of the strip off square with a saw, and then whittled the joint surface with a sharp utility knife. To make this beveled face match the strip that it will join with, I used a short piece of strip placed where the next strip will lie as a guide. Proceeding by trial and error, I kept slicing off bits of cedar until the fit was right. Making a cut like this (more of a ripping cut than a cross cut) with a saw, with the strip glued over the mold, is next to impossible because the saw slips sideways on the grain of the wood.

The opposing strip to the one in the last picture is glued and clamped in position, on the other side of the mold. Note the scrap of cedar wedged up under the black web clamp in the foreground. The scrap is placed to effect a localized point of pressure where it is really needed. This was the last of the strips that were added on the "alternating sides scheme." From this point on, one side of the bottom was stripped up, then the remaining half was closed in.

As the stripping operation progresses along and the area where the end of the canoe rounds over to the bottom is reached, a change must be made in the way the strip ends are joined. The method of letting one strip end bypass the other no longer works. The strip ends start to meet at a tilt to each other. The solution is to cut and bevel the ends of *both* partnering strips so the joint between them is on the midline of the stem. (If up until now you have been cutting the strip ends off even with the inside stems, you need to start letting the strip ends extend past the inside stem, so they meet each other along the centerline of the hull.) I glue the first strip of a pair on as usual, and cut and bevel the ends when the glue is dry. However, the second strip of the pair must have its ends cut to fit before it can be glued. This is easiest to do with the strip clamped or tacked in position as it would be for gluing, but with the last 18 in. or so at the ends free. Place a block of

wood underneath the strip before you saw the end off to ensure that you don't gouge the hull by accident with the saw. Then work on the end of the strip with utility knife and small plane to get the bevel right, trial fitting frequently. When the first end is done, clamp it in place (no glue yet), and work on the other end. When you are satisfied with the fit there, start gluing and clamping/nailing/stapling the strip from that end. I undo a few clamps at a time, apply glue between strips, and then re-clamp before moving to the next section. This is to prevent the strip being glued from snapping out of place and potentially damaging fragile edges during the rebellion.

Since I haven't tried building a canoe of every design in existence I can't say for sure if all of them have a transition zone where the strip ends need to be joined along the midline (regardless of hull bottom stripping pattern), but I suspect this is the case in at least a great majority of designs. Even in the canoes that I stripped with a zigzag joint pattern in the bottom, there were two or three pairs of strips that had to be joined as just described.

Here, on a different canoe from that pictured previously, the fourth and fifth pairs of strips (down from the top) were joined right on the centerline of the canoe. Upon reaching the flatter part of the hull bottom, another pattern of joining strip ends was initiated. The strip ends were cut to fit against the upper edge of the previously placed strip. This works well when using square or beveled-edged strips, but not bead-and-cove-edged strips.

Stripping the Bottom

The Wee Lassie II hull I am building is to have a straight joint running from stem to stem down the keel line of the canoe. Furthermore, one side of the hull bottom will be stripped first, then the second side will be filled in. Not having to fit and trim the ends of the strips on the first side makes for rapid assembly of the pieces.

On the Wee Lassie II, I have started to strip the first side of hull bottom. Two strips have been added to the same side. The ends of the strips must completely overlap the centerline of the mold.

Two-inch finishing nails were driven into both ends of one of the strips right at the centerline of the mold, and twine strung between them. Using the tautline as a guide, make markings at frequent intervals along the keel line. Measure distances from outer strip edges to the centerline of the stations, and compare those figures to measurements from strip edges to the tautline markings. They should be the same, but if not, either make adjustments or ignore the differences. Differences of up to 1/8 in. may dismissed as measuring errors, but more than that calls for investigation. When drawing a line along a straightedge connecting the tautline markings, average the markings to yield a straight line, and check this by sighting down the line. Re-mark the line where necessary to make it straight.

Same view, minus clamps.

Continuing to fill in one side of the hull bottom.

If, as you add more strips to the bottom the way the Wee Lassie II is being done here, you begin to have trouble with getting the strips to bend as sharply as you need them to, stop. Leave part of this side "unstripped." Cut the strips you have already glued on along the keel line as shown in the next series of photos, and then add strips to the other side up to point where you left off on the first side. Then, fill in the bottom with strips running straight, parallel to the keel line. Remember that if bead and cove strips are being used, the upper shaped edges of the last pair of strips that wrap around the hull must be removed to permit the fitting of the length-wise strips. See photos describing the placement of the second-to-last strip for this canoe for an illustration of what I mean. Changing your plans for stripping the middle of the hull bottom is easier than having to fight stubborn strips into position. Note that the last few strips on the second side not only have to bend into the same curves as those on the first side, they also will have long, tapering, breakage-prone ends to deal with as you work on fitting and gluing them. So, if you are having trouble with the first side, expect more trouble with the second side and bail yourself out of a frustrating situation by putting the last strips on another way.[9]

A utility knife works well for rough cutting strip ends. Starting from the middle, work toward the stems. The cut face needs to be plumb, not square to the strip surface, so hold the utility knife vertical. Trim the strips to about 1/8 in. from the centerline; the rest will be cut away with a plane. This trimming process goes fairly quickly.

One side of hull bottom filled in.

Use a small plane to finish trimming the strip ends down to the keel line. It works well to pull the plane toward you here, so you can see where the cutting edge is in relation to the centerline.

One half of the keel line cut finished.

The keel line cut is done, and now the other side of the hull bottom can be closed in.

Strip end pulled into place and glued.

Working your way to the flatter part of the hull bottom, you do reach a point where it is helpful to draw cutting lines on the strips. The illustrated method of marking strips which follows works for short cross cuts that can be made with a Japanese saw, as well as for long tapering cuts that have to be made with a utility knife and plane.

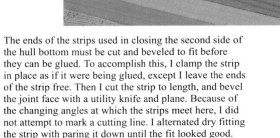

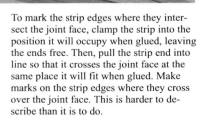

The ends of the strips used in closing the second side of the hull bottom must be cut and beveled to fit before they can be glued. To accomplish this, I clamp the strip in place as if it were being glued, except I leave the ends of the strip free. Then I cut the strip to length, and bevel the joint face with a utility knife and plane. Because of the changing angles at which the strips meet here, I did not attempt to mark a cutting line. I alternated dry fitting the strip with paring it down until the fit looked good.

To mark the strip edges where they intersect the joint face, clamp the strip into the position it will occupy when glued, leaving the ends free. Then, pull the strip end into line so that it crosses the joint face at the same place it will fit when glued. Make marks on the strip edges where they cross over the joint face. This is harder to describe than it is to do.

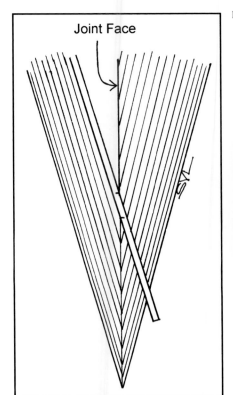

Joint Face

Reference marks for cutting line.

To draw the cutting line, simply place a straightedge so it connects the two reference points and mark that line.

Finish off with a plane. Trial fit the strip often as needed to see where more work is required. With bead-and-cove-edged strips like the one here, care must be taken when rolling the strip into and out of the joint to protect the very thin corners on the strip.

Remove most of the excess wood with the utility knife. Place a piece of scrap wood under the strip to prevent digging into the hull.

The strip fitted and glued into place.

In this photo, which shows a different boat under construction, the strip ends are cut at a wider angle so the cut is more of a cross cut than a ripping cut. In this situation, the Dozuki saw is a better choice for the initial cut than whittling the wood down with a utility knife. The strip end is being finished with a plane, the same as for the long tapering cut previously shown. The plywood scrap under the saw blade is to support the strip and protect the hull while making saw cuts.

The last strip will have to drop into place like a puzzle piece; working it into place around a shaped edge would be close to impossible. So, before doing any fitting of the second-to-last strip, remove its bead edge with a plane.

The second-to-last strip is glued and clamped. The last two strips that are placed can be a drain on one's patience, but perseverance pays off. If you break a corner off a strip that is otherwise fitted and ready for glue, save the broken piece, and glue the strip in anyway. You can glue the other piece in later, and no one will be the wiser.

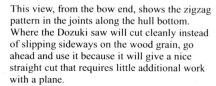

This view, from the bow end, shows the zigzag pattern in the joints along the hull bottom. Where the Dozuki saw will cut cleanly instead of slipping sideways on the wood grain, go ahead and use it because it will give a nice straight cut that requires little additional work with a plane.

Clamping a beveled-edged strip. Since the edges of these strips do not interlock, they sometimes need extra encouragement to stay in place while glue dries. The near end of the strip being glued has a homemade clamp holding it flush with the strip it is butted up to. The location of a station underneath the hull precluded the use of a conventional clamp, so I made a clamp of a 1/4 in. carriage bolt and nut, with two plywood "washers" strung on the bolt. Be alert to possibilities for simple and cheap solutions to clamping "problems." Most of the time you can devise what you need of ordinary stuff you have around. Other things I have used include a strategically placed bag of tire chains on the hull bottom, and a piece of cord tied off to another object in the shop to pull a strip over against the inside stem.

Fitting the last strip is very much a trial and error process, but there are ways to abbreviate it. The first step in that direction is to cut a strip to about the right size before going to the "fine tuning" phase. Select a strip and plane one edge flat to match one side of the opening, along the keel line. Make markings along this planed edge at one-inch intervals. Then, make markings on the hull on one inch intervals along the keel line side of the opening. These markings will serve as reference points for the next step.

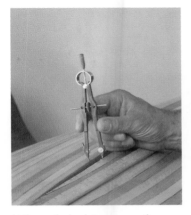

At the marked points, measure the opening width with a compass.

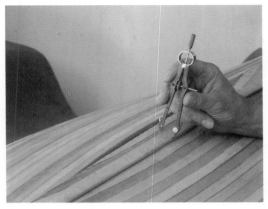

Transfer width measurements to the strip at the corresponding points.

Draw a cutting line on the strip connecting the width markings. Then, saw the strip ends off as usual and whittle the strip down with the utility knife. Leave a little excess wood outside the cutting line, and work that down with the plane, checking the fit frequently.

As the strip gets closer to actually fitting, you may want to sand the edges down the rest of the way. Use a sanding block or longboard so the strip edges don't get rounded over. One reason I finished the job by sanding is that the strip is coarse-grained and getting a smooth cut with the plane at an oblique angle was not possible.

Last strip glued and clamped.

Stripping completed.

Now that the wood strips that distinguish *your* canoe are assembled to form a complete hull, stand back and admire your work. Clean up the shop (so you can at least present the illusion of respectability) and invite your friends over to join you in marveling at your accomplishment. This is another important milestone in the project, made especially significant by the fact that you no longer have to explain to people what you're doing. It is completely obvious that you are building a canoe, and from the casual observer's viewpoint it is essentially done. However, if the hull looks great now, it just keeps getting better as it is brought to actual completion. So, when a little break has fully recharged your reservoir of ambition, read on for more canoe-building adventure.

Chapter Seven

Preparing for Fiberglass

The next major step in the construction of your canoe is to bind all those wood strips into a single structure by covering the hull with a skin of fiberglass cloth and epoxy. Before that step can commence, however, there are some important things to do in preparation.

In this chapter a series of smaller steps are presented collectively as "prep work." Actually, some of these steps are optional. Some are not; for instance, if you have used staples during the assembly of the wood strips, those staples have to come out before fiberglassing the hull. (From a philosophical standpoint, you really don't *have* to take the staples out, but it is interesting to imagine what it would be like to get the hull off the mold if a person were to put the fiberglass over the staples. I'm guessing that it is easier to pull the staples beforehand.) One of the steps detailed in this chapter has little to do with readying the hull for fiberglass, but is related due to the timing of the work. The installation of the outer stem pieces, if that is on your list of features to add, is done at this stage of the project.

A pleasant aspect of preparing the hull for the application of fiberglass is that the various steps can each be done in a few hours. The exception is the fairing of the hull, but that activity can itself be broken down into stages of a few to several hours each, depending on how smooth the hull surface is to begin with. These steps move along reasonably quickly, and I think are rather enjoyable, because of the transformation in the appearance of the hull. A good measure of care has gone into the construction of the canoe thus far. By extending that level of care through the preparation process, you can look forward to professional quality results in your fiberglass/epoxy work.

Pulling Nails and Staples

The first thing to be done is to pull all the nails and staples out. With nails, break the wooden pads away from the shanks of the nails, and pull them out with pliers or end-cutting nippers (so long as you don't cut the nails!). Pulling the nails with a claw hammer is apt to dent or otherwise mar the wood strips, so avoid that. Staples can be pulled with a commercially manufactured tack puller, or else a screwdriver that is bent near the tip. The bent part of the shank is braced against the hull as you pry the staples out, so wrap that part of the screwdriver shank with multiple layers of tape to pad it. If you have assembled the hull without using any such through fasteners, you can smile as you skip straight to the next step.

Fairing the Hull

The process of refining the shape of the hull by removing the ridges and humps, leaving a smoothly rounded surface, is called fairing the hull. The fairing process serves to make the hull not merely pleasing to look at, but more importantly, streamlined for efficiency in the water. A fair hull is one of the hallmarks of quality. Canoes are not driven at great speed by paddle, so drag is not an immediately obvious detractor, but over an accumulation of many hours a paddler will appreciate a canoe that moves through the water easily, tracks and turns as expected, without unnecessary drag induced by irregularities in the shape of the hull. (I suppose an argument could be made that a fair hull offers better gas mileage for the transport vehicle also, but that might be a bit of a stretch. At freeway speeds, it just might make a difference, who knows?) The smooth, graceful curves we are after are mostly achieved by sanding. That is also true of a fine quality finish. However, the overall shape of the hull is more important than how nicely the wood strips are finished, because the shape affects the function of the canoe, and any sanding beyond that point is only for visual effect. According to that order of priorities then, we concentrate on the hull shape first, and after we are content with that, we do whatever sanding is needed to achieve the desired finished appearance.

This is a great time to take advantage of good weather and work outside. Lots of chips and dust are generated during this process. This material can be added directly to the soil if you work outside. Otherwise, you have to collect it and dispose of it. But if you are not blessed with agreeable weather, outfit yourself with a decent dust mask (which you should do even if you work outdoors) and go ahead on the project indoors. You would hardly be the first person to experience a dusty shop.

One of the ways I keep the hull fairing process enjoyable is to break it down into segments, which I spread out over several days. Trying to hurry encourages sloppy work, which I end up regretting later. Some of the sanding can be physically tiring, though not unpleasantly so. It is easier to maintain high standards and a critical eye if you take breaks as needed and knock off working on the hull for the day at the conclusion of each step. This makes the process take longer, but I think it is more important to hold out for good results and enjoyment of the work.

Start out by using one or two different planes and a spokeshave to remove the grossest and most accessible ridges. The areas where the strips meet edge-to-edge going around a curve have many ridges which can be reduced with cutting tools. A long plane is used along the keel line to straighten it up, because it is less affected by minor irregularities in the hull surface than a short plane. A small plane may be used to smooth up other very accessible areas. The spokeshave is perhaps the most useful tool because it can be used in places a plane won't fit due to the contours of the boat. Even so, there are areas that can't really be reached. This is no cause for concern; what can't be planed off now will be sanded off later. Planing mostly serves to reduce the amount of sanding required.

Remove the high spots with cutting tools. Planing off the ridges is faster and makes less mess than sanding, so it makes sense to remove the worst of the irregularities that way. Also, it reduces sanding time later, for the benefit of those who don't love sanding. Don't worry about achieving perfection at this stage; this whole job can be done in an hour or two. If you start to pull pieces of wood up due to cutting into the grain, try working the opposite direction. If the grain is crazy and difficult to work without damaging the wood, the best thing to do is just leave those spots for sanding down. You will probably find it hard to do much on the sides of the hull near the stems without denting the wood with the corners of your tools. If that is the case, sand it instead (next step).

The next phase of fairing the hull amounts to sanding. I commit a day for this, but not all of that time is spent sanding. A goodly amount of the time is devoted to evaluating progress and determining how much to take off where. The goal is to get the hull smoothly rounded and the keel line straight while removing a minimum of wood. That means you do have to pay attention to what you're doing. I use a dual action sander with 80-grit disks for most of this work. The cedar is soft and can be removed fairly rapidly with this tool. When you are getting started and developing a feel for what the sander will do, pick a flat area of the hull to work on. The pressure of the disk will be distributed over a broader area that way, so it is less likely you will "oversand" a particular spot. As you get more proficient and the disk dulls a little, move into the more rounded areas. The sanding pressure will be more concentrated at the point of contact with the hull, so these areas call for extra care. Keep the sander moving; don't allow it to rest in one spot. Also, move the sander up and down *across* the strips. My natural inclination is to work the sander along the strips lengthwise, but that is not very productive; it smoothes the strips but does a poor job of fairing the hull as a unit. Keep the sander flat against the hull except for the areas where you need to use the edge of the disk to sand down a small spot. You will discover that some strips resist sanding more that others. Stay away from the keel line of the boat with the power sander, at least at this point. That area of the hull is best faired up with a longboard.

The sander is a dual-action, variable-speed sander with a 1/2 in. thick foam pad behind the sanding disk. The self-adhesive disks used for this step are 80 grit. If you are not comfortable with the idea of using such coarse grit disks, use 120-grit instead. The work will take longer, but there is less risk of taking off too much wood. The hull shows evidence of the trimming previously done with the plane and spokeshave.

Begin sanding in a flat area. Here, the sander has its optional handle removed to make it easier to rotate the sander as needed to keep the disk flat against the hull while moving it over the hull surface, and also to eliminate interference from bumping the handle into the strongback. I run the sander at a medium speed setting.

Move the sander up and down across the strips to smooth the hull. Keep the sander moving, so you don't sand an area flat that is supposed to be rounded. Pay attention to the direction the disk is turning and capitalize on it; some areas you can reach one way but not another. Do most of the sanding with the middle of the disk, but small areas near the ends of the boat and along the keel line sometimes require pressure from the edge of the disk. I do the flat areas of the hull with new disks, and sand the turn of the bilge with slightly worn disks. This offsets the changes in concentration of disk pressure. Sand just enough to smooth the hull and remove most of the humps and glue, then move on.

One thing to beware of is sanding a hole through the hull. The strips are only 1/4 in. thick to begin with, which means there's not a lot of margin for errors. If you think the wood may be getting thin, press it with your fingers and compare the flex there with that of the surrounding area. If the wood gives appreciably more, stop sanding there. An unfair hull is better than one with a hole in it.

The keel line deserves special attention, because it is an obvious landmark in the topography of the craft and is something even casual observers will notice, *especially* if it is irregular. I find that I spend around half of the time that goes into fairing the hull on the bottom of the boat, making the keel line straight and flat (or smoothly curved if it is supposed to have rocker). One thing I can't accept is a depression, or hollow, in the keel line. Since the way you get rid of these is to sand away the high spots all around the depression, usually other irregularities are gone by the time the apparent hollow is. Again, a hole through the hull is really the ultimate in undesirable, so if you still have a dip after sanding away a lot of wood, stop. If you have to, you can fill in a low spot with extra layers of fiberglass. This can be almost impossible to detect if well done.

I don't try to get the hull perfectly smooth using the DA sander. Rather, I make sure the hard edges of the strips and glue blobs are gone and the hull is "pretty smooth;" flat where it is supposed to be flat and rounded where it's supposed to be round. The fairing of the hull is not yet complete, but the improvement in appearance is already remarkable.

Installing the Outside Stems

Outer stems make a nice finishing touch at the ends of a canoe. These pieces provide additional impact resistance for the boat where impacts are a common occurrence. Also, if you want to put metal stem bands on the canoe, hardwood stem pieces will hold the screws for the stem bands much better than the end grain of softwood strips.

On the other hand, many fine canoes have also been built without outer stems. Not only that, a good many of these have been routinely used for running rivers and other heavy-duty activities.[1] This provides ample evidence that outer stems are not necessary to the survival of a wood strip canoe. If you have joined the strips at the ends of your canoe the same way as shown in the photos of the Wee Lassie II, then the choice of adding outside stems or not is entirely up to you. You can save yourself some time by omitting this step, and reinforcing the ends of your canoe with an extra strip of fiberglass along each stem instead. Just shape and sand the ends of the canoe so they are smoothly rounded, and continue on with the other steps in preparation for fiberglass. The only instance where outer stems *must* be installed is if you have planned for them from the start and cut the ends of the strips off flush with the inside stems.

If you're planning to add outside stems, now is the time to do it. The sides of the ends of the boat are smooth and even enough to see where the centerline is without variations in strip thickness or alignment creating optical illusions.

The outer stems are made up of two or sometimes three laminations of the wood of your choice. Spruce for lightweight boats and ash for stouter boats are popular selections because both bend and glue well. The outer stems may already have been steamed and bent to shape earlier on, at the same time the inside stems were bent. The alternative (to be shown here) is to bend and glue the laminates right on the hull. The length of the outer stems (how far inboard they extend on the bottom of the boat) is determined by the length of the inside stems. (If there are no laminated wood inside stems, there is no practical way to put on outside stems. In the process of fitting and attaching the outer stem pieces, the extreme ends of the strips will be sawn, planed, and sanded away, so that if there were no inner stem present to hold the strip ends in place, the ends of the canoe would probably spring wide open.) A good rule to follow is to make the outer stems slightly shorter than the inner stems; one inch shorter is sufficient. For bending the outer stem pieces right on the hull, the laminates are cut 1/8 in. thick for good flexibility, and pieces are 1/2 to 3/4 in. wide. For a canoe having a very fine entry (like the one under construction in these photos), 1/2 in. is wide enough. For a canoe with stouter, blunter stems, laminates up to 3/4 in. wide are typical.

The outer stem laminates can be glued to each other and to the hull with either carpenter's wood glue or thickened epoxy. For the more substantial epoxy joint, there are a couple of important items to know. For a strong joint, the joining pieces must only be clamped tightly enough together to make them touch. If more clamping pressure is used, too much of the epoxy is squeezed out of the joint, leaving an insufficient amount to form a good bond. This is aggravated if the parts being joined are porous and have not soaked up some epoxy before being clamped together. The epoxy will wick into porous wood, leaving a glue-starved joint. Also, epoxy continues to strengthen as it cures over a period of days. The glue will harden within a day (usually) but doesn't achieve full strength until the epoxy is fully cured. That can range from three days to one week.

What that means for this application is that epoxy is probably best used in cases where the outer stem laminates are steam bent and glued together prior to installation on the hull. The outer stem is only composed of one unit at this point, and it already is of the shape required to fit well. It is easy to handle, does not need heavy clamping pressure to conform, and when the clamps (or screws) are released, the outer stem laminates will not stress the joint by trying to spring out straight. The surface that the pre-laminated outer stem mates to is prepared as shown in the next series of photos, down to the point where the strips are cut off even with the inside stem. From that point down to the sheer, the base for the outer stem is already made. The problem of the resin wicking into porous wood is eliminated by "painting" mixed, unthickened epoxy on the pieces to be joined and letting it soak in. The end grain cedar of the strip hull is especially thirsty and will usually soak up three or four applications of epoxy before a shiny film remains on the surface, indicating that the wood has taken up all the resin it is going to. Put the resin on the wood and let it soak in, and then add more coats as needed until the wood stops taking it up. A thickening agent is then added to the remaining epoxy to make a paste (of about peanut butter consistency), which is spread on one side of the joint. Then the outer stem is fastened to the hull, usually with screws. The thickeners used in the epoxy must be of a type that is recommended for use as an adhesive filler. Usually colloidal silica is used because it makes the epoxy spread smoothly, and some wood flour or sanding dust is added to color the resin brown. You can just use wood flour if you want; the epoxy won't spread as smoothly, but that isn't critical here. The screw holes are drilled during a trial fit just before gluing the outer stem on, and when the epoxy has cured the screws are backed out and holes plugged with pieces of dowel.[2]

The means I have used for adding outer stems is perhaps more primitive appearing, but has produced pleasing results. It would be risky to recommend epoxy for this, because the conditions for producing a strong epoxy joint may only be partially met. The clamping pressure in certain areas would probably be too great, and the resulting weak joint might not hold when the clamps holding the laminates are released the next day. Wood glue used in combination with thin, flexible strips of wood stock produces outer stems of acceptable strength, especially considering that the outer stems will be bonded permanently in place when fiberglass and epoxy are applied to the hull.[3]

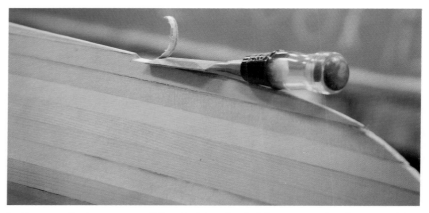

Making a seat for the outer stem. Where the inboard end of the outer stem is to be, saw straight down into the strips, perpendicular to the centerline, to depth of 1/4 in. If a saw cut that deep would result in a base at the bottom of the cut wider than the outer stem pieces you will be using, then only cut down far enough to make a base as wide as your outer stem stock. It is neither necessary nor desirable to cut down through the strips to the inside stem here. Next, use a chisel to cut away the strip edges to make a flat place for the outer stem to rest.

Plane the strip edges smooth and flat. As you move down the end of the hull, you have to cut across the end grain of the strips. A sharp spokeshave is helpful there. What is even better is a belt sander, if you have one. This is one of the few places in the whole project where I think a belt sander is the best tool to use, so I'm hesitant to list it as an essential tool. I didn't have access to a working belt sander, so what I used for this boat (besides the chisel, plane, and spokeshave) was a longboard with 100-grit paper for sanding the ends of the strips flat. Exercise care in keeping that seating face flat; otherwise the outer stem pieces won't fit well.

End of hull, ready for addition of outer stem. For the best finished appearance, the flat edge at the extreme end of the hull needs to be of even width, and it should gradually broaden out to the widest point at the inboard end on top. Additional sanding on the sides of the hull alongside the stem may be necessary to achieve this. I've tried sanding out irregularities after gluing on the outer stems, and it didn't work very well, so my recommendation is to take care of that now.

The outer stem laminates are nailed and clamped in place. Clean up all excess glue before it dries where you don't want it.

When the glue has dried, pull the nails and trim the stem edges down to blend in with the hull sides. Most of this work was done with a plane and spokeshave.

The outer stem laminates being added here are 1/8 in. thick by 1/2 in. wide ash. On the outer piece, small holes for the nails were drilled at 2 in. intervals along the midline starting 1 in. from the inboard end. I opted for wood glue for this operation because it is strong enough, easy to use, and easy to clean up. I spread glue on all the surfaces to be joined (about 6 inches at a time) and then started putting both laminates on at once, similar to the way the inside stem was made. With both pieces held in position by hand, I drilled through the lower strip using the endmost hole in the outer strip as a pilot hole, and then drove a small nail through the ash pieces and the cedar strips into the inside stem. I

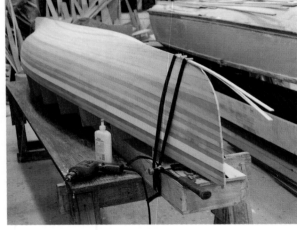

The final shaping was done with the hooked edge of a "gooseneck" scraper and a piece of 80-grit sandpaper. (The scraper appears in the photo showing filler being sanded, a couple steps away.)

didn't want the nail to go all the way through the inside stem, so I only drove it in far enough to hold the outside stem pieces in place. (The nails didn't hold as firmly as I would have liked, so web clamps were added to help secure the laminates. Another solution would have been to use screws instead of nails.) The rest of the nails were driven the same way, drilling holes in the lower strip just before each nail was put in, moving down the end of the hull toward the sheer. Keep the row of nail holes right on the centerline of the stem as much as possible. The glue made everything slippery, and the ash pieces put up something of a fight, so the fact that wood glue is easy to clean up was very relevant here.

Fairing the Hull, Continued

This is where the lines of the boat are advanced to perfection. The indispensable tool for this important step is the longboard. This tool can easily be homemade. The board needs to have a little give when pressure is applied, so it will round over the high spots on the hull. The longboard I have and like is 15-3/4 in. long by 2-3/4 in. wide, and has a 1/8-in. thick foam pad on the face of it. Sticky back paper doesn't seem to be available in the grit I use, so I use an adhesive similar to contact cement to attach the paper to the longboard. (The tool I use as a longboard doesn't have clips for the ends of the paper as is often the case with longboards sold at auto body supply outlets.) Another "tool" not to be without is a brush to remove the dust from the hull, and don't forget your dust mask.

While sanding the wooden hull with the longboard does involve physical labor, I don't mind the work because the boat really improves in appearance, and I get completely absorbed with the process of smoothing everything up, looking for irregularities, checking progress, and so forth. I allow perhaps six to eight hours for this step. Here again, some of that time is actually spent looking for high spots and dips, so not all of the time is spent sanding. I concentrate especially on the bottom of the boat along the keel line, but no part of the hull goes unsanded. When you get to the point where the hull is mostly fair, brush the dust off each time you stop to look the hull over because accumulations of dust can make things look different than they really are. Also, it's a good idea to look at the hull critically at different times of the day because the light can affect how well irregularities show up. The pattern of the wood strips can fool you, so a strong light contrast between the hull and the background you view it against is helpful.

As you go along there is a good chance of finding difficult areas where sanding with the longboard doesn't seem to produce much of a result. Plug in the DA sander (80-grit disk) and use that on those extra hard strips. Once in a rare while there will be a small hard spot that you can't get at by sanding without affecting adjacent areas that don't need it, so a sharp curved scraper can come in handy. That is only for the worst places; the longboard is generally very effective.

Beginning of "power stroke." Hold the longboard at an angle across the strips so you can apply firm pressure to three (or more) strips at a time. I use 100-grit paper for this.

End of "power stroke." The long board is still oriented the same way across the strips, but the sanding stroke actually runs mostly parallel to the strips. This technique not only smoothes the hull, but replaces the swirl-shaped sanding scratches from the DA sander with straight scratches running lengthwise of the strips. Lengthwise scratches are less visible in the finished boat than scratches that run across the strips or in curlicues, and those that are visible are less distracting. When there is a high spot to sand down, I do sand at an angle across the strips because more wood comes off that way, but then I finish sanding that area parallel to the strips to get rid of the crosswise scratches.

Remember how it was to get the strips to do what you wanted in the stem area? Sanding out those irregularities with a longboard makes it look like the strips just fell into place. It also blends them in perfectly with the outer stem, giving the end of the canoe a finished appearance. Spend some time here; the flat sides spread the sanding pressure out over a fairly large area so progress isn't as fast as other places. (Switching to a new piece of sandpaper helps.) Where the strips have considerable twist you may find that certain neighboring strips form low ridges where they responded to twisting unevenly. Reduce these ridges by sanding at an angle across them, rocking the longboard as needed over the curves to fair the hull. Keep an eye on hull thickness—a slight ridge is much better than a hole.

Filling Gaps and Holes

After the admirable job you have done of giving your canoe hull the finest curves around, you know this boat really well. Part of what you know is that there are gaps between strips here and there. (If your hull has no gaps, you may take a bow, and skip ahead to the next section.) These gaps don't have a lot of impact on the strength of the hull once it is fiberglassed, yet they are of more than cosmetic importance. They must be filled in order to keep the resin that you use to bond the fiberglass to the outer hull from running elsewhere, leaving a bubble under the cloth, or a resin-starved area in the glass. Resin-starved spots and bubbles are both visible and weak, making them quite undesirable.

There are a few choices available in terms of fillers. A number of well-known strip canoe builders use a paste of mixed epoxy resin with wood flour or a fairing material to fill cracks. Wood putty mixed with water also works well. The filler I have been using lately is a premixed putty that has a petroleum-based binder. Whatever of these you use, either mix or select a color compatible with the color of the wood used for the hull.

I have never used the putty that is mixed with water, but I have used an epoxy filler and the premixed putty sold as Wood Patch.™ The reason I changed fillers is that my experience with the epoxy mixture was unpleasant enough that I never want to repeat it. I was not yet adept at handling epoxy at that time, and after filling the cracks in the hull I was working on, I did not get the excess filler cleaned off before it hardened. I found out that sanding epoxy blobs off a bare cedar hull (if I'd left them on, there would have been dark stains) is a difficult proposition at best. The epoxy is so much harder than the wood (when mixed with wood flour anyway, instead of a fairing filler such as phenolic microballoons) that you can take a lot of cedar off next to a blob before the epoxy finally comes off. In fact, I nearly sanded a hole through the hull in one place. The canoe was a 17-1/2 footer, built with square-edged strips (lots of gaps), so it took me forever to clean up the mess. I'd read of a suggestion to spread a mixture of epoxy thickened with wood dust to the entire exterior of the hull to seal all the staple holes and gaps. After my experience, I would say to *never* do that!

Most new hulls, especially if built with bead and cove strips, don't have enough gaps to really benefit from filling with an epoxy paste. I concede that epoxy will strengthen the area being filled better than any of the other fillers. This may be of interest if you have used square-edged strips and have a lot of cracks between strips, particularly at the turn of the bilge. If you do decide to use epoxy, mix the resin and hardener together well first, and then add the filler(s) that color and thicken the epoxy. Load the filler into a syringe and force it into the gaps with that rather than a putty knife. Put small batches of filler in the syringe, because the stuff will set up in the syringe if you don't apply it all fairly quickly. Scrape off any unintended drips right away. Sand the excess filler off within a day or so. You don't want to have to sand this material after it's rock hard, with soft wood right next to it.

My preference is to use a soft, easily sanded filler that is premixed, dries quickly, and comes in the colors I want. There may be other good brands, but Wood Patch is the locally available one that I use. It needs to be worked with a metal putty knife because it dissolves the plastic ones. The problem with putting it on the hull with a putty knife is that it dries in the can the whole time you are dipping the filler out and applying it, so it may need to be thinned before you are done. A better way to apply it is to use a syringe, because then the filler doesn't dry before it's on the wood, and you only put the filler where you want it, so there's much less waste and less sanding to do later. The syringes that are used for epoxy will resist the solvents in Wood Patch. (For pictures showing how to get the filler into the syringe, and application of filler with a syringe, see the section in the following chapter on making a fillet along the keel line inside the hull.) This filler is dry enough to sand in only an hour. It takes longer than that to dry completely though, and it contains acetone, which dissolves epoxy, so wait until it is fully dry before applying epoxy over it.

Filler color warrants some coverage. Before you choose a filler color, you need to know what color the wooden hull will be under a coat of epoxy. Some woods darken only slightly; others darken drastically. Western red cedar is one of the latter, and it continues to darken with age. If you select a filler color based on the color of the bare, sanded wood, you will be in for a big surprise when epoxy is applied because the filler will not match then. Take a few strips representative of the color of the hull you've built and sand them smooth. Then mix up a very small batch of epoxy resin and brush it on the sample strips. Use these for matching filler color. If you want to be doubly careful, you could put epoxy over a sample of dry filler to see if the filler color changes. Wood Patch in the redwood and walnut colors doesn't seem to.

There are varying recommendations regarding choice of filler color. I follow the basic principle that lighter colors draw attention and darker colors recede. With the color variation in western red cedar, unless the filler is matched to the darkest wood, it is inevitable that a dark strip will end up with lighter filler next to it. It is obvious that there is filler there, and even calls attention to it. However, it hardly registers if a darker filler is next to a lighter strip. The light strip draws attention away from the dark filler. My practice now is to use a filler that is as dark as the darkest wood, or even one shade darker.

For filling nail or screw holes, there is an additional option. Round toothpicks are manufactured with not one, but two "multi-gauge" ends suitable for plugging small holes of varying sizes. Clip the toothpicks in half with side cutting pliers, dip the toothpick tips in glue and poke them into the holes. After the glue dries, cut the ends of the toothpicks off and sand them down flush with the hull. Don't even bother filling staple holes. There are so many of them and they are so small that it's not worth the effort.

This is a good time for a break. Everything that must be done in preparation for fiberglassing is done. The hull will perform as it was designed to whether or not you do any more sanding. For many builders, that is good enough, especially if the threshold of tolerance for sanding has already been exceeded.

Apply filler to cracks in the hull, and glue toothpicks in the nail holes in the outer stem. Gaps between strips don't have to go all the way through the hull to need filling. Any avenue larger than a staple hole will wick resin away from the surface and should be filled. I fill even what appear to be fairly shallow grooves left from the joints between strips because when the fiberglass cloth bridges those small depressions, air bubbles can be trapped there.

Sand off excess filler. A scraper and hand sanding pad are shown here, but what was even more useful was the longboard with 100-grit paper. The toothpicks were clipped off to about 1/16 in. long, and then I filed them down flush with the outer stem with a small, fine-toothed file. I haven't had the occasion to deal with toothpicks in the hull but the longboard should smooth up the clipped off ends satisfactorily.

Going for a Flawless Finish

If you are really into visual effect or else love sanding (either condition may cast doubt upon your sanity) some more attention to the hull is called for. Although the canoe looks terrific now, the application of epoxy resin will reveal quite a few scratches and possibly areas of uneven sanding, which will show up as light and dark blotches. My first canoe looks like that. (The shape of the hull has turned out to give great performance, and besides, I'm kind of attached to it, so I still take it out in public.) For a finish that will really showcase your craftsmanship you need to sand with finer grit papers, and actively search out and eliminate bad scratches. This takes less time than one might expect. The three or four hours it takes goes by quickly for me, anyway.

Sanding with a hand-held pad. Going over the hull with 220-grit paper makes deep scratches show up if they are there. Such scratches are most quickly removed with the longboard, using 180-grit paper.

First, change the paper on the longboard to 180-grit, and longboard the whole hull using sanding strokes that run parallel to the lay of the strips. Since the hull is already fair you don't need to pay attention to that except to avoid sanding a flat where one doesn't belong.

Next, hand sand with a flexible foam pad using 220-grit paper.

Brush the hull clear of dust frequently so scratches can be seen.

When the sanding job seems complete, assure yourself that it is by doing one last test. Get a bucket of plain water, and a clean sponge, and wipe down a section of the hull at a time with the wetted sponge. The wood should just get wet, not soaked. This raises the grain of the wood. Poorly sanded areas and residual scratches will appear darker than the well-sanded places.

With the last rough spots sanded out, go over the hull one final time with the hand pad to knock down the raised grain. By now, you have probably noticed one

of the nicest surprises that come with sanding to this degree, and that is having secondary grain patterns show up in the wood surface. These fancy patterns, if present, are hard to see or appreciate if the wood is not sanded with a fine-grit paper. It is exciting to see unexpected patterns appear, and is one of the greatest delights of working with wood. With softwoods like red cedar, there is no real payoff for sanding with paper finer than 220-grit. So, with this step accomplished, you are ready for the next step, which is the application of fiberglass and epoxy.

This is the final result of resanding the hull with 220-grit paper. Note the variations in strip color and grain pattern.

Hull of Wee Lassie II design, fair and sanded for a fine furniture finish.

Wet the hull using a sponge and look for dark scratches or patches that indicate a need for more thorough sanding. Do a section of the hull at a time, and mark the areas that need more work by circling them with chalk. Chalk easily sands off and doesn't dent the wood.

A tandem canoe, ready for fiberglass.

Chalk markings around scratches. When the wood dries the scratches don't show up as much, but the chalk does. Resand these spots as needed.

Chapter Eight

Fiberglassing the Hull

The application of woven fiberglass cloth to the hull with a resin binder is commonly known as "fiberglassing." That term seems to downplay the role of the resin in the resulting matrix. In reality, the fiberglass is absolutely useless without the resin, which bonds the glass to the hull, locks the flexible cloth into a solid structure, and makes the composite waterproof. Nevertheless, the term is a convenient one, so I will continue to foster that misrepresentation by using "fiberglass" in keeping with casual convention. The term "layup" also refers to the act of applying fiberglass and resin, as well as to the resulting cured composite. Though less commonly used, that term is actually more correct because by definition it includes *all* the ingredients.

The fiberglassing stage of construction brings out an interesting paradox. Until the glass is applied, you really don't have much of a boat. If you were to put your bare wooden hull in the water, you would shortly have a lot of cedar pieces sailing independently of each other. (That is, unless you have chosen to use a waterproof glue to edge-glue the strips.) Once the crucial step of bonding the wood together with the fiberglass and resin into a single unit is completed, it will *look* like you have done little more than apply a clear finish. Most boat builders would be happy to skip straight to the varnishing phase without fiberglassing. The main drawback to that strategy is that you would end up with a beautiful wood sculpture that would make a very poor boat. Even if the glue joints between strips held fast, the hull would still be fragile. The strength of the wood lies lengthwise of the grain, but crosswise of the grain, wood is relatively weak. Traditionally built wooden boats have interior frames to support the planking across its grain. Strip hulls built over a removable mold have no permanent transverse wooden frames to hold them in shape. If you want your canoe hull to resemble a boat more than a basket, something must be added to tie the strips together crosswise, and support them. That requirement is fulfilled by the application of fiberglass-reinforced epoxy. With the fiberglass cloth laid out over the hull one step hence, you will see that while half of the cloth fibers run lengthwise, the same as the strips, the other half of the fibers run around the canoe, across the strips. Those strands may be small, but there are thousands of them distributed over the length of the hull. All together, they add up to a lot of strength.

Both the inside and outside of the hull are fiberglassed. It would seem unnecessary to do this to the inside of the hull, since the exterior is the part that strikes rocks and is in constant contact with water. Besides, additional epoxy and cloth means additional cost and weight. There are good reasons to fiberglass the inside, however. For one thing, there is usually at least some water in a canoe. Also, the inside bottom of a canoe takes quite a beating from feet lubricated with sand and mud. The best reason to fiberglass the inside is perhaps the least obvious, though. The strength of the hull is greatly enhanced by the presence of two layers of fiberglass separated from each other by a core material, specifically, the wood strips. Fiberglass-reinforced plastic has more strength in tension than in compression. That means the material resists being ripped apart by stretching better than it withstands crushing. Because of this characteristic, the inner and outer skins of fiberglass complement each other. Pressure brought directly to bear on one of the skins would have to be sufficient to cause the skin on the opposite side to stretch in order for the hull to distort. For example, when the canoe is in the water, and you step into the boat, you are putting pressure directly against the inside skin of fiberglass. The inside skin would have to stretch a little under this localized pressure to allow the hull to bend out of shape. The outer skin, being separated from the inside skin by the wood strips, would receive less pressure per unit area, because the strips distribute the load over a larger area. Also, because the outer skin would be on the outside curve of the "distortion," it would have to stretch more than the inside skin for the hull to give due to pressure from inside the boat. Both of the fiberglass skins resist stretching, but the outer skin would provide more support for the hull in this case. In contrast, if you were paddling along and the bottom of the canoe came to rest on a submerged stump or boulder, the direct pressure would be against the outer skin of fiberglass, so the skin of fiberglass *inside* of the hull would provide most of the resistance to distortion. If a builder were to construct a canoe hull with fiberglass only on the outside, the boat would probably stand up to abrasion of the outside, and resist being pushed out of shape due to pressures coming from the inside reasonably well. Unfortunately, that would leave the interior of the hull more vulnerable to wear from gritty feet, and flat areas of the hull would tend to flex excessively in response to pressure against the exterior of the hull. Also, a wood hull that has fiberglass on one side but not the other is an example of an unbalanced laminate, and is subject to problems related to different properties of the different materials as they respond to exposure to water, heat, and perhaps other influences.[1]

The way I have taken to doing my fiberglass work involves using two different formulations of epoxy resin. The two resins have distinct characteristics that make them better suited for some applications than others. The resin I use for sealing bare wood, saturating fiberglass cloth, fixing blemishes and actual damage, and any other situation where I need a resin with extra clarity, low viscosity, and/or a long window of workability is System Three's Clear Coat.™ The resin I use for gluing pieces together, filleting corners, building up the last layer(s) of resin over fiberglass, and other times when I need faster curing or greater viscosity is System Three's regular resin with the "fast" hardener for low-temperature curing. (System Three has another resin that is promoted as having these characteristics and also better clarity, called Crystal Resin.™ I have not yet tried it, so I can't comment on it.) It may seem like a complication to stock up on two different resins, but I find the benefits far outweigh any inconvenience. After all the work that has gone into the canoe hull so far, coming up with a rough-looking fiberglass job would be very disappointing. Most of the people I've talked to who have the woodworking skills to feel confident in tackling a boat building project hesitate when they consider the prospect of fiberglass work because they have little experience with that. And the hesitation is justifiable. If you use the regular epoxy resins that are in general use for boat building, you have to have some experience to do a really nice-looking job. You probably do not want to experiment on your canoe. The main reason I advocate the use of a low-viscosity, slow-curing resin for the application of fiberglass is that it is extremely forgiving to use, and even a rank novice can produce stunningly beautiful results. If for some reason you can only buy one type of resin, buy the low-viscosity resin. (I do *not* recommend using solvents to thin the regular resins.) However, there are definitely times when a thicker, faster-curing resin is to be desired, so get some of each if you can. In my projects, I use about two-thirds Clear Coat epoxy, and one-third System Three general purpose epoxy.

Before beginning any fiberglass work, you need to take a moment to consider some important conditions. These will have a large influence on how your fiberglass job turns out. First, make sure that your canoe hull will not be exposed to direct sunlight while it has curing resin on it. Wood which is in direct sun heats up, and the air naturally present in the wood expands and escapes. If there happens to be a coating of fresh resin on the wood, that expanding air will be trapped in the resin as bubbles. Arrange a way to work in the shade. A second condition to monitor is temperature. The epoxy resin and hardener are formulated to cure properly within a certain temperature range. The System Three resin and low-temperature hardener I use for certain things tend to cure faster than I want them to if the temperature is much over 70°F. On the other hand, Clear Coat resin cures very slowly at temperatures below 60° or 70°F. Also, the wood responds to temperature by expanding and contracting as just mentioned, but not as dramatically if out of the sunshine. That means if the temperature is rising when you apply the first coat of resin, you are apt to have those infernal air bubbles trapped in the epoxy. You can get around this by waiting until the temperature is beginning to drop when you put the first coat of epoxy over the bare wood hull. As the air in the wood contracts, it draws the resin into the wood so that not only do you not have bubbles in the resin, you get better penetration of epoxy into the wood in the bargain. The third condition you need to arrange for is good light. It's too easy to miss a problem spot if the light is inadequate. The really frustrating aspect of that is that these problems usually are easily taken care of while the epoxy is runny, but a lot of work to deal with later when the epoxy is hard. So, you don't want to wait until the resin is rock hard to look at the job in bright light. The fourth condition to attend to is your own. Only when you are awake and alert can you do your best work with epoxy, particularly if you are just learning to use it. While this book describes the simplest, easiest way I know of to get top quality results, you do need to be sharp so you don't make careless mistakes in measuring the resin or overlook some small thing that could be permanent later. I find that fatigue markedly increases my problems when applying fiberglass, so I just don't do this when I'm tired.

Fiberglassing the Outer Hull

One of the things about this project that works out really well is that the outside of the hull is the easiest to fiberglass, and that is the part we do first. Thus, we get to buff up our skills on a part that is not too demanding. By the time the inside needs to be done, you will be experienced enough to be able to carry that off with confidence as well.

To start, look over the wooden hull and ask yourself how much stroking that nice smooth wood has received since it was last sanded. It is nearly impossible for people to look at such a fine surface without also running hands over it. The problem is, epoxy resin is fairly sensitive to certain contaminants, and oil from hands on the wood can cause the resin to not stick or not cure normally. So, if the wood has been petted, give it a light sanding with 220-grit paper to remove any accumulated oil, and vacuum off the hull.

Vacuum the dust off the hull. A brush attachment for the hose improves your ability to remove all loose dust. You should also dust off the wood with a dry, fairly lint-free white cloth such as an old T-shirt. If you use a colored cloth and it leaves fibers on the wood, the colored fibers will show up under the fiberglass. White fibers generally turn transparent when soaked with resin.

The next step is an optional one. You can either go straight to laying the fiberglass cloth over the hull, or seal the hull with a coat of epoxy resin first. I like to seal the wood because then I don't have to worry about the resin being drawn out of the glass cloth later by the wood as it absorbs resin. If you wet out fiberglass over bare wood, you need to tend the work for some time after that to add resin where the glass has become dry. Otherwise, you will end up with resin-starved areas and small bubbles where air has gotten into and through the glass fibers. These will not go away with the addition of subsequent coats of resin after the saturation coat has hardened. It is not difficult to get a good saturation coat when bonding fiberglass to bare wood, just a commitment of a little more time and attention. If you have done a good job of filling all gaps in the wood, that goes a long way toward a successful saturation coat.

I prefer to seal the wood before wetting out the cloth because that saturation coat of resin is the most critical one in the layup, and I don't want to take *any* chances with it.

Materials for application of seal coat of epoxy. I use Clear Coat™, a low viscosity resin, because it soaks into the wood really well and it is easy to spread with a brush. Also, because it is thin it doesn't go on the wood in a heavy layer which is likely to sag or run before hardening, and then have to be sanded smooth. This epoxy is mixed in a 2:1 (resin:hardener) ratio. I mix resin in graduated cups rather than using the pumps that are available. For the amount of epoxy work I do, measuring the resin isn't that inconvenient. Besides, I find that I mix a lot of really small batches of resin for which the pumps would dispense too much. Since epoxy migrates all over the place, prepare yourself for that and wear expendable clothes, get stray hair out of harm's way, always wear gloves (latex is better than vinyl), and apply a barrier cream (not under gloves) to exposed skin if you think it prudent. To "paint on" the epoxy, I use inexpensive natural-bristle brushes. Another item that should have been included in this picture is a plastic squeegee, often called a spreader. A squeegee that is two or three inches wide serves nicely for trowelling flat any resin runs that do develop before they harden.

Measuring resin. Dispense the resin first, and then match the quantity of hardener to the quantity of resin (according to the proper mixing ratio), not the other way around. I want a 6 oz. batch of mixed resin, so I poured 4 oz. of resin into the cup.

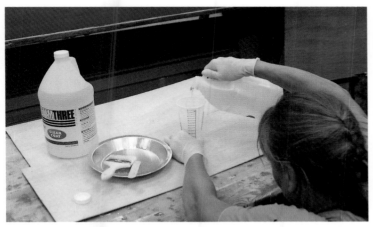

Measuring hardener. I added 2 oz. of hardener to the cup containing the resin, bringing the total up to 6 oz., with the resin to hardener ratio at 2 to 1. Use a clean stir stick (no loose debris on it; old hardened epoxy is OK) to mix up the epoxy in the cup. Mix thoroughly without whipping a lot of bubbles into it. With Clear Coat, bubbles aren't much of a problem to deal with, but you will find that with heavier resins, bubbles can be difficult to eliminate. The best plan is to avoid creating them in the first place.

Pour the mixed resin into a wide container. This extends the pot life of the mixed epoxy. The pot life is the amount of time you have before the epoxy begins to gel, losing its ability to wet out cloth, allow bubbles to escape, and spread easily. Gel time is influenced by the temperature of the resin and hardener before mixing, with higher temperatures speeding the reaction up. The curing reaction itself is exothermic, meaning that heat is given off during the process. So, if the mixed resin is in a container that doesn't permit heat to dissipate, the heat produced as the epoxy begins to gel actually causes the reaction to go faster. The epoxy will reach a point where it solidifies rapidly in the cup, causing the cup to get so hot that you can't hold it, and visible fumes come out of the cup. To avoid this, mix epoxy in small enough batches to apply fairly quickly, put the mixed epoxy in a wide container so that heat will dissipate, and get the resin on the boat as fast as possible while minimizing waste from run-off.

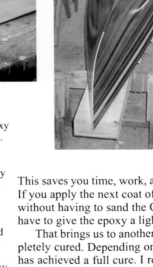

Moving toward the opposite end of the hull, on the first side. I am still using up the first 6 oz. batch of resin here. At about 70°F, 6 oz. of mixed resin is all I can spread very well before it starts to gel.

The entire hull has been sealed with epoxy. It took approximately 26 oz. of mixed resin to seal this 13 ft. 3 in. hull. Examine the hull, looking for runs in the epoxy. If you find some, brush them out, or squeegee them flat. Otherwise they may have to be sanded out later, depending on the size of the ridge they create.

Start on one side of the boat, and brush the epoxy on as evenly as you can. Begin at the stem and work your way to the other end of the boat. By applying the epoxy that way, the resin you are brushing on will be blended into resin that has just been spread and has not had a chance to gel yet. That allows the brush marks in the epoxy to level out nicely. Watch for loose bristles from the brush in the resin and pick them out.

Once the seal coat of resin is on the hull, let it cure at least a day before putting the fiberglass cloth on. That gives the resin time enough to harden so that the fiberglass won't stick to it as you lay the cloth out, and the resin surface won't be marred if it gets bumped during handling. Something to keep in mind as you plan the work is that epoxy takes as much as a week to cure fully, and there is a window of time where subsequent coats of resin will bond chemically to previous coats *without* sanding. This saves you time, work, and dust, and if you can escape having to sand, take advantage of it! If you apply the next coat of resin over Clear Coat epoxy, you have up to seven days to do that without having to sand the Clear Coat. (I don't wait more than three days.) After that, you will have to give the epoxy a light sanding to get the next coat of resin to stick.

That brings us to another important fact about epoxy. Epoxy *can* be sanded before it is completely cured. Depending on your sanding equipment, it may be easier to sand epoxy before it has achieved a full cure. I recommend doing a little testing on your own. Wait until the epoxy seems hard, and see if you can sand it without the epoxy forming little balls of resin on its surface, and without the sandpaper loading up almost immediately. If those things happen, you need to wait longer and try again. Besides ease of sanding, there is another potential benefit here. If you can sand just the spots that need it and apply the next coat of resin before the original coat cures completely, that saves you the trouble of sanding the entire hull just to get the next coat to stick. You can skip sanding the places that are already smooth. Using Clear Coat as an example, it *can* be sanded after two days, but doesn't *have* to be sanded until it has cured for seven days. So, if you ended up with some runs in the seal coat of epoxy, you should be able to sand them out between two and seven days after application, and not have to sand the whole hull. Remember that the temperature of the work area affects cure time, so if it's over 70° or 75°F you should anticipate that the Clear Coat epoxy will cure in less than seven days; adjust your plans for the next application of resin accordingly if you don't want to sand.

Shortly before putting the fiberglass on the hull, make sure the canoe is dust-free. If you are fiberglassing the day after sealing the hull, you may not even have to dust it. Check to see if there are bugs, brush bristles, or other undesirables in the epoxy coating and scrape them out. Do not use a rag dampened with water or anything else to dust the hull. One of the shortcomings of Clear Coat is that water will cause milky spots to appear on the surface of the resin. These spots can be sanded out, but then you have more dust to get rid of. Other solvents (and hand oils) can leave residues that cause problems when subsequent coats of resin are applied, so keep them off the hull.

Now that it's time to put the fiberglass cloth on the hull, some choices need to be made regarding how the layers of cloth will be applied. These choices relate to the order in which the layers will be put on, and how much time will elapse (if any) between application of layers. The basis for your decisions will be:

1. What degree of clarity do you want in the finish?
2. How much time do you have to spend on it?
3. Will the process of smoothing the cured layup damage the integrity of an important layer of cloth?

The most important of these is the strength of the fiberglass covering on the hull. The largest pieces of cloth placed on the boat are generally the most important because they unify the largest areas of the hull into a single entity with the most uniform physical properties, promoting even distribution of loads over the hull surface. Therefore, the large pieces need to be protected from breaks that might occur during the sanding of the layup surface.

There are incentives to layer the cloth as in example A, however, especially if you want to save time by applying the saturation coat of epoxy to both layers of fiberglass at the same time. The cut edges of glass cloth stay much neater during the process of wetting out if there is another layer of cloth over them, so having the full-width cloth over the partial layer prevents fraying of the edges of the partial layer.

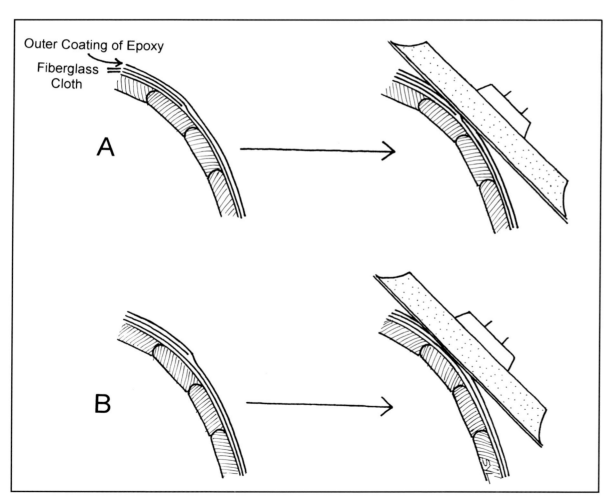

Possible damage to a fiberglass cloth covering as a result of layering sequence and smoothing the finished layup. In example A, where the largest continuous layer is placed over a partial layer, there is potential for the main layer to be broken by sanding through it during the fairing of the hull later. This is prevented by layering the cloth as in example B or by putting enough resin on the hull that the transition from the area having two layers to that having a single layer can be made smooth without sanding down into the cloth at all. In example B, the largest continuous layer is located under the partial layer, placing only the edges of the partial layer at risk. (Curve of hull exaggerated for purpose of illustration.)

Partial layer of fiberglass cloth laid out and trimmed. The cloth was trimmed in place on the hull, even with the strip that is at the 4 in. waterline. Note that this hull was not sealed before application of the glass cloth.

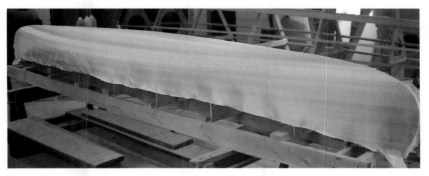

The full length and width layer of cloth laid over the hull and partial layer of cloth. The partial layer is still visible. Both layers used on this 17-1/2 ft. canoe are 6 oz. cloth.

Fiberglass cloth wet out with first coat of epoxy resin. System Three's regular resin with the low-temperature, fast-curing hardener was used here. I could not have accomplished this job (my first try at epoxy work) without the assistance of a friend who was quite familiar with epoxy handling and application. Even with someone else mixing the epoxy and coaching me, I did not get as uniform a coating as I would have liked. Due to my inexperience, I overworked the epoxy in some places, which trapped microscopic bubbles in the resin and resulted in cloudy streaks on the boat, and I also made the mistake of putting on some resin that had begun to gel, so that it did not wet out the cloth completely. I think these problems are typical of those encountered by novices using regular viscosity epoxy for the first time, and I shudder to think of the mess I might have made were it not for my assistant's help. At the very least, I should have used a slower curing hardener to allow more time for the resin to soak into the cloth and to give me more time to spread the stuff around. I have never been as happy with the general purpose resin for wetting out cloth as I am with Clear Coat; now I only use Clear Coat for this application.

When there are only two layers of cloth being put on the hull this way, the risk of sanding through the main layer is not overly great if you are generous with the resin in the area of the edge of the partial layer and then don't sand more than necessary when smoothing up the fiberglass later. Sanding through the main layer is more likely if there are three layers of cloth with two partial layers under the main one in an area that will probably be sanded heavily. If you do go through the major layer of cloth, you will have a weak spot in the fiberglass sheath unless you put a patch over it that overlaps the edges of the break by at least an inch all the way around. (It *is* possible to make a repair if necessary, it's just aggravating to have to do so.)

As far as the time commitment goes, it is faster to put on all the layers of cloth and wet them out at one time where possible. You can wet out two and even three layers of cloth at a time in many areas of the hull. One place you will probably be able to do only a single layer at a time is along the stem, because the cloth will not want to cooperate there. This will be discussed more later.

With respect to the final clarity of the fiberglass, my experience has been that application of only one layer of cloth at a time yields the most transparent results. Even using lightweight cloth, which wets out readily, and the super-thin epoxy resin, I still seem to end up with a pattern of tiny air bubbles trapped in the interface of the layers of cloth if I apply the saturation coat to multiple layers at a time.

Equipped with this information, plan out how you want to apply the glass cloth. For the Wee Lassie II I am constructing, the designer suggests only a single layer of 4 oz. fiberglass over the whole hull. It is, after all, supposed to be a lightweight canoe. However, I know who will be using this canoe, and recognizing that the V-bottom may take a beating along the keel line, I decided to add two more layers of glass there. I also know that I may either intentionally or accidentally sand the boat heavily along the keel line once all the epoxy has cured, so to best protect the main cloth layer, I will put the extra cloth pieces on top of the main layer instead of underneath. And for clarity of finish, the extra cloth strips will be put on after the first coat of resin on the main cloth layer is tack-free.

Rolling out the glass cloth over the hull. This lightweight model canoe is being covered with 4 oz. cloth. Keep the cloth as clean as you can, and try not to weaken the fabric by kinking the glass fibers in a tight fold during handling.

Fiberglass cloth draped and smoothed over the contours of the hull. Leave the fabric at least 3 in. "too long" at both ends. You can trim the extra fiberglass off about 2 in. below the sheer and save the pieces for later projects. Don't trim too close to the hull because the cloth may move around a bit as you apply the resin, and you could come up short on one side.

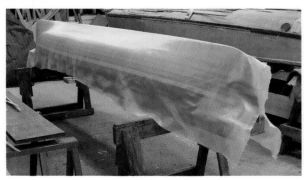

Wet out the cloth with low-viscosity epoxy resin and a natural bristle brush. Do one side of the canoe, then the other. Begin with a section of the cloth about three feet back from one end of the hull to anchor the cloth in place. Then do the area between the first section and the nearest stem. Follow that by applying resin from the first section to the far end of the hull. I mixed resin in 6 oz. batches for this step. Here, I left the resin in the cup because it is easier to pour out of,

Redistribute excess resin with a squeegee. Rather than throw excess resin away, move it to where it will do some good. Be very watchful of how the resin behaves. As long as it still flows easily, you can work it to a limited extent. If you notice it acquiring a frothy appearance, you are trapping bubbles in it that will not come out. If it's not essential to move the resin, stop doing so. If there is just plain too much resin, scrape the surplus off and discard it.

and I was getting the epoxy on the hull quickly this way, so there was little heat build up in the cup. Where the hull bottom is flat enough to pour the resin directly on the cloth and spread it with the brush, do that because it goes faster than "painting" it on a brushload at a time. For much of the surface, you will need to dip the resin out of a tray (as for the seal coat) and brush it on so that the epoxy soaks into the cloth before it runs off the hull. Normally a brush at least an inch wider than this one would have been used, but I was out of wide brushes when I wanted to do this. Wrinkles often form in the cloth along the sheer. These are sometimes rather persistent. It may help to gently raise the edge of the cloth and move the fullness toward the middle of the boat, and lay the cloth back down. As the resin becomes tacky, use a squeegee to press the wrinkles flat. If you simply can not get the wrinkles out, use scissors to cut upward along the highest ridge of the wrinkle, and then lay the two sides down in the resin with one side overlapping the other. This is called a dart, and can be used to encourage cloth to conform in other situations as well.

Making a dart. This example shows a strip of fabric placed over the stem area. A. The fullness in the cloth forms a wrinkle that can't be worked out flat. B. Make a cut along the top of the wrinkle. C. Lay one flap down tight to the hull. D. Lay the other flap down so it overlaps the first.

A

B

C

D

Discarding excess resin. The goal is to bond the glass cloth tightly to the hull without squeezing too much resin out of the cloth. Make sure the cloth appears transparent, but without the satiny, glassy look that indicates resin starvation.

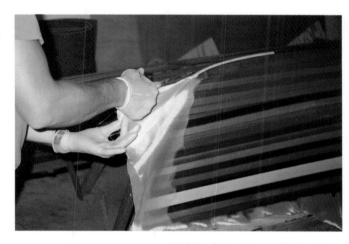

Making cloth at the stem lie flat. First, hold the fiberglass straight out as shown so that a fold forms along the top. Use scissors to cut the top of this fold back to where the cloth hugs the stem.

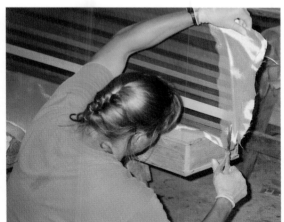

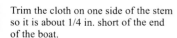

Trim the cloth on one side of the stem so it is about 1/4 in. short of the end of the boat.

Cloth on one side trimmed, ready to wet out. Next, trim the second side the same way. This trimming is done now, rather than before putting any epoxy on the fiberglass. If it were done earlier the cut edges of the cloth would almost certainly slip out of position before it was time to apply resin along the stems.

Brush resin on the cloth, avoiding distortion of the fabric.

Squeegee the cloth tight against the hull.

Fiberglass cloth with first coat of resin. Try to hold the shop temperature steady in the optimum range for curing (around 70°F for Clear Coat). If the cloth was applied over bare wood, and you can't control the temperature very well, apply the epoxy at a time when the temperature is gradually dropping. That discourages the formation of bubbles (caused by gas escaping from the wood as it heats up), and having them be trapped in the fiberglass layup. Sealing the wood before applying the fiberglass eliminates this problem. The saturation of the glass cloth required about 25 oz. of mixed Clear Coat resin.

If you have put the fiberglass on a bare wood hull, check the fiberglass for air bubbles and dry spots every ten minutes or so for half an hour to an hour, and paint on more resin as needed to properly wet the glass. This will probably necessitate mixing small batches of resin. I use small 3 oz. graduated cups for this, but you could also measure small amounts of resin by drawing it up in a graduated syringe. The smallest amount of resin I ever mix is 3/4 oz., because trying to mix less than that could introduce more error in measuring than the resin will tolerate, in terms of an incorrect mixing ratio, and not cure. After half an hour, the wood should have absorbed all the resin it is going to. When you are satisfied that no more dry spots are going to appear, the best thing you can do is leave it alone while the resin cures.

Let the epoxy cure until it is tack-free and rubbery. This will take at least twelve hours. At that time, you can cut the excess cloth away from the sheer with a utility knife. It is much easier to cut through the resin drips while they are still "green" (pliable) than later when the resin has hardened completely.

Cut excess cloth away from the sheer. After the epoxy has cured to a rubbery condition, the extra fiberglass cloth can be easily cut away with a knife. Be careful to not pull the cloth up off the hull in the process.

Allow the epoxy to cure to the point of being hard enough to sand. This may be 1-1/2 to 2 days from the time the resin was applied, in the case of Clear Coat. The cut edges of the fabric at the stems will have hardened into rough ridges with sharp stickers on it. If you use 6 oz. cloth rather than the 4 oz. cloth shown in these pictures, you will probably find that the 6 oz. cloth frays along the edges much more than the lighter cloth. (It is also not as flexible.) This is normal. Just be extra careful not to snag yourself on the ragged edges. These must be smoothed down before the stems can be covered with fiberglass cloth strips. A piece of coarse sandpaper and a sanding block are usually the best bet for that job. Sand the edges of the fiberglass down smooth and dust the area clean with a dry rag.

Now, you need strips of fiberglass cloth cut on the bias to put on the stems. These strips can be purchased from fiberglass and resin suppliers, but I always cut them from scraps of cloth leftover from projects. Bias cloth means that the lengthwise orientation of the piece is diagonal to the woven fibers of the cloth.

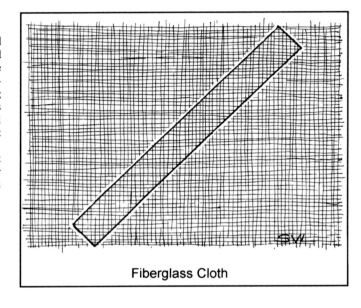

A cloth strip, cut on the bias.

Fiberglass Cloth

The reason bias cloth is used for this step is that it will conform to contours that cloth cut parallel with the weave will not. (Those who have experience sewing clothing will be familiar with this.) I love bias cut cloth because it will give a very neat and tidy covering in areas that would be a headache to do with straight cut pieces. Measure along the stems to find out how long an area you need to cover. Since the stems seem to be magnets for solid objects when the boat is in use, I always put on at least two layers of cloth and extend the ends of the strips back on the bottom of the hull by about a foot or 18 inches. On this particular boat I plan to put strips along the entire length of the keel line, but this is a special case. For most canoes this practice would be a waste of time and materials. If your fiberglass scraps aren't large enough to cut out strips the length you need, cut short pieces and overlap the ends when you apply them to the boat. Make the strips wide enough to overlap the edges of the cloth that is on the hull already by at least 1 in. If you follow my lead and put two layers of cloth on the stems, I suggest making one layer wider than the other so all the edges don't end up in the same place, and you can grade the thickness of the layup more easily at sanding time.

You can either cut strips of fiberglass cloth freehand using scissors, or do it this way. The cloth is laid out flat, and a metal straight-edge placed over the cloth diagonal to the grain. Bear down on the straightedge to hold the cloth in position and cut along the straight-edge with a sharp utility knife. This is easy and works really well. Here, a 2 in. wide strip is being cut, which is the same width as the 4 ft. rule placed over the strip.

Preparing to cut a 3 in. wide bias strip.

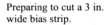

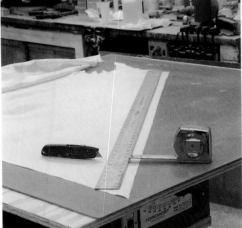

Lay the strip in place. A little Clear Coat epoxy resin has been brushed on the stem to help stick the cloth in place, although adherence is weak before it starts to get tacky. Handle the cloth with care so it doesn't stretch out long and narrow before you have it where you want it. In this photo the 2 in. wide cloth is being put on as a first layer, and the 3 in. wide cloth is to be placed over it. The cloth could just as well have been put on in the reverse order. I did it this way so the wider second layer would keep the edges of the first layer from fraying out and looking nasty. This only works if both layers are put on in the same session, rather than allowing the resin to cure between layers.

"Tack" the bias strip down along the keel line with resin. I do this before trying to smooth the edges down.

Three-inch wide bias strip, with ends trimmed square.

Brush the edges down against the sides of the hull.

Anchor the strip in place with resin so it doesn't slip out of position while brushing down the fuller edges of cloth on the sharp bend of the stem. The big ruffles in the cloth look hopeless as prospects for smoothing down against the hull, but this lightweight fabric cut on the bias is amazing stuff. With a little fiddling, the cloth laid down as smooth as I'd wished for. The cloth will slide around in the resin, and you work that to your advantage in getting it to conform to the hull in areas like this. If this were 6 oz. cloth, the ruffles might need to be snipped, and the cut edges overlapped in a dart to get them to lie flat.

Add the second layer of bias cloth. It is put on the same way as the first strip, before the resin in the first layer gets past the tacky stage. (That is, unless you are intentionally putting the strips on in two separate sessions.) I wanted the second (wider) layer of cloth to hold the edges of the first layer down flat, so it was necessary to make sure the edges of the second layer extended over the edges of the first strip. The only negative result of putting these two layers of cloth on in the same session is that tiny (but visible) bubbles were trapped between the two layers of bias cloth, and I was not entirely successful in getting them all out. Some builders prefer to wet out the bias strips in a tray, then lift them out of the tray and put them on the hull. I have not tried that because it seems like it would be too easy to stretch the cloth out of shape getting it from the tray to the boat, but it might eliminate the bubble problem.

Brushing the first layer back into position. The bow and stern of this canoe are very sharp, and the fiberglass has to go around a very tight turn here. The cloth kept lifting away from the stem along the leading edge, causing an air bubble to form under the cloth. When the resin finally began to get tacky, it held the cloth down where it belongs. It's a good idea to monitor areas where problems seem persistent so you can correct them while it's easy to do so (before the resin hardens).

Place the next strip on the keel line. Unless your canoe hull also has a sharp V-bottom, you don't need to extend the bias cloth layer all along the keel line as is being done here. This 2 in. wide strip is placed end-to-end with the neighboring one (rather than overlapping) because another layer of cloth will be placed over the joint, tying it together. If I were adding only one layer of cloth, I would overlap the ends of the strips by an inch.

A second application of Clear Coat resin on the rest of the hull. Once the bias strips were on the hull, I brushed another coat of epoxy over the rest of the canoe. It takes only about two-thirds as much resin to cover the hull now as for the saturation coat. The glass cloth looks much glossier with more resin on it, and you will find that more sags and runs form in the epoxy. You can save yourself some sanding time later by squeegeeing these flat before they harden.

If you had some dips in the keel line (or elsewhere) of your canoe hull that you could not get out before fiberglassing, you may want to consider adding a layer or two of cloth in those areas to bring them up even with the surrounding contours. Then, when it's time to sand the layup smooth later, you can fair the edges of the "patches" in with the rest of the hull. Extra layers of fiberglass will make the those places slightly less transparent than areas having fewer layers of fiberglass, but you have to look for such a minor difference to find it. It will certainly be less obvious than a hollow in the finished hull.

With all the additional pieces of fiberglass cloth on the hull, let the resin harden for a day. Meanwhile, you can decide how you want to go about filling the weave of the cloth the rest of the way. The critical step of wetting out all the cloth is done; most of what you can do for the clarity of the fiberglass/epoxy layup is behind you. The options are to put a lot of coats of Clear Coat epoxy on the hull to fill the weave, two or three coats of regular resin on, or some combination of those possibilities. Clear Coat will provide a little more transparency and give up bubbles more easily. However, it cures much more slowly, builds less than half as quickly as regular resin (meaning twice as many applications are needed to get the same build up), and also runs off the hull. Regular System Three resin builds more quickly (fewer coats needed), cures faster, and runs less readily, although it certainly will sag and run, just not as bad. The regular resin is not quite as clear, but for me the main drawback is that it traps bubbles much worse than Clear Coat. You can pop most of the bubbles by dragging a foam brush over the resin surface, provided you do it before the resin really starts to gel. (The technical manual for System Three resins indicates that fanning the epoxy surface with a heat gun will also pop the bubbles.) Don't wait until the whole hull is coated to do this; brush out bubbles after covering each quarter of the boat. An alternative I haven't tried yet, but plan to, is to mix Clear Coat with regular resin to come up with a blend having intermediate characteristics. This can be done, according to the manufacturer, as long as the two different resins are mixed with their own hardeners before they are poured together.

I apply all coats of resin with a natural bristle brush and sometimes a squeegee. Many epoxy users argue that resin can be applied more quickly with a roller. I've tried using a roller a couple of times and have not been impressed. The problem I've experienced is that the roller whips air into the resin as I put it on, and the microscopic bubbles persist as a cloudy spot after the resin has hardened. If I intended to paint the boat, I guess that would be acceptable, but I don't want to do that. Using a brush and mixing the resin in small enough batches to apply to the hull before the epoxy gels is fairly trouble free, it just takes longer.

A phenomenon to be aware of as you add more resin to your hull is print through. Print through is the term used to describe the appearance of the fiberglass cloth texture in the varnished or painted outer surface of the boat. The glass fibers don't actually show, but in light conditions where the finished surface is highlighted, you can see a woven pattern in the surface. There seem to be two causes for this. One is that the wood part of the hull expands and contracts (due to environmental conditions) at a different rate than the fiberglass over it, creating stress at the wood/fiberglass interface. We will be eliminating that possibility by fiberglassing both the inside and outside of the hull, preventing the wood from absorbing moisture and also holding the wood firmly in place on both sides. That restricts the wood's ability to contract and expand in response to temperature changes. The other cause of print through is not enough resin over the glass cloth. If you sand down to where you can see the glass fibers in your layup, the application of varnish will make the cloth look transparent, but you definitely will have print through. A resin film that is too thin will also result in print through. I have been fooled by a glossy smooth appearance in Clear Coat resin right after it was applied, only to come back later and find that the epoxy shrunk in thickness as it cured, leaving the texture of the fiberglass visible in the surface. (Some shrinkage is to be expected with most, if not all resins.) I dealt with that by slathering on a coat of the regular epoxy, which builds up in thicker layers.

If you want to be extra confident that you will not experience this problem, apply two to three more coats of the thicker epoxy over the entire hull before you sand. (Remember that a coarser

weave cloth requires more resin to completely cover it, so if you have used 6 oz. cloth you might consider three coats or resin, while two more coats would be plenty for 4 oz. cloth. If you use another brand of resin, this should be interpreted to mean a liberal application of epoxy, however many coats it takes.) This goes quickly if you apply the successive coats over a short enough period of time that you don't have to sand between coats. In fact, you only need to wait until the preceding coat is firm before you can apply the next coat. The whole operation can be done in one day if you start early enough and you use a fast-curing hardener. The other thing this heavy application of resin buys you is that it makes it easier to sand the hull smooth later without getting down into the glass cloth. Even so, something to expect as you sand the hull is to sand into the edges of the bias cloth strips that you put on at the stems. This is one of the more challenging areas for layering cloth and then making the surface smooth and fair after the epoxy has cured. You can either ignore the exposed cloth and accept print through after finishing, or brush more resin over the area and sand it again later. I prefer to brush on Clear Coat, which wicks down into the exposed fibers better, and then apply regular resin over that to bury the cloth.

If you are trying to keep your boat light in weight, the addition of so much resin makes it heavier than it really needs to be and also more expensive to build. Knowing that I would expose the edges of the bias strips when sanding the hull fair, and then "have" to put more resin over those spots, I decided to do some of my sanding before applying the last coat of resin to the whole hull. I put one more coat of Clear Coat epoxy on the hull, and then allowed it cure for three days before giving it a light sanding in preparation for the last coat of epoxy.

The third coat of Clear Coat resin over the fiberglass is being given a light sanding with the DA sander (using a 120-grit disk) to knock off the edges of the bias strips and the worst of the runs before putting the last coat of resin on the hull. Clear Coat does not produce an amine blush (a waxy residue) on its surface as it cures, so there is no need to scrub anything off this type of epoxy before sanding. (More on that later.) Wear a dust mask or respirator when sanding epoxy that is not completely cured, so you don't become sensitized to epoxy by inhaling the dust.

Sand between the epoxy runs with sandpaper or an abrasive pad (such as Scotch-Brite™), and then dust off the hull. To make sure the last coat of resin adheres well, you need to raise some tooth on the whole surface. Vacuum the hull and dust it with a dry rag. The toothbrush in the photo is for getting the dust out of bubble craters in the epoxy. The most annoying thing about bubbles in epoxy at this stage is that if the resin hardens with bubbles in it, and then you sand the tops off the bubbles later, dust instantly accumulates in the residual pock marks and can be hard to remove. Sometimes the next coat of epoxy wets out the dust to transparency, but sometimes it doesn't, and you won't find out until it's too late to do much about it. I try to get as many of the bubble holes clear of dust as possible.

Even though I have put a total of four applications of Clear Coat (including the seal coat) and one coat of regular epoxy on the Wee Lassie II, there really is not much resin on this boat. This is equivalent to about 2-2/3 coats of regular resin. What allows this to work adequately is that for such a small canoe, lightweight cloth, which requires less resin to fill the weave, will suffice.

Now that you have the fiberglass on the hull, you have to admit that that job was not so difficult after all, and besides that it even looks good except for the ripples in the surface, which you will get rid of shortly. Using the thin, slow-curing resin for the more particular parts of the work essentially eliminates the problems commonly faced by novice (and experienced) boat builders.

Most epoxy resins produce a waxy residue (usually referred to as a blush) on their surfaces while curing, especially in humid conditions. Clear Coat does not do this, but regular System Three resin does. This blush will cause sandpaper to clog up like crazy and prevents varnish from drying properly, so it must be removed. Luckily, it is water soluble and easy to wash off.

Scrubbing the amine blush off the last coat of epoxy. This residue is supposed to rinse off with clear water, but I use some detergent in the water and scrub the hull with an abrasive Scotch-Brite pad. Then I rinse the whole works using a garden hose. Abrasive pads are good for cleaning and sanding situations where sandpaper would clog up. The pad will perform well for much longer than the sandpaper because it can be rinsed free of dust and put back to use.

For the last coat of epoxy, I need a substantial coating to really cover the fiberglass cloth, so I used System Three regular epoxy and put it on with a 3 or 4 in. brush. The temperature was around 80°F, so I had to mix the resin in small (3 oz.) batches in order to get it on the boat before it started to set. (The hardener I used was the low temperature, fast curing type.) Stop every 15 minutes or so and lightly brush the surface of the epoxy with a wide *foam* brush to pop any bubbles before they become permanent. You can minimize the incorporation of bubbles in the resin by being careful how you mix it up, but there will still be some.

Now you can set about smoothing up the hull. The hull will never be as well supported once it is off the mold as it is on the mold, so it's best to capitalize on having that solid support. The DA sander and longboard are the most effective tools for this work. One thing you will find is that epoxy, even without the blush, tends to plug up sandpaper. Your best options for dealing with this are to use the DA sander for as much of the work as possible, because the action of the sander seems to kick the dust out of the sandpaper better than anything else, and use high quality open-coat paper on the both the DA sander and longboard. You will probably still have to extend the life of the paper by using an abrasive pad or wire brush to scratch off the accumulated dust.

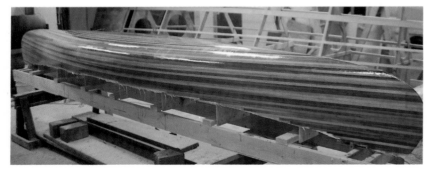

A 17-1/2 ft. canoe with three coats of general purpose System Three resin over 6 oz. fiberglass cloth. There are two layers of cloth on the bottom of the hull. There is more resin applied to the cloth (per unit area) on this boat than the Wee Lassie II, and that is appropriate for two reasons. One is, the wooden hull was not sealed before fiberglassing, so some of the epoxy applied to the cloth was absorbed by the cedar. Second, because of the size of the canoe and the stresses that will be placed on the hull when in use, a heavier cloth was used for more strength. Heavier, coarser textured cloth requires more resin for wetting out and filling of the weave. The fact that two layers of this cloth were wet out at once, below the waterline, really increased the volume of resin required for the saturation coat.

Expect to use up to twice as many pieces of paper to sand the epoxy surface as it took to go over the wooden hull the first time. Sanding the fiberglassed hull with dull paper only generates heat and additional work for you.

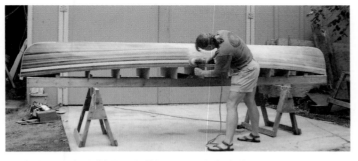

Use the DA sander (with 80-grit disk) to smooth the hull. Moving the sander up and down across the strips seems to work best, but is not as important as it was when sanding bare wood. Don't sand an area more than is needed to get it smooth; you don't want to expose the surface of the fiberglass cloth. You may want to use a sharp scraper to remove the worst runs because they will be hard for you to sand out without "oversanding" the areas nearby.

Fiberglass layup sanded mostly free of drips and sags, and ready for longboarding.

Use the longboard with 100-grit paper to eliminate any lingering irregularities in the hull surface. This is the last substantial sanding the outer hull will receive before varnishing, so be as critical in evaluating the condition of the surface as suits your standards. One thing you need not be too concerned with is the pattern of scratches in the surface. These will disappear when varnish is applied. Sand in whatever direction works best to get rid of humps and bumps. You may want to sand out the worst scratches, but a silky smooth surface is not necessary. Scratches in the cured resin offer a good base for varnish to bond to.

You may, during the last step, have either sanded down to or through the fiberglass cloth. If you have exposed the cloth fabric, but not made a hole in it, there is no damage to the structure of the canoe. In that case, you can either ignore it or re-coat the area with resin to prevent print through, and re-sand the area later, feathering the edges of the resin patch down to blend in with the surrounding area. If you sanded through the cloth, a fiberglass patch needs to be put over the area to restore the integrity of the layup. Cut a piece of fiberglass cloth to a size that will give an inch of overlap with the cloth around the damage on the hull. Make the corners of the patch broadly rounded rather than square, and then put the patch on the hull with the same succession of epoxy coats you used for the main job. After the resin has cured, sand the area smooth, and you are ready to go.

When epoxy resin is brushed onto a smooth hull, the resin will run. If the runs are allowed to harden, it will be a challenge to sand them smooth, and there is a risk of sanding down into the fiberglass cloth in the process. This problem can be minimized by squeegeeing the runs flat while they are still soft, or using tape to control the flow of the resin.

Using tape to catch runs. The epoxy does settle in a little ridge along the upper edge of the tape, but it is much easier to deal with a straight, even edge at sanding time than irregular runs. Remember to peel the tape off as soon as the epoxy has set to the rubbery stage.

Taking the Hull Off the Mold

This is a big day for the project! You will finally get to see your canoe hull right side up, the way it will sit in the water.

The shape of the canoe will affect how you take it off the mold. I built one canoe, a Wee Lassie model, that slid right off the mold without unfastening anything. Another canoe, a modified version of Hazen's Micmac model, which has recurved stems and sides tilting inward along the sheer, had to be taken off the mold by unfastening all the stations from the strongback, and then removing the stations from the hull one by one.

Wee Lassie II hull, off the mold. The stem forms are held tight by a combination of pinching between the hull sides, and excess wood glue. These forms were pried loose using a long screwdriver and some judiciously applied water to soften the glue.

A tandem canoe with recurved stems, and sides with tumblehome, off the mold. The middle mold was rotated out of position for removal. The other stations were freed by tapping them toward the middle of the boat. The stem forms were rolled up out of the ends of the hull. There should be no trouble getting these loose, provided the station edges were well taped. If wood glue seems to be causing a hang up, try putting a little water on the problem spot and letting it soak until the glue softens enough to let loose.

Hull minus stem forms.

Lifting the hull off the mold with the stem forms still attached. The shape of this canoe is such that it doesn't grip the stations. The stem forms seem to be stuck, so they were unscrewed from their cleats on the strongback.

The hull you have constructed will need trimming along the sheer line if the wood strips were not laid parallel to the sheer. Find or make markings on the outside of the hull indicating where the sheer was at each station location. This gives you a series of dots to connect on the outside of the hull. Then, get a batten that bends evenly along its length, and clamp it to the side of the hull so it makes a curving sweep that connects the sheer line markings. Draw a line along the edge of the batten, which will serve as the cutting line.

Here the sheer is half cut. A coping saw with the blade turned to one side was used for this job.

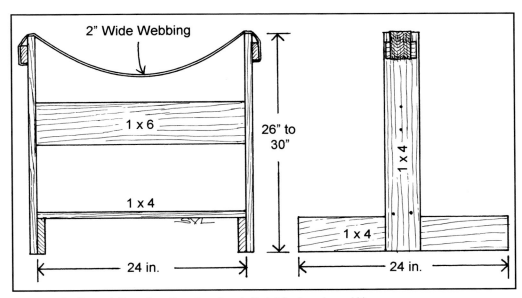

Cradle stand dimensions. Carpet can be substituted for the nylon webbing.

Preparing the Inside of the Hull for Fiberglass

Once you have come back to Earth and recovered from the elation of having righted your canoe, it's time to get to the business of working on the inside of the hull. The concave surfaces of the inside of the hull are somewhat harder to work on due to limited space, and also the limitations in the application of most tools. The DA sander with the foam backing pad will be your best friend here, but even it won't work everywhere. You will also want to have a curved scraper and a foam hand sanding pad. Another indispensable item is a vacuum cleaner for removing accumulations of dust.

But first, you need to come up with some type of cradle to hold the boat while you work on it. My favorite "cradle" is a pair of independent stands with sling straps on the top. These stands can be moved closer together to hold the hull upright, or slid farther apart to allow the hull to rest on its side.

Cradle stand. This stand is 26 in. high. It is built of 9-ply flooring plywood that was left over from another project. The sling is 31 in. long between the two uprights.

When you have devised a means of supporting the hull, you are ready to get on with the fun. The general scheme is to first remove the worst of the ridges, sharp edges, and glue blobs with the scraper. That is followed by sanding with the DA sander where you can use it. The rest of the smoothing up is done by hand sanding.

Scrape down high spots and excess glue. There are a lot of areas on the inside of the hull that are best worked with a sharp, curved scraper. Some builders modify the blade of an ordinary paint scraper just for this job. One of the advantages of this tool is that it offers the ability to really concentrate on a small, localized spot without affecting adjacent strips. For glue removal, a drop of water added to excess glue will soften it up for easier scraping.

Do most of the sanding with the DA sander (with foam backing pad). You will be able to get most of the way out to the stems and all but the tightest concave curves with this sander. To get the foam pad to conform to these contours without digging into the soft wood at the edges of the disk, start the sander in a flat area, and the press the pad down firmly against the hull as you move into a concave area. If the edge of the disk starts to tear at the wood, retreat. In certain areas, you may actually want to do some shaping using the edge of the disk. You can even up the surfaces of strips in some hollows that are about the same shape as the edge of the disk if it's tilted at the right angle. This technique is only for the early stages of sanding where you're smoothing the surface, not finish sanding. I do most of the work with 80-grit disks, and with the sander operating at a medium speed for good control. Once the wood surface is mostly smoothed up, I switch to 120-grit disks for sanding out scratches and any remaining irregularities. Probably the most important tips here are to pay close attention to what is happening where the disk meets the wood, and keep the sander moving.

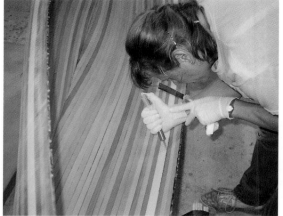

Wood Patch filler is being applied with a syringe to fill cracks. This makes for a much neater job than using a putty knife, there is far less waste, and less sanding to do later, and the filler does not dry out in the container. The syringe is the same type used for dispensing wood glue earlier in the project, and is of a plastic that resists deterioration from the solvents in Wood Patch. To get the filler into the syringe, scoop the filler into a plastic bag (a Ziplock sandwich bag is great), squeeze the filler down into a corner, snip a hole in the corner of the bag, and the squeeze the filler into the syringe through the hole.

Here, a putty knife is used to drive the filler into the cracks.

I do some of the heavy sanding by hand with an 80-grit disk stuck on a foam pad. Near the stems where no other tool will reach, I sand crosswise of the strips to even up their surfaces, and then lengthwise of the strips to get the crosswise scratches out. I hand sand places where the DA sander won't work, and to get scraper marks out. The DA sander doesn't do a perfect job of smoothing the hull interior, so I improve the regularity of the surface by hand sanding. This is also the time to shape and sand the inside stems if your canoe has them. When I'm happy with the fairness of the inside of the boat, I go over it with 120-grit paper to eliminate deep scratches and swirl marks left by the DA sander. How much sanding you do once the boat is essentially smooth inside is up to you.

Sand the dried filler smooth. Next, the whole inside of the hull will be resanded with 220-grit paper for a top quality finish. That and the next step are optional.

Wet the wood with water to make rough spots show up. Mark scratches and other poorly sanded areas with the chalk, and when the wood is dry, resand the hull, concentrating especially on the areas that are still rough.

The inside of the hull is ready for the application of fiberglass.

The inside of the hull is a pretty sight, sanded smooth. This is a good time to pause, to appreciate the results of your efforts.

Fillets and Joint Reinforcement

A fillet is a putty of epoxy and thickening agents that has been added to the inside corner of an angled joint. Fillets are used to improve the strength of a joint, provide a rounded corner that fiberglass can conform and adhere to, and/or give a joint a more finished appearance.

There are only a few instances where fillets are really necessary in the construction of a strip canoe, but lots of places where they *can* be used. It is mostly dependent upon the judgment and taste of the builder. It is quite possible to build an entire canoe without making a single fillet.

The Wee Lassie II hull has a V-bottom that I felt might experience a lot of stress were it run aground with a 210 lb. person in it. The outside of the hull has already been reinforced, but a fillet needs to be made along the inside of the keel line to strengthen the joint, and also round out the corner of the joint so fiberglass cloth will bridge that area without having air bubbles form under the cloth. The application of this fillet is shown as an example of how to make a fillet, but this is actually a very unusual situation. Few canoes have enough of a V-shape along the keel line to make a fillet that runs from one stem to the other. Most "stem area" fillets do not extend more than 1-1/2 ft. inboard from the extreme ends of the craft, because the hull bottom broadens out to a rounded shape unsuitable for filleting.

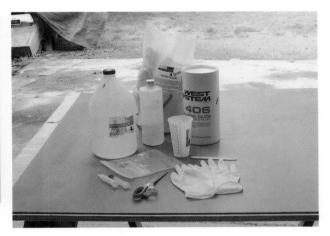

Materials for mixing filleting putty and applying it. The resin is the regular System Three epoxy. Usually it is desirable to have a fillet cure quickly, reducing the likelihood of it sagging from its own weight. Also, you can tool (shape) a fillet made with faster-curing epoxy sooner. The two fillers used to thicken the epoxy are colloidal silica, to give the putty a smooth texture, and wood flour, for brown coloring and more bulk. The only item missing is a tool for shaping the putty after it is applied.

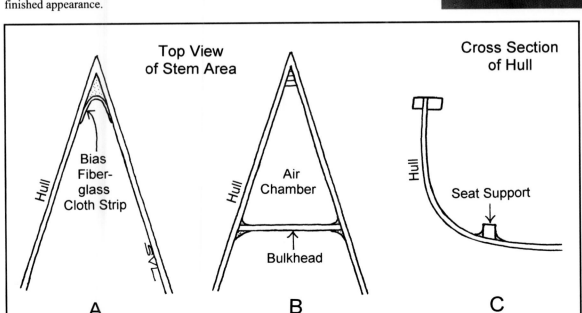

Top View of Stem Area

Cross Section of Hull

Hull

Bias Fiber-glass Cloth Strip

Hull

Hull

Air Chamber

Bulkhead

Hull

Seat Support

A   B   C

Examples of fillets used in strip canoe construction. A. Fillet used to substitute for a built-in wooden stem. The fillet supports the hull sides where they join in the stem area. It also provides a rounded surface for a strip of bias-cut fiberglass cloth to bond to, which adds more strength. B. Fillets added to joints between bulkhead edges and inside hull. Bulkheads offer excellent support for the ends of the canoe, with the bonus of creating a sealed air chamber for extra flotation. The fillets give the joints a more finished appearance and also spread out stresses over a larger area of the hull. C. Fillets added to improve visual appearance of joint. The seat support illustrated here doesn't need structural support from a fillet, but the fillet does make the joint look better.

Mix the resin in the proper ratio, and then add the fillers. I use small amounts of mixed resin, generally 3/4 oz. to 1-1/2 oz. for making the putty; that way the stuff doesn't set up before it's applied. The colloidal silica and wood fillers are added until the mixture has the desired consistency. As can be seen here, measuring filler is not a closely regulated operation in my shop. The amount added was one handful.

Pouring thickened epoxy into a syringe. This material is actually too runny to use for a fillet, because it would sag before it cured. I want to force this mix into some tight joints, and for that it will work fine. The syringe can also be used for applying a stiffer mix; see the section on installing bulkheads for pictures of that.

Apply thickened epoxy to the joint along the keel line. I didn't mix a new batch for this; this was just a good way to use up the "leftovers." When you are done with the syringe, you can clean it out by drawing acetone up into it and flushing it out a few times. The barrel of the syringe can be left to soak in acetone, but the plunger should be washed off and dried, as the acetone causes the rubber tip on the plunger to swell. System Three offers a cleaning solution concentrate that is a safer material than acetone and could be used instead.

Adding wood flour. I usually end up with about equal amounts of colloidal silica and wood flour in the filleting mix. Stir up the mixture and check its viscosity. How stiff the mix needs to be depends on how you want to use it.

Forcing thickened epoxy into the gap between the inside and outside stem. This is an example of an area where a runny mix works well. I want the epoxy to flow downward as far as possible.

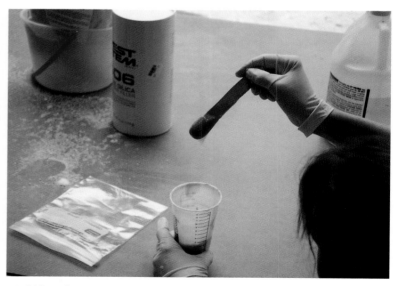

A thicker mix. More filler was added to this batch. This is a good consistency for filleting; it is similar to mayonnaise.

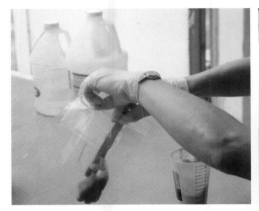
Put the putty in a sturdy plastic bag.

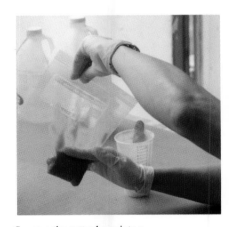
Squeeze the putty down into a corner. Next, snip the corner off the bag, creating an opening about 1/4 in. in diameter to force the putty through.

Apply the putty to the joint. This technique is amazingly mess-free. Be aware that the epoxy mix is all together in a mass here, and surrounded by your warm hands, and that both factors promote quick gelling of the resin. Don't waste any time getting the putty on the boat.

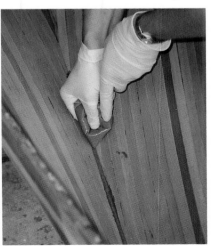
A bead of filleting putty all along the keel line. To be extra neat I could have placed masking tape on each side of the keel line (perhaps 1/4 in. to each side) to pull up after shaping the fillet. (The tape is best put in place before applying the putty to the joint.) That would leave a fillet with nice straight, even edges. This is shown later, in the section on installing bulkheads and decks.

Tooling the fillet. Before you can shape the fillet, you must let the putty start to set up a little. If you tool it too soon, you find that the putty is too soft and ends up sticking to everything (especially the tool), and the fillet surface will be anything but smooth. Keep checking the fillet and when the tool leaves a smooth depression when dragged over the surface, the time is right. Try to get it done fairly quickly, as the fillet is continuing to harden. Small fillets take 20 to 30 min. for the putty to gel enough to be tooled; large, bulky fillets take less time because the mass of the mix encourages quicker curing. All kinds of things can be used to shape fillets; the only requirement is that whatever you use leaves a smooth concave surface on the fillet. I cut round flexible pieces out of the sides of used mixing cups or empty milk jugs. These are useful in situations like this one where the breadth of the fillet varies with the shape of the joint. Wipe off excess resin accumulated on your shaping tool frequently.

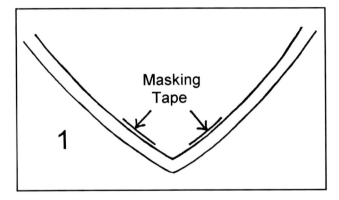
Masking Tape

1

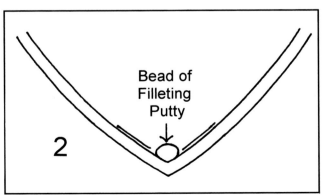
Bead of Filleting Putty

2

continued on next page...

...continued from previous page

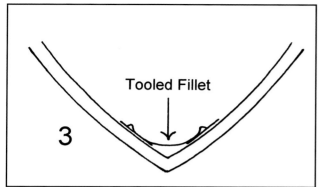

Tooled Fillet

3

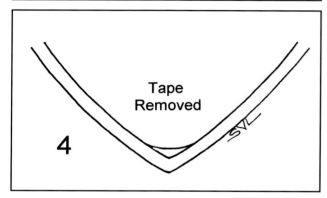

Tape Removed

4

A method for making professional-looking fillets. This works for vertical as well as horizontal joints. 1. Prepare the surface by sanding it to raise some tooth. Then, keeping in mind the width of the fillet to be made, attach strips of masking tape along each side of where the fillet will be. 2. Apply a bead of putty along the joint, and let it set up to the point that it can be shaped. 3. Shape the fillet with a smooth, rounded tool of your choice. The tool usually leaves a ridge of putty on each side of the fillet. If you have matched the amount of putty applied to the desired size of the fillet, these ridges of putty will be on the masking tape. 4. Peel off the masking tape promptly, before the putty gets stiff, so the edges of the fillet will lay down smooth. The fillet edges are often lifted and left slightly ragged by removing the tape, but they will lay back down if the putty is still soft enough.

Strips of bias cloth are laid over the fillet along the keel line. The ends of the strips don't overlap, because another layer of cloth will be laid into the whole inside of the hull, tying everything together.

Such a strip of bias cloth was laid over the fillet along the keel line of the Wee Lassie II. The addition of the fiberglass cloth strip contributes a lot of extra strength to this joint. I chose to put these strips under the main layer of cloth because the shape of the inside of the hull lends itself to that scheme.

Position the fiberglass cloth strip with a dry paint brush. The cloth doesn't cling to the paint brush bristles as it does to fingers, especially in tight spaces. For areas where the cloth needs to be massaged into pronounced contours, a brush is the tool of choice.

Fillets are easy to make once you are familiar with the process. Nail together some scraps of wood in a T-shape so you have some practice joints to play with and experiment with putty consistency, and application and tooling techniques. You will quickly master this basic method of strengthening and finishing joints.

A joint commonly filleted is the inside stem area in canoes constructed without wooden stems. That area requires a substantial fillet. This fillet becomes an important part of the structure of the canoe and warrants special attention. The tooled surface of the fillet may easily be as much as an inch wide, which is at least four times wider than most fillets. Also, the joint surface itself is apt to be vertical for much of its length, which presents a problem for such a bulky fillet. If you were to apply the fillet all at one time, two things would probably happen. One is that the fillet would sag out of shape before it gelled due to its own weight. The other is that the fillet would set up so suddenly that you might not get it tooled before it was too late. The solution is to apply the fillet in layers, allowing each layer to set up before application of the subsequent layer. It is only necessary to wait until the last layer is firm to add the next one. You would actually not need to tool the first layers, but you could do that just for the practice. After all, if they turn out lumpy that's all right because they will be buried anyway. The structural strength of the fillet can be enhanced by placing a bias cloth strip over it so the cloth extends an inch or more onto the inside surfaces of the hull. A smoothly concave surface on the fillet provides an excellent base for the fiberglass cloth strip.

Wetting out the bias strip with Clear Coat epoxy.

Fiberglassing the Inner Hull

The sequence of steps in fiberglassing the inside of the hull is essentially the same as for the exterior. But because the hull is now right side up, the effects of gravity draw the resin down into the boat, and the limited space within the hull requires us to be creative in fitting the fiberglass cloth smoothly to the surface of the strips.

The inside of the hull may (or may not) be sealed before the application of the glass cloth. As with the outside of the hull, I elected to seal the wood inside, and proceeded straight to that step as soon as the bias cloth over the fillet was saturated with resin.

Sealing the bare wood with Clear Coat.

Allow the epoxy to cure until it can be sanded. Hopefully, you don't have any runs to get rid of, but now is the time to work on them if you do. Sand down rough spots along the edges of any pieces of fiberglass cloth you've applied. You may at this point still have stalagmites of epoxy resin along the sheer. (They were stalactites until the hull was taken off the mold and turned over, right?) These will snag the glass cloth during the next step if not removed. You can file them down, or if you are a little daring, use a grinder to eliminate them. The hull should be strapped firmly into the cradle so that it won't move while this is being done; it would be all too easy to damage the sheer strip if

Inside of the hull, after the application of the seal coat.

Getting ready to trim away extra cloth at the stem. After fiberglass cloth has been smoothed neatly into the hull, there will still be a wad of extra cloth at each stem. Organize the cloth into one large fold, with equal amounts of cloth on each side of the fold.

Cut straight down the fold to the bottom of the hull. This separates the cloth at the end of the hull into two sides, which can now be trimmed to fit into the stem area. Trim one side at a time, with the cloth for the other side folded out of the way. Arrange the cloth for the first side so it lies smoothly against the vertical hull side, and mark the cloth with a line traced as close to the inside stem as possible. Then cut the cloth along that line with scissors and press the cloth back in place. Repeat for the other side.

the hull shifted. It's not necessary to make the sheer perfectly smooth right now, just get most of the resin drips off.

Next, lay out the fiberglass cloth so that the whole interior is covered. Begin at one end of the hull and unroll the cloth to the other end. Retain an extra 6 in. of cloth at each end, just in case it's needed later. Starting in the middle of the boat, work the cloth down into the hull. Work toward the stems, letting the excess cloth hang over the sheer, while avoiding snags that will disrupt the weave of the cloth. The fiberglass conforms to the inside of the hull remarkably well. As you get near the stems, there will be a lot of fullness in the fabric to smooth and adjust out. Take your time getting the cloth to lie flat against the hull. Do not leave any "tailoring" of the fiberglass on the inside of the hull for later, when resin is being applied.

The fiberglass cloth is ready for the saturation coat of epoxy. It is often helpful to clip clothes pins in a few places along the sheer to hold the cloth in position.

resin mostly filled the weave of the lightweight cloth, and there were large areas where little texture was left showing. An additional caution is that the regular resin is harder to get a good, evenly transparent saturation coat with. Don't attempt it unless you have an assistant to help you get the job done quickly, because the resin has a much shorter window of workability (if you use the fast-cure hardener, as I did).

If you try for a textured surface and end up with glossy spots in patchy distribution, just keep adding coats of resin as if you were after a glossy interior in the first place. There are significant advantages to the smooth finish, so remind yourself of those as you work along.

A larger canoe with 6 oz. cloth fitted into the hull.

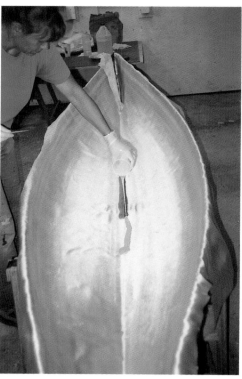

The amount of resin applied to the fiberglass cloth can be varied to produce different textures inside the hull. One option is to fill the weave of the cloth completely. This produces an even glossy surface. The other option is to only partially fill the weave of the cloth, so that the texture of the cloth surface is still partially retained. Selling points for this approach are that less resin is required, and because of that the boat will be a little lighter and less expensive to build; the surface texture will cut down on glare when out on the water, and also offers "nonskid" footing; and there is less sanding to do in preparation for varnish. The advantages of filling the weave are that the glass fibers in the cloth are better protected and supported, resulting in a more durable surface; the boat interior is easier to clean; and if you ever have to refinish the inside of the hull, it is *much* easier to remove old varnish from a smooth surface. (You have to sand old varnish out, because chemical strippers damage the fiberglass layup by stripping the epoxy as well.)

My preference is for the textured surface. I have found two ways to get the results I wanted and one way to not get the desired result. The critical thing about making the textured surface look great is that the cloth needs to be evenly saturated with resin all over the interior of the boat; not patchy, where puddles of resin have created smooth, glossy places in the otherwise textured surface. The key to getting an even distribution of resin is to apply all the resin needed in *one* coat. If you have to add more resin in a second coat, there is a good chance the epoxy will run or puddle somewhere, spoiling the uniform appearance of the surface. The weight of the cloth and the thickness of the epoxy resin used will affect your success to a major degree, due to the relationship between the amount of resin required to saturate the cloth and the ability of the resin to build up in a single coat. Two cases where I achieved the desired texture were when I applied a single coat of System Three regular resin to 6 oz. fiberglass over bare wood; and when I applied a single coat of Clear Coat to 4 oz. fiberglass over sealed wood. The Clear Coat experiment gave a slightly better appearance, but the fiberglass has been more susceptible to damage than that in the general purpose resin experiment. One instance where I did not get the result I wanted was where regular System Three resin was applied to 4 oz. fiberglass over sealed wood. The thicker

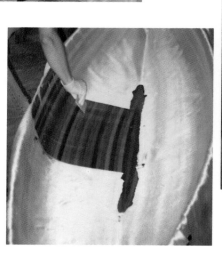

Start by pouring a 6 oz. batch of mixed epoxy along the keel line. The cloth needs to be anchored here first to minimize the possibility of it scooting out of position as the resin is applied.

Draw the resin up the near side of the hull to the sheer. You can use either a wide natural bristle brush or a new squeegee for this. You may want to have both on hand. Be organized about distributing the resin. Try to wet out a section all the way to the sheer before going to a new area, and avoid leaving unwetted streaks between sections. Also, press the fabric as tightly against the hull as you can without pulling the cloth; it seems to be easier to float the cloth over an excess of resin on the inside of the hull than on the outside. Floated cloth has an unsightly ridged or rippled appearance, and the only way to get rid of these irregularities after the epoxy has hardened is to sand them out. Since the fiberglass is on the surface of the lumps, you will have sanded a hole in the fiberglass in the process of getting rid of the lumps; then the cloth layer has to be patched. Not a happy picture. It is quite easy to avoid, however, by squeegeeing away excess resin after the cloth is wet out, but while the resin is still runny. Good light is essential to spotting these things before they have a chance to become a problem.

To wet out the cloth along the inside stem, start at the bottom of the hull and use a brush to tack down the trimmed edges of the fiberglass cloth with resin. Tack the cloth in place up to the sheer. Now the last section of dry cloth will stay put as you wet it out. Notice that the cloth on the near side is folded back out of the way for now.

After wetting out a fairly broad area on one side, switch sides and repeat the same procedure. Pour another batch of epoxy along the keel line, and drag it up the other side of the hull. Keep an eye on the fiberglass cloth at the keel line. As you pull resin up the sides, the fiberglass may lift away from the hull bottom. If that happens, be sure to work the cloth back down against the hull.

Below and right: Having saturated the cloth in the middle of the hull, the ends of the craft remain to be done. It is important to not allow the resin along the edges of a saturated area to set up before wetting out the cloth adjacent to it. The surest method is to mix smaller batches (3 oz.) of resin, and apply it to both sides of the hull next to one end of the first area (until you run out of resin) and then switch to the opposite end of the first wetted area and apply a new batch of resin there. Keep alternating ends of the boat as you work your way toward the stems.

Fold the remaining side down into place and apply epoxy.

97

The stem area with fiberglass wet out. It will probably be necessary to reach into these tight quarters as far as possible with a squeegee to press the cloth against the hull and remove excess resin. That done, evaluate the possibility of placing bias strips over the inside stem (or fillet) successfully before the epoxy hardens. Most canoes have enough room at the stems that bias strips can be applied. If such is the case with yours, go ahead with that step because it will ·save you the trouble of having to sand the ragged edges of the cloth along the inside stems in order to add the bias strips later. This canoe is so narrow at the ends that it was not possible to get the cloth strips down to the stem surface while the hull sides were still sticky. I waited until after the epoxy hardened, then sanded the rough spots near the stems before adding the bias cloth strips.

In order to work a 4 in. bias strip down into a very narrow stem area, the strip is folded in half lengthwise and pushed down into the hull until it touches the stem surface. The brush is used to spread the strip edges to conform to the hull.

When the epoxy has cured to a rubbery consistency, but not yet hard, trim off the cloth scraps with a utility knife.

The bias strip is in position and ready for epoxy. Note that the corners of the strip are rounded for a "finished" appearance.

Wet out the cloth with epoxy resin. (I used Clear Coat.)

The application of strips of bias cloth over the inside stems (of either wood or epoxy putty) is optional. I recommend doing this extra step, because it contributes additional strength to the stems of canoe, and at small cost in terms of time, materials or effort. I would only consider omitting this step if I were building a canoe with really substantial laminated hardwood stems, and the shape of these large structural members made it impossible to lay cloth over them.

Anchor the cloth strip to the inside stem with resin before spreading epoxy along either side.

Preparing for the last coat of epoxy resin. The fiberglass has three coats of Clear Coat resin over it at this point. Since the inside of the hull is harder to work on than the outside, I figure I will accidentally sand down to the glass cloth while smoothing the interior layup and then have to recoat those areas to prevent print through, so I might as well do some of the necessary sanding before the final coat of resin. The DA sander (with 80-grit disk) is being used to lightly sand as much of the surface as I can get to.

The last coat of epoxy is applied to the inside of the hull. The choice of resin used depends on how much build up is desired. I opted for Clear Coat, but heavier resin gives you more material to work with if you have a lot of surface irregularities to smooth out.

The interior of the hull is recoated with resin after wetting out the bias strips. The bias cloth "tails" were left attached until the epoxy firmed up to avoid disturbing the bond with the hull.

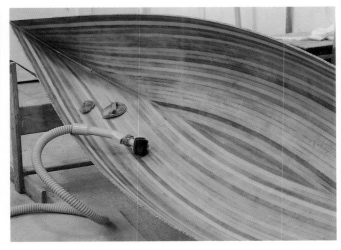

The hand-held pad with 80-grit paper is used to sand areas the DA sander can't fit into. The steel wool is for roughening the low spots that the sanding disks won't reach, to make sure the next coat of resin will stick.

Sand the last coat of epoxy in preparation for varnish and attachment of structural parts. This is an extensive sanding, with the goal of making the inside of the hull as smooth as possible. Tools used are the DA sander with 80-grit disk, sanding block with 60-grit paper, hand-held pad with 80-grit disk, and vacuum cleaner. The sanding block turned out to be of somewhat limited utility on this small canoe; I could have gotten along without it. Take special care to not sand down into the fiberglass at this stage. After the contours of the hull are smooth, the whole inside of the hull will be resanded with 120-grit paper to remove scratches which might show up under the varnish. The epoxy surface doesn't have to be as finely sanded for varnish as the bare wood hull was in preparation for the fiberglass. Varnish fills most of the scratches in the epoxy in two or three coats, rendering them invisible. If you do sand down to the fiberglass, deal with it the same way as on the outside of the hull; recoat with resin, patch it if necessary, or ignore it.

Applying the first (and last) coat of epoxy to the interior of a 17-1/2 ft. canoe. As the photo suggests, the procedure is the same as for the smaller craft. The middle of the hull is wet out first, and then subsequent batches of epoxy are spread toward alternating ends. System Three's general purpose resin with "fast" hardener was used on this canoe. To move along quickly enough to maintain workable edges on the wetted areas with this type of resin, an assistant who can and willingly agrees to mix epoxy is indispensable.

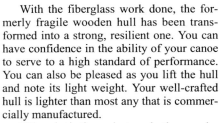

With the fiberglass work done, the formerly fragile wooden hull has been transformed into a strong, resilient one. You can have confidence in the ability of your canoe to serve to a high standard of performance. You can also be pleased as you lift the hull and note its light weight. Your well-crafted hull is lighter than most any that is commercially manufactured.

This point in the project marks the completion of the most important part of the canoe, the hull. It also marks a change in the magnitude of the individual steps in the building process. The addition of the framework and other support and trim pieces consists of a series of discreet "subprojects," each of which offers its own satisfaction for the builder. The builder can finish these one at a time, or work on several concurrently. The completion of each item makes a solid contribution to the finished appearance of the canoe and also the builder's sense of accomplishment. For now though, pause to enjoy what has already been accomplished, and cross one more item off the list of steps in the construction of a wood strip canoe. Completion of this step is sufficient excuse to dispense with moderation; celebrate to your heart's delight!

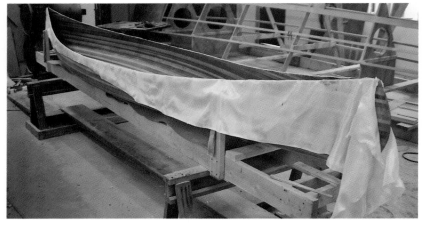

Saturation coat complete. This canoe has fillets in the ends of the hull rather than laminated wooden stems. As soon as the principal layer of cloth was wet out, bias cloth strips were applied over the fillets in the stems.

Epoxy work on the inside of the hull is completed. A single application of resin produced a uniform "burlap" texture on the interior of the hull. The winning combination was a bare (unsealed) hull, one layer of 6 oz. cloth, and regular System Three resin. The only preparation required for varnish is to scrub the hull out with soapy water and an abrasive pad (such as Scotch-Brite™), and then hose it clean. The relatively minor amount of labor involved in getting the hull ready for finishing makes this treatment a really attractive alternative. The key to success is the right combination of fiberglass cloth weight, resin viscosity, and hull preparation (the absorbency of the wood). If you'd like to try for this textured surface, it might be well worthwhile to do some experiments with scrap wood, fiberglass, and a little resin to see what works for you.

Chapter Nine

The Framework

As you admire the fine lines of your new hull and imagine how it will handle on the water, an almost irresistible urge to put it in the water will probably begin to overtake you. And you could go ahead and put it in the water. But would you be able to do that and not step into it for a quick paddle around? While the hull can support itself, it needs a framework to be able to retain its proper shape while carrying a paddler.

The most important framework pieces are the gunwales. After that come the thwarts and decks. The seats are also framework pieces, but they support the paddler, not the hull.

Builders who are anxious to upgrade their status to "paddler" as soon as possible can speed up that process by doing some steps concurrently. For example, work on the inwales and outwales can be underway at the same time, and the seat frames and thwarts are natural companion projects. Another advantage to this plan is that supplies can be conserved. You will use a lot fewer disposable brushes if you varnish two seat frames and two or three thwarts in one go, rather than treat each piece as a separate project. The same is true of small gluing operations. The smallest batch of epoxy glue you can mix will sometimes be too much for one small job, but if you have two or three things to glue you can use it all up instead of having to throw part of it away. The key to success here is to plan out the order of operations and actually post the list somewhere so you don't lose your place.

There is a range of alternatives in the way the various pieces can be crafted, allowing the builder to satisfy his or her own fancy in adding details that really make the boat unique. I have experimented with more variations with some pieces than others, but in no case have I exhausted the possibilities. In this chapter a sampling of these possibilities is presented, so readers can select what they like, or use these ideas as a foundation for something different. Let your imagination play a little, and with the basic information provided here, you may even come up with an innovation all your own.

The Gunwales

The support system made up of the inwales and outwales is the first to be installed, not only because it is the most important, but also because nearly all the other pieces attach to it.

The gunwales may be very simply constructed or somewhat more elaborate. The inwales can be designed with drainage holes in them (or not). The ends of the inwales may be set into decks, or they may be run all the way to the inside stems. All of the treatments have their distinct advantages. See the following illustrations for examples of popular gunwale designs.

Example A shows what is by far the simplest and fastest way to make the inwales. There is no need to figure out seat and thwart locations before installing the inwales, because those items can be placed anywhere along the length of the inwale. The main disadvantage of this alternative is that the canoe will not drain very well when overturned. Also, this inwale

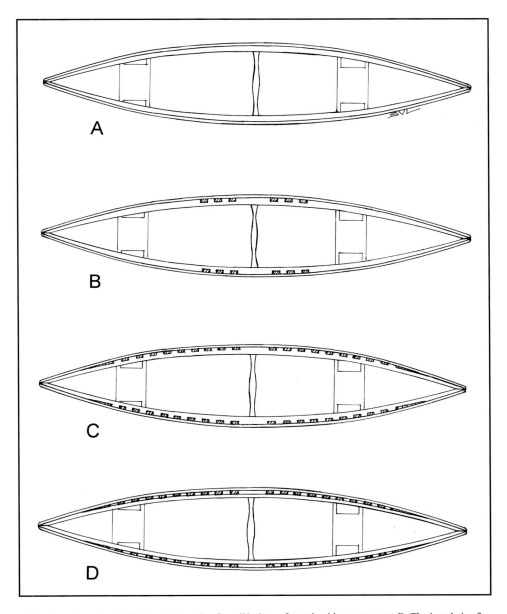

Inwale treatments. A. The inwale is made of a solid piece of wood, with no scuppers. B. The inwale is of a solid piece of wood, with some scuppers. C. The inwale is of solid stock with scuppers along most of the length of the sheer. D. The inwales are of narrow stock, with spacer blocks glued between the inwale and inside hull. (Not drawn to scale.)

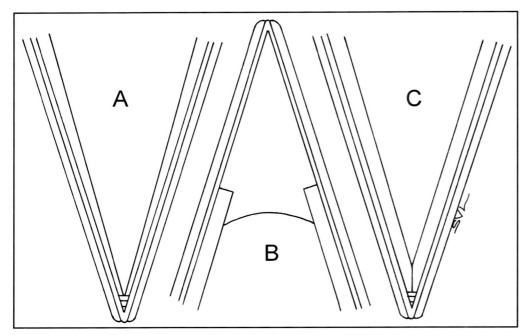

Joining of inwale ends. A. The inwales are tapered from full width at about 32 in. from the ends down to whatever half the inside stem surface is at the tips of the inwales. The beveled off edges on the inwales would be next to the hull if you are planning to fit a deck between the inwales, because that makes deck-fitting easier, particularly if the inwales are scuppered nearly to the ends as in C and D of the previous illustration. Otherwise, it makes no difference which side of the inwale is beveled. B. The ends of the inwales are set into a deck. The inwales are installed first, and the deck (more properly termed a breasthook in this case) is made to fit into the opening between the inwales and the extreme end of the hull. C. The inwales are run at full width all the way to the point where they cross the centerline of the canoe. There, the ends of the inwales are joined to each other as well as to the inside stem surface.

Gunwales in cross section. A, B, and C are outwales; D, E, and F are inwales. A. This outwale has the lower edge beveled. The bevel can be cut using a table saw.[1] B. This outwale is a standard for canoes of all sizes. Longer canoes (over 16 ft.) usually have the larger, more substantial outwale for greater strength. C. A trimmer outwale for small, light weight canoes of 14 ft. or less. D. A solid wood inwale of popular dimensions for canoes of all sizes. Scuppers 1/4 to 3/8 in. wide can be cut into inwale stock this size. E. A narrow inwale sometimes used on tandem canoes and more often used for small, light canoes. Inwales this size need to be of hardwood to provide much support. A limitation with these inwales is that they are so narrow that it is difficult to use them for attaching seats. F. An inwale structure made up of a continuous inwale piece with spacer blocks attached. The combination of the two usually totals about 3/4 in. wide. The spacer block and inwale can both be 3/8 in. wide, or the block can be 1/4 in. wide and the rail 1/2 in. wide.

design has the least stiffening effect on the hull for the weight of the inwale pieces. The inwale can be made of material as narrow as 3/8 in. by 3/4 in. on up to as wide as 3/4 in. by 3/4 in. If your goal is to make a light canoe, then this style of inwale will be unnecessarily heavy if you use hardwood of the more standard 3/4 in. by 3/4 in. dimensions. If you shave the wood down to 3/8 in. by 3/4 in. to conserve weight, the inwale will be too narrow to hang a seat from, and you would have to mount the seats on risers attached to the hull sides; or for a small solo canoe, put the seat on a support structure attached to the hull bottom. A weight saving alternative would be to use a softwood such as spruce for the inwales and make them 3/4 in. by 3/4 in. to provide for seat installation. Example B is an intermediate design which provides for drainage, yet is still simple to make and offers the additional benefit of tie-down points for securing gear. The inwale stock does need to be 3/4 in. wide to allow for the 3/8 in. wide cutouts, so that means the inwales still could be fairly heavy if they are of hardwood rather than softwood. In example C, how far fore and aft the cutouts are carried is up to the builder. Advantages of this variation are that stiffening along the sheer is comparable to that of the solid wood type, but for significantly less weight; with better drainage, and plenty of tie-down points. Disadvantages are that more figuring is required to make sure the holes don't end up where you wanted to place a thwart or hang a seat, and that in the process of carving out the holes you waste some wood by turning out a lot of chips and dust. In example D, the spacer blocks can be of hardwood or softwood, and block size varies from 1/4 to 3/8 in. wide x 3/4 in. thick x 2 to 4 in. long. Leftover cedar from hull construction, or a contrasting hardwood, or wood matching the inwales can all be used for the spacer blocks for distinctive visual effects. Using these blocks eliminates the need to remove wood to create the scuppers. The intended placement of thwarts and seats will dictate the locations of the blocks. Advantages of this type of inwale construction are the same as for C.

After settling on a gunwale design that appeals to your notion of practicality and good looks, it's time to start cutting the pieces. Measure along the sheer from stem to stem to see exactly how long the pieces need to be. Always leave the pieces 6 in. to a foot longer than that for starters. You may need to adjust them fore or aft a bit during the fitting process, and you can't do that if there's no margin to work with. If you need spacer blocks, cut those too. See the section on inwale installation for more information on block size and spacing.

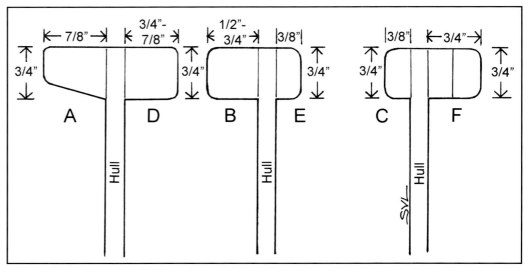

Making gunwale pieces. The designer of the canoe I am building recommends 3/8 in. by 3/4 in. hardwood inwales and outwales, with 3/8 in. by 3/4 in. by 3 in. spacer blocks placed 4 in. apart on the inwales. For this canoe, that means I need 42 of the blocks (plus a couple extras in case of mistakes). These gunwale pieces were ripped from a 3/4 in. thick ash board 16 ft. long. I really only need 14 ft. long pieces, so I used the extra 2 ft. at the ends for making spacer blocks, which are being marked off here. The ends of the gunwale pieces did not yield as many of the blocks as I needed, so a fifth 3/8 by 3/4 in. strip of ash was ripped for the remaining blocks.

Cutting the spacer blocks.

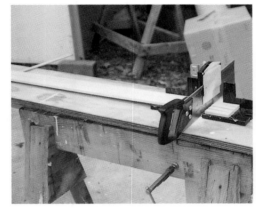

Before putting the gunwales on the canoe, ask yourself how often, if ever, the gunwales will have to come off. If there is some certainty that they will have to be removed in the foreseeable future, then they should be put on with screws. Epoxy forms a permanent bond (except with oak), and once the parts are epoxied in place, the gunwale pieces have to be destroyed to get them off. It is unusual for gunwales to have to come back off a wood strip canoe. I thought I might want to remove the inwales of one of my canoes for refinishing the interior of the hull, so I installed the inwales with screws. I found that it's not necessary to take the inwales off to work on the inside of the canoe, and so never have. In retrospect, I should have glued the inwales on. Gluing the gunwales to the hull gives a stronger attachment and stiffens the sheer more, providing better support for the hull. So unless you are sure they will have to come back off, I recommend gluing the inwales on.

Different builders seem to have differing opinions and preferences on the order of operations for gunwale installation. Some install the inwales first, others install the outwales first, and yet others put the inwales and outwales on at the same time. I doubt I could do a decent job of the latter. I like to put the outwales on first because it goes quickly, and I'm ready for a step that goes quickly. If you think it is a better plan to put the inwales on first, skip ahead to that and then come back for the outwales.

Installing the Outwales

The first step in attaching the outwales is conducting a clamp roundup. Find every clamp on the claim, and put it in the canoe hull. C-clamps are best, followed by spring clamps, followed by bar clamps, Vise-Grips, and anything else that will work. At least a dozen clamps will be needed; thirty is better.

Then, do a trial fitting of the first outwale piece by clamping it to the sheer. That will help you organize your clamps before you have wet epoxy to deal with. Let the ends of the outwale extend past the end of the hull for now. They can be cut off later. Also, arrange for a way to hold up the

loose end of the outwale while you start clamping at one end and progress to the other. An assistant is helpful; so is a large cardboard box, properly placed.

Now that you have these details in order, it's time to do the deed.

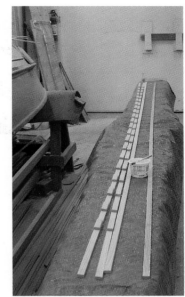

Applying unthickened epoxy to the outwale. Mix a small batch of the faster curing epoxy (about 1 oz. for this 14 ft. piece), and brush a thin film of epoxy on the outwale. An inexpensive brush made for use with soldering paste works well for applying epoxy to these smaller parts. The unthickened epoxy wicks into the wood fibers to improve the bonding of the wood with the sanded epoxy on the exterior of the hull.

Colloidal silica and wood flour were mixed into the remaining resin to make it about the consistency of peanut butter. The ratios of the two fillers were adjusted to get a color close to that of the ash outwale. Spreading the mix around the sides of the cup as shown in this picture slows down the curing time of the epoxy by preventing heat buildup in the resin mass.

Spread thickened epoxy on the outwale. The stir stick works better for this; the brush would leave too heavy a coating. The wood grain will still show through the glue, which is only about 1/16 in. thick. The idea is to get enough glue on the outwale to allow a little excess to squeeze out of the joint, but not so much as to create a mess and waste epoxy resin. Now that the epoxy is spread out on the outwale piece, it will cure slowly enough to allow adequate time for clamping.

The first outwale is clamped to the sheer. Support the free end of the outwale somehow while you begin putting clamps on at the other end. As you clamp the outwale on, let it run about 1/8 in. to 1/4 in. below the sheer. There are usually some bumps and dips along the

sheer, which are most easily eliminated by sanding them down to the surface of the gunwales after those are attached, so install the gunwales a little low. After you have the outwale clamped firmly enough to keep it in place and a little glue has squeezed out along the edges, pick up the excess glue with the corner of a putty knife. Wipe the putty knife clean on a paper towel or rag often as needed so the epoxy doesn't get all over. It's much easier to get rid of unwanted epoxy at this stage than after it has cured, so do as much clean up now as you can, particularly along the underside of the outwale.

The second outwale is clamped in place. Notice that the sheer shows above the outwale by about 1/8 in.

A tandem canoe at the same stage of construction, for comparison.

Cut off the ends of outwales. Stay clear of the end of the hull.

There are several ways to make attachment points for ropes to a canoe. One of them involves drilling holes in the hull right behind the inside stem and gluing in a section of pipe for a rope to pass through. If you would like to do that, see Chapter 10 for instructions now. It is easier to accomplish this before the inwales are installed, because they further limit your working room.

Installing the Inwales

If your canoe is to have solid wood inwales with no drainage holes, the installment of the inwales is nearly as simple as for the outwales. The only real difference is that the ends of the inwale pieces need to be cut off *before* installing them.

If your inwales are going to have holes in them, there are some things you need to do to ensure that you don't come up with a hole where you really need solid wood. If you want to hang seats from the inwales in the traditional manner, you need to plan ahead for that. Thwarts must also be located where there is wood enough to hold them, so plan for that, too. There are some differences in the priority of placement considerations between solo canoes and tandem canoes. Solo canoes are the simplest to plan out, so we will cover them first.

In a solo canoe, there is only one seat (a definitive feature), and usually one but sometimes two thwarts. In order for the canoe to be correctly trimmed, that is, set level in the water, the paddler's center of gravity must be in the center of the boat. (An exception to this rule is in the case of asymmetrically shaped solo canoes. They are shorter and broader in the stern than in the bow, so there is more buoyancy per unit of length in the stern. The paddler's center of gravity will be a little aft of the center of the boat when the canoe is trimmed for cruising. See the section on seat installation for information on how to allow for this, or refer to your boat plans for specifications on seat location.) Placement of the seat and thwart are established according to where the paddler's center of gravity needs to be, with the thwart placement subordinate to the seat. In other words, the seat goes exactly where it needs to, and thwart has to go somewhere else, so it doesn't interfere with use of the seat. If there are to be two thwarts, their placement isn't critical, as long as they are out of the paddler's way, yet far enough toward the middle of the canoe to render support to the midsection of the hull.

Depending on the canoe's depth and shape, the seat may be either suspended from the gunwales or supported by wooden pieces from underneath. Follow the designer's recommendation on that, and if the seat is to be hung from the inwales, make sure inwales will accommodate the attachments.

To figure out seat and thwart locations, start by measuring the actual length of the hull, from end to end. Then, divide that figure in half. Measure half the length of the hull and place a stick across the hull there, clamping it to the outwale. Make sure the stick is perpendicular to the centerline of the hull by measuring the distance from the end of the hull to where the stick crosses the sheer on both sides of the boat. Those measurements must be the same. (See illustration.) This marks where the paddler's center of gravity needs to be. Now, consider whether the paddler will usually be in a kneeling position with knees braced against the hull, or sitting with feet extended toward the bow. If the paddler will be kneeling at least some of the time, put the leading edge of the seat frame where the crosswise stick is clamped to the sheer, and mark the sheer and inwale to show that. Then, determine where the aft edge of the seat will be (you need to know the size of the seat), and make markings for that, too. Finally, mark the thwart location. The thwart would be a short distance behind the seat, at the next spacer block back if you are using them. Where the paddler is to sit on the seat with feet extended forward, the seat should be *centered* on the location marked by the crosswise stick, because the paddler will always be sitting squarely on the seat. In this case, the seat will usually be situated near the waterline, and supported from underneath rather than hung from the inwales. That means the seat frame location need not be marked on the inwale, but the thwart location does.

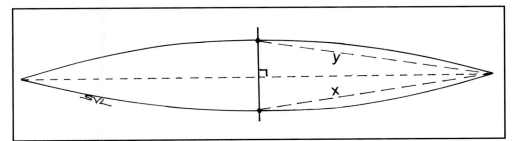

When the crosswise stick is perpendicular to the centerline, then *x* equals *y*.

Mark spacer block locations on inwales, using the first inwale as a pattern for the second. The same type of markings would be used on solid wood inwales which are to have scuppers (holes) cut into them. The thwart and seat locations are reference points for the locations of all the blocks.

In tandem canoes, there is no seat in the middle of the boat to displace the center thwart or carrying yoke. (The yoke and thwart serve the same purpose of stabilizing the hull, but a carrying yoke is also specially shaped to fit around a person's neck and shoulders, while a thwart is not.) Therefore, the location of the center thwart will be the primary influence on the placement of drainage holes in the middle part of the canoe. However the seats, which are to be placed near the ends of the canoe, must be taken into account. The seats in a tandem strip canoe are almost always hung from the inwales. There does exist an alternative method of installing seats by attaching them to cleats, which are glued to the inside of the hull. See the section on seat installation for more on that.

Tandem canoes may or may not have additional thwarts, besides the center one. The need for additional thwarts is based on expected use of the canoe. Lightly loaded canoes of up to 18 ft. with only a center thwart will be fine with a crew of two paddlers on lakes. For canoes over 16 ft. long that are likely to be heavily loaded and used on whitewater or stormy lakes, at least one more thwart is in order. Add two for extra strength. A nice thing about the question of whether to put in secondary thwarts is that it doesn't necessarily *have* to be answered until the canoe has been tested a few times for performance. I used one of my canoes for several years before deciding to add a second thwart. These thwarts are located according to the paddler's convenience and where inwale construction offers a place for them. In other words, block spacing along the inwales needn't be adjusted for secondary thwarts. If a second thwart is added, it usually goes about midway between the stern seat and the center thwart. If a third thwart is added, it generally is placed just aft of the bow seat. A consequence of that is that it makes it near impossible for a solo paddler to sit facing "backwards" on the bow seat to paddle a tandem canoe. Instead, the paddler has to kneel in the midsection of the hull or sit on the stern seat with a weight in the bow to trim the canoe for decent handling.

Tandem paddlers often paddle from a kneeling position, perched on the leading edge of their seats. Since that is where their centers of gravity are, those are reference points in determining seat placement. The weight in the stern needs to balance that in the bow for the canoe to rest level in the water with paddlers aboard. In most cases, it is assumed that the paddlers are about the same weight or that the gear aboard can be adjusted to trim the canoe. This is practical, since paddlers may trade positions, and a canoe may also be used by several different people. Based on these assumptions, the seats are placed so that the leading edge of the bow seat is the same distance from the middle of the canoe as the leading edge of the stern seat.

Mark the thwart location on the inwale piece *and* on the upper edge of the hull. First, clamp an inwale piece to the sheer with a little extra length extending over both ends of the hull. Then, either follow the designer's instructions for seat and thwart placement, or figure them out yourself. Mark the thwart location, and if the seat is to be hung from the gunwales, mark the location for that also.

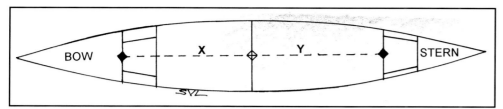

Bow and stern seat placement. If the bow and stern paddlers are the same weight, or if gear onboard can be moved to trim the canoe, the seats are placed so that distance X equals distance Y. If the weights of the two paddlers are significantly different, and these two people will always occupy the same seats, then the seat positions can be "custom located" for proper trim. Use the equation (X)(Bow paddler's weight)=(Y)(Stern paddler's weight). Determine how far one seat will be from the midpoint of the canoe, and after that has been established, figure out where the second seat goes by solving the equation for the remaining variable. Usually the placement of the bow seat is subject to the most conditions, so it might be best located first.

Now we must decide how far toward the ends of the canoe to locate the seats. Factors for consideration are adequate leg room for the bow paddler, ease of reaching over the gunwale while paddling, lateral stability, buoyancy of the hull, and foot room under the seats. Characteristics that are enhanced by moving the seats toward the middle of the boat are buoyancy (the canoe's ability to ride up over waves instead of cutting into them), leg room for the bow person, lateral balance (due to the bottom of the hull being wider under the seats), and indirectly, foot room under the seats. Foot room is affected by the distance of the seat above the hull bottom. The boat is more stable if you hang the seats low, closer to the waterline. This is something you would do if the hull is round and narrow under the seats. However, it can make extrication of large feet a difficult maneuver. By moving the seats toward the middle of the boat, where the hull is wider and flatter, the seat can be raised higher above the hull bottom (and waterline) without unduly compromising stability. Also, depending on the paddler's arm length, the paddling position may be more comfortable with the seat placed higher, near the gunwales. Characteristics that are improved by moving the seats toward the stems are a shorter distance to reach over the gunwales for paddling, and increased leverage and range of motion in turning maneuvers.

In weighing these choices, consider the shape of the canoe and paddler(s). If the canoe is wide and flat-bottomed relative to its length, the seats can afford to be placed fairly close to the ends of the boat. If the canoe is narrow and round-bottomed, the seats should be put farther inboard. Long-armed, big-footed paddlers will probably be happier farther inboard, while shorter-armed paddlers will prefer being seated closer to the stems.

If all this is too complicated to take in, take measurements off a canoe similar in shape to yours, or contact the designer for advice. At any rate, don't be immobilized by fear of making a mistake. You can move the seats later if you need to. When I built my first canoe, I built the hull based on one designer's plans, but followed another builder's advice on seat placement. I ended up with a canoe that was really hard to keep up-

right! I immediately lowered the seats by at least 2 in., and later moved the bow seat a whole seat width inboard. (I had to make a new seat; the original seat frame did not reach the hull sides in the new position.) I probably should move the stern seat too, but haven't yet.

With all this figuring done, we can get on to spacer block size or, viewed another way, the size of the holes in the inwales. The rule is, let your good taste guide you, as long as there is a strong connection between the inwales and the hull, and appropriate attachment points for thwarts and seats. There can be many short, closely spaced openings in the inwales, or longer openings spread farther apart. The spacer blocks for the inwales of the canoe in the photo series are of intermediate design: 3 in.-long blocks placed 4 in. apart.

The way I am creating openings in the inwales of the Wee Lassie II is by attaching spacer blocks at regular intervals to a narrow rail of inwale stock. Another way to achieve the same effect is to start with a wider piece of inwale stock and bore or cut the holes into the inwale edge. This can be done in several ways. One of them is to clamp the two opposite inwale pieces together so the sections to be cut out face each other, and markings for the openings are on the upper edges of the inwale stock. Then, bore a series of holes with a 3/4-in. Forstner bit where each opening is to be. That done, unclamp the inwales and use a rasp to smooth up the insides of the holes. Other means of making these holes would include use of a table saw or radial arm saw outfitted with a dado blade or, alternatively, a plunge router.

Place spacer blocks over markings on inwale pieces. The work surface is covered with plastic to prevent an unwanted epoxy bond.

Plan for scupper placement. Sticks can substitute for the actual seat frames and thwart pieces. The final placement of the center thwart in a tandem canoe is established when the rest of the canoe is essentially finished. The balance point in the middle of the finished canoe is located by picking the canoe up by the thwart (wedged under the inwale) and adjusting the thwart's position until the canoe hangs level. Then, the thwart is moved forward an inch or two (so the canoe will ride a little low in the stern while portaging) and fastened in place. That means you need to leave and inch or two extra space between scuppers at the midpoint of the canoe to allow for some fore and aft adjustment of the center thwart. Remember to make reference marks along the sheer to help you line up the inwales correctly when it's time to install them.

Place plastic tape over the block edges that will not be glued. This is partly to prevent accidental bonding of opposing blocks during gluing, and partly to speed up the repositioning of the blocks later when time for doing so is limited. The tape being used here is 3/4 in. wide filament tape. Don't attempt to pull the tape tight between blocks; a little slack is helpful.

Flip the rows of blocks back over and adjust them into position on the inwales.

Flip the rows of blocks glue surface up and brush on unthickened epoxy. This gluing process required a total of about 1-1/2 oz. of mixed resin (the faster setting type). Both surfaces being joined are bare wood, so both surfaces of all the joints are coated with unthickened epoxy.

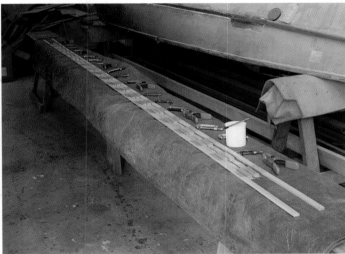

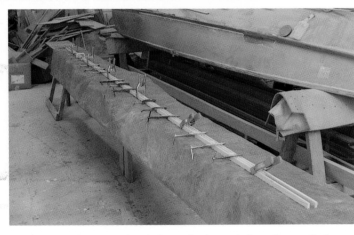

Turn the inwales up on edge, facing each other, and clamp. Do any final adjusting of blocks now.

Add colloidal silica and wood flour to the leftover resin from the preceding step and spread a thin layer of the mix to one surface of each joint.

Close-up view of clamping arrangement. The clamping pressure is enough to squeeze a little glue out. Use a putty knife, screwdriver, or another scraping device to remove as much excess epoxy from the outsides of the joints as possible.

File cured epoxy blobs from the joints.

Use a router to round the inside edges of the openings in the inwales (top and bottom sides). This is an optional step. This could also be done with a file and/or sandpaper, but would be time consuming. The only difficulty I've encountered with using a router for shaping the edges of these openings is that the end grain of the spacer blocks seems to burn. This may be due to the limitations of my equipment.

Sand epoxy off the undersides of the inwales. It is easier to take care of this now, before the inwales are installed. The upper sides will be readily accessible after the inwales are on the canoe, so those can be postponed for the time being.

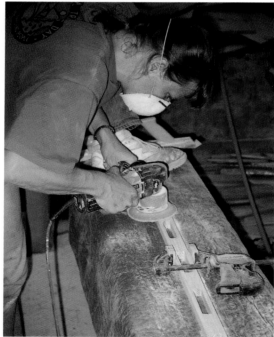

Round over the lower edge of the inwale. This is another step that is much easier done now than later. The last thing I did before putting the inwales on the hull is remove the burn marks from the spacer blocks with a round file and coarse sandpaper.

Clamp one inwale to the sheer, matching the thwart markings. The location of the thwart is the only reference mark on the sheer of this canoe.

Cutting lines are marked on the inwale. The crosswise cutting line is determined by sighting straight down on the inside stem and estimating where the inwale end needs to be cut to fit. The tip of the inwale needs to be half the width of the inside stem surface, so a mark to that effect is made on the crosswise cutting line. A straight-edge is used to draw a long bevel that extends back from that width marking at least 2 ft. Trial and error fitting will establish the final bevel.

The first inwale is glued and clamped in place. Wipe the dust off the fiberglass along the appropriate edge of the hull and carefully work the inwale into position. Clamp as you did with the outwales, with the inwale 1/8 in. to 1/4 in. below the sheer. Clean up stray epoxy with the trusty putty knife, paying special attention to the scupper openings.

Second inwale fitted, glued, and clamped.

Bevel the side of the inwale that mates to the sheer. I used the plane as much as possible and the angle grinder with a 24-grit disk the rest of the time. Trial fit the inwale as often as necessary to get the bevel right. Resist the urge to pull the inwale against the hull in an unnatural curve; work on the bevel until the inwale tapers smoothly along the hull. Repeat the process for the opposite end of the inwale.

Remove the worst irregularities with a coarse rasp. Choose your tools according to the workability of the wood. This ash is really hard and demands the use of tools that would destroy a softwood.

Mix up a small batch of epoxy and coat the joining surfaces of the wood, first with unthickened resin, then thickened epoxy. This will become a familiar routine.

Use a longboard to smooth the upper surface of the gunwales. Coarse 100-grit paper was the best option here. A belt sander can also be used for this, if you have one.

Shape the upper edge of the outwales with the router. A plane and coarse sandpaper can be used instead, if necessary.

Turn the hull upside down and round over the lower edges of the outwales. Also, shape the ends of the outwales so they are smooth and match each other. This may require a rasp or file since the end grain of a hardwood like ash is abrasion resistant.

Rounding over the upper edge of the inwales. If you plan to put decks on the canoe, don't shape the inwale edges where the decks are to go. Leave the inwale edge square for better joining with the deck pieces. If you haven't decided exactly how far inboard the decks will go, then leave a few extra inches of inwale unshaped. It can be finished up with a file and sandpaper later, as needed.

In theory at least, the gunwales are permanently fixed to the hull, and should not need further fastening. I've not convinced myself that real life conditions bear this out as fact, however. Mechanically attaching the outwales and inwales to each other by means of screws through the hull seems like a prudent measure. The hull is then clamped between the gunwales, whose parts can support each other because they are linked together.

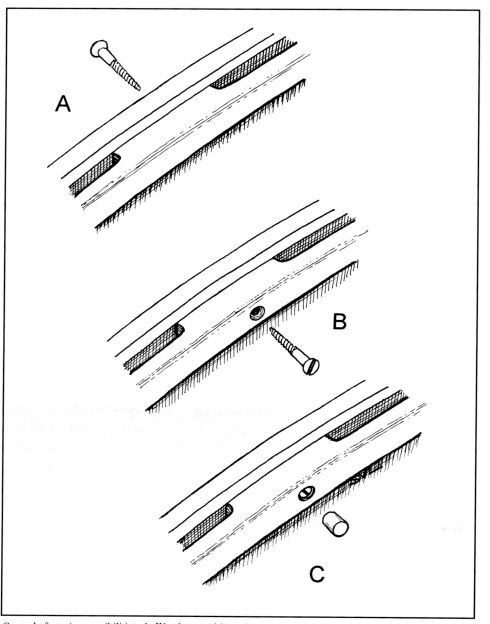

Gunwale fastening possibilities. A. Wood screw driven through the outwale into the inwale. B. Screw driven through the inwale into the outwale. C. Screw hole counterbored to accept a wooden plug.

For those not already familiar with wood screws, the unthreaded shank of a wood screw is the same diameter as the outside diameter of the threaded part. If a hole is drilled to fit only the threaded part of the screw, the unthreaded shank will not go into the hole because it is too big for the hole. On the other hand, if a hole is drilled to accommodate the unthreaded shank, it will be too large for the threaded part, and the threads will not grip the wood. What this means to the builder is that the holes must all be drilled to two different diameters, to two different depths. (Also, a recess will have to be made for countersink screw heads.) This could get to be quite tedious if you were to drill all the holes to the required diameters and depths in separate steps. There is, fortunately for us, a special type of drill bit which will do all of these things in a single step. Combination countersink drill bits which are adjustable to the depth needed are great labor and time-saving devices. They are made for each nominal wood screw size, and are priced affordably. Considering the improvement in efficiency that they offer, they are one of the best bargains in the tool section at the local hardware store.

Driving brass wood screws through the inwales. Number 6 screws 1-1/4 in. long were used here. One screw was placed in each spacer block except where the thwart belongs; I put two screws there, located so as not to interfere with the carriage bolt that will hold the thwart.

Close-up view showing combination countersink drill bit. Rubbing the threads of the screws on a piece of wax or moistened soap greatly facilitates the driving of the screws.

Thwarts

Making the Thwarts

The thwarts are the next items to which we direct our attention. The thwarts are the last pieces to be fastened more or less permanently in place, but they are needed to help hold the canoe in its proper shape while fitting deck pieces, seats, and also bulkheads, if you decide to put those in. The thwarts will usually stay put when wedged into position, but if they don't, they need to be clamped to the inwales while all these other pieces are being fitted and installed.

Thwarts can be as plain or as finely sculpted as the builder wants to make them. The grain in the hardwood stock you want to use may even suggest a special design. Hardwood blanks for making thwarts can range from 1-1/2 in. wide for a narrow spindle-shaped thwart, to as much as 6 in. wide for a carrying yoke. Carrying yokes are usually made wide enough at the ends, where they attach to the gunwales, to accommodate two bolts at each end. All other thwarts have just one bolt at each end.

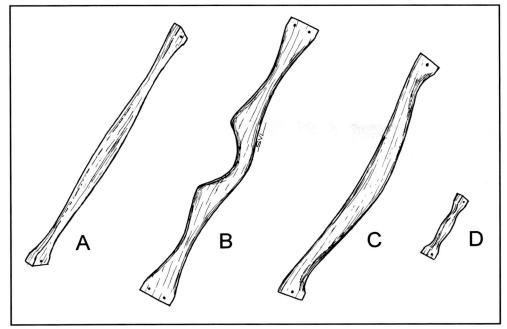

Examples of different thwart designs. A. An elegant spindle-shaped thwart. B. A combination carrying yoke/center thwart for a tandem canoe. C. An asymmetrical thwart for a solo canoe. D. A carrying thwart, for placement near the stems of the canoe.

Thwart patterns can be drawn freehand by the builder, or traced from parts from another boat.

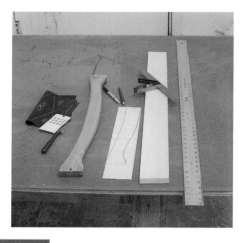

Tools and materials for making a thwart. The thwart shown to the left is one that was made for another solo canoe, which I want to copy. I traced the shape of that thwart onto a piece of paper by drawing around it. The Wee Lassie II is a slightly wider canoe than the one this thwart came from, so the new thwart pattern needs to be stretched out a bit. The ash blank is 3/4 in. thick by 3-1/2 in. wide by 32 in. long.

Tracing the thwart pattern onto hardwood stock. Mark the crosswise centerline on the hardwood blank, line up the centerline on the pattern with it, and tack the pattern in place. Slide carbon paper under the pattern and trace the outline of the pattern with the tracing wheel. Then flip the pattern over and trace the outline of the remaining half. Cut around the outline with a jigsaw or bandsaw.

The half-round file and longboard (with 100-grit paper) were the weapons of choice for refining the shape of the thwart. Later, after I was happy with the shape of the piece, I sanded the flat areas with the DA sander (120-grit disk) and hand sanded the rounded contours. I hand sanded the whole thwart with 220-grit paper to prepare it for the first coat of varnish.

Installing the Thwarts

Thwart installation takes place after the inside of the canoe hull, the thwarts(s), and the gunwales have been varnished, although more varnish is applied over the thwart bolts after installation. The main reason for postponing installation is that the presence of thwarts makes access to the interior of the canoe inconvenient. A little creative spark will generate variations on the method of attaching thwarts shown here. I use this method because it is simple, strong, and I like the finished appearance.

Locating the hole for the thwart bolt. The washer for this 1/4 in. stainless bolt is the same diameter as the hole that must be made to recess the bolt head. That makes the washer a useful tool for determining where the middle of the hole should be. While I like to have the bolt head overlap the edge of the hull a little bit, the main concern is that the bolt shank hangs far enough inboard to have a solid purchase in the end of the thwart. Move the washer around until the position of the proposed hole looks right, and then mark the center of the hole.

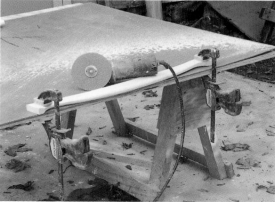

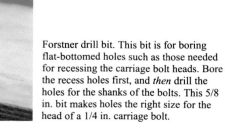

This ash piece is quite hard (as advertised), so to speed up the shaping process I used the angle grinder, with a 24-grit disk.

Forstner drill bit. This bit is for boring flat-bottomed holes such as those needed for recessing the carriage bolt heads. Bore the recess holes first, and *then* drill the holes for the shanks of the bolts. This 5/8 in. bit makes holes the right size for the head of a 1/4 in. carriage bolt.

Bore the hole for carriage bolt head. The carriage bolt will tilt slightly with its shank toward the keel line of the canoe, so angle the drill somewhat to allow for the way the bolt head will rest.

Clamp the thwart in place, with a block of wood underneath.

Thwart installed. If the bolt holes are angled in enough, the washers will fit over the ends of the bolts (under the thwart) without hitting the inside of the hull. If the washers touch the hull, you can file the edges down to fit. The ends of excessively long bolts can be a safety hazard. If the bolts extend more than 1/4 in. below the nuts, take them out, saw off the unneeded length, and file the sharp edges of the cut ends smooth.

Seats

Making Seat Frames

There are a few variations on the basic canoe seat, but all seats have one thing in common: a sturdy frame. Such a frame is made from a durable, abrasion-resistant hardwood like oak or ash, in lengths of stock 3/4 in. thick and 1-1/2 in. wide. The seat itself can be of whatever dimensions the builder likes. An average seat size is 15 x 12 in. (outside measurements). Here is one place where additional size and comfort cost almost nothing in terms of additional weight, so you might as well make the seat however large you like. (The weight of the frame, which makes up most of the total weight of the seat, varies little as you move the pieces closer or farther apart to change the size of the seat.)

Drill a hole for the carriage bolt shank. Choose a slightly larger bit than the size of the bolt, so the bolt will be easy to put in. This is a 5/16 in. bit for a 1/4 in. bolt. Drill all the way through the thwart, angling inward slightly. The block under the thwart helps keep the edges of the bolt holes crisp.

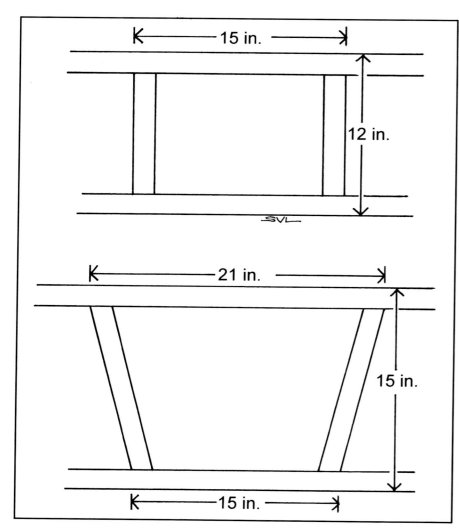

Seat frame parts. These ash pieces are 3/4 in. thick and 1-1/2 in. wide. The long pieces, which will be crosswise in the canoe, are longer than the hull is wide. The ends will be cut off later when it's time to install the seat. This seat will be 12 in. by 15 in. (outside frame measurements). The dowels are a sturdy 5/16 in. diameter, of birch.

Seat frame clamped together and marked for drilling dowel holes. First, the middle of the two long frame pieces were located, and then markings were made 6 in. to either side of the middle. These are where the inside edges of the side pieces will join with the long pieces. All the other markings are referenced from these points.

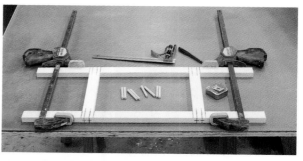

Drilling dowel holes. The drill bit has a band of tape wrapped around it to indicate adequate hole depth. This drill bit is 5/16 in., and makes very tight holes for the size dowel used here. The pairs of lines drawn on top of the frame right above where the dowel holes go are there to assist in drilling straight into the ends of the side pieces. I sight along the drill bit and lines, keeping one straight with the other. Another way to do this would be to use a doweling jig.

Two different seat designs. The rectangular seat is of an "average" size, and is the easiest to make. The trapezoidal seat is large and comfortable, but is a little more complicated to make. Of course, the dimensions can be varied; either seat can be made larger or smaller. Both seats are visually attractive, but the trapezoidal seat has an especially nice "custom look" to it in a tandem canoe. In figuring how long to make the long pair of frame pieces, measure the width of the hull where the seat is to be installed, and add a few extra inches to that measurement for insurance.

The seat frame joints must stand up to the demands placed upon them. I've had excellent success with seats having doweled joints, and I also like the appearance, so I continue to favor that method of joining pieces. Other means of joining seat frame parts include mortise and tenon, and lap joints.

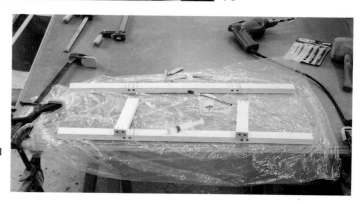

Applying epoxy to joint surfaces. Unthickened epoxy was painted onto the joint surfaces (especially the end grain of the side pieces) with an acid brush. After allowing the first coat of epoxy to absorb into the wood a bit, a coating of thickened (with colloidal silica plus a little wood flour for color) epoxy was brushed on.

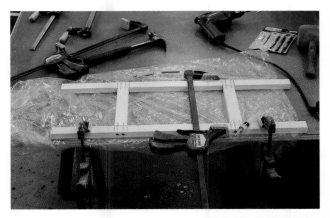

The frame pieces are clamped into position for doweling. The syringe was used to squeeze a little unthickened epoxy resin into the dowel holes.

Since my router was out of commission, I shaped the corners of the seat frame using a spokeshave, trimming plane, and longboard (with 100-grit paper). I also sanded the flat sides of the frame with the longboard.

Dowels are driven into place. The dowels were dipped in unthickened epoxy before driving. Because these dowel joints are so tight, there is actually very little epoxy in the joint. As a result, the epoxy is a minor contributor to the strength of the joint, but it does serve to seal the wood surfaces inside the joint.

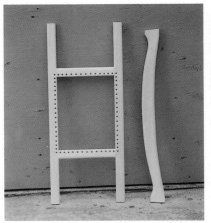

The seat frame and thwart were hand sanded with 120- and 220-grit paper and are ready for varnish.

The dowel ends are trimmed off and holes are drilled for caning. This seat will be finished with hand-woven caning. To lay out the placement of the holes, begin by marking a line all the way around the perimeter of the seat, 3/8 in. from the inside edge. Then, mark the middle of each side on the line. These midpoints and the corners are reference points for all the other holes. Starting at a midpoint on one side, mark hole locations at 3/4 in. intervals to one corner. The last two holes will probably not be exactly 3/4 in. apart. In that case, adjust the hole spacing near the corner to even out the distance between them. Lay out the hole locations the same way going from the midpoint of the same side to the other corner. If the seat being built is rectangular, mark hole locations for the opposite side on the same spacing as the first. Repeat this process for the second pair of sides. If your seat is trapezoidal, and opposing sides are of unequal length, figure hole spacing for those sides independently of each other. The hole spacing needs to be the same, therefore the opposing sides will have different numbers of holes. The holes are drilled with a 1/4 in. bit; I used a drill press, but a hand drill could have been used. I did use a hand drill with countersink bit to relieve the sharp edges of the holes.

Supplies for varnishing the seat frame and thwart. The twine is for suspending the pieces, so that all sides can be varnished in a single session. The pipe cleaners are useful for applying varnish to the insides of the holes. The seat frame needs to be varnished now, before the caning (or other seat material) is in the frame, because the caning will interfere with varnishing if it is put off until later. The one exception is if you decide to put natural cane on your seats; then you need to varnish the caning *and* the frame. (I think plastic cane looks just as good and is more practical, so that's what I use.) For the first coat, the varnish is thinned to promote better penetration into the wood. See Chapter 11 for more on varnishing.

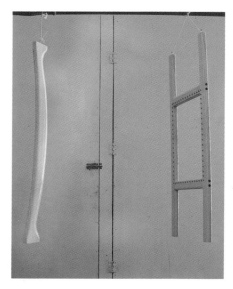

Thwart and seat frame with fresh varnish drying. Small nails were driven into the ends of the pieces to provide attachment points for suspension. These items received three coats of varnish each.

The seat surface itself can be made using any of a whole range of possibilities for materials. Nylon web material can be tacked and woven over the frame, wooden slats can be screwed to the frame, a non-stretching lace material can be woven over the frame snowshoe fashion, or a solid rectangular piece of fabric with grommets along two opposing edges can be stretched over the frame and lashed tight underneath with a boot lace. Pre-woven natural caning can be purchased and pressed into a routed groove around the perimeter of the seat. My favorite way to make a seat is to hand cane it with plastic lacing sold at leather shops. Instructions for that style of seat are in Chapter 10. Hand-caned seats are second to none in appearance and comfort. They do take some time to weave, so if you are anxious to get out on the water, another alternative may be more appealing. Finish the seats according to your needs and desires. You may want to do some of the seat installation work before completely finishing the seat. Read ahead for more on that.

Installing Seats

The seats are installed after the last coat of varnish inside the hull is dry, because like the thwarts, the seats really limit access to the inside of the hull. There are two ways of supporting the seats in a wood strip canoe. One way is to attach the seat to wooden risers that support the seat from underneath. The other way is to suspend the seat from the inwales. Each method has the advantage in certain situations. The key is, how low in the boat is the seat to be placed?

In tandem canoes and many solo canoes, the paddler often propels the boat from a kneeling position, braced against the forward edge of the seat and with the feet under it. For this type of canoe, the widespread practice is to hang the seat from the inwales. As awkward as it appears from an engineer's standpoint, the system has worked for several generations, ever since seats (rather than just thwarts) began being put in canoes. There is nothing under the seat to interfere with the paddler's feet, and there are no structures bonded to the inside of the hull, creating stiff places in the hull.

In contrast, some solo canoes have the seats placed so low in the hull (at or near the waterline) that the paddler sits with the feet extended out ahead of him- or herself. It is impractical to hang the seat that low from the inwales. Rather, one or two wooden supports called risers are bonded to the bottom of the canoe, and the seat is placed on top. This arrangement works well in a very small canoe.

There has been some discussion of bonding risers to the inside of tandem canoes for attachment of seats at the standard height.[2] For seats this high, the risers would be glued to the sides of the hull. This practice has not been embraced by many builders, but it's not clear whether that is due to its departure from tradition or actual problems with performance. Something to consider is that where the risers are bonded to the hull, there will be extra rigidity in the hull, so the hull

would not flex evenly over its surface. To what degree this is a problem, I don't know. I suspect that in a canoe that receives moderate use, it isn't much of an issue. If I were to experiment with this, I would use pieces of hardwood 3/4 x 1 in. by the length necessary to hold the ends of the seat frame, on each side of the hull. I would bond the wide side of the risers to the hull for more glue surface to spread the load over, with the 3/4 in. edge up. The seat frame would be screwed to the upper edge of the risers.

Regardless of exactly how the seats are attached to the hull, the support system needs to hold the seat level. The canoe used to illustrate this book is unusual in that the seat is placed very low in the boat, but many other elements of the installation process are the same as for other canoes.

Establish the approximate location of the seat supports. First, a long level is placed across the gunwales, and the canoe adjusted in the cradle stands until it is level. Then, the rule on the combination square is extended and locked at the distance the bottom of the seat is supposed to be from the bottom of the hull (plus the thickness of the stick the square is sitting on). Then, the two seat support pieces (these are cedar, for lightness of weight) are moved apart until the combination square is the right distance from the hull bottom and sits level. The cedar pieces are 1 in. wide by 1-1/4 in. high by 20 in. long. They are longer than the seat to allow for fore-and-aft adjustment of the seat position.

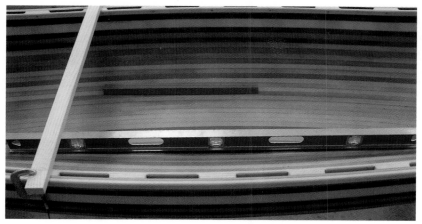

Ensuring that the canoe is level along the centerline. Place the long level so the middle sight glass is at the balance point of the canoe. In symmetrical canoes, that will be the midpoint between bow and stern. In this asymmetrical solo canoe, it is where the widest station was located. Adjust the cradles so the canoe rests level.

Use a compass to scribe the curve of the hull onto the seat support stock. This only needs to be done on the outside edge; the inside edge can be shaped as needed later after trial fitting.

Rough shape the bottom of the riser. A utility knife gives quick results.

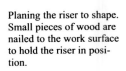

Planing the riser to shape. Small pieces of wood are nailed to the work surface to hold the riser in position.

Trial fit the seat supports. Keep working on them until they are level lengthwise and crosswise, when placed equidistant apart.

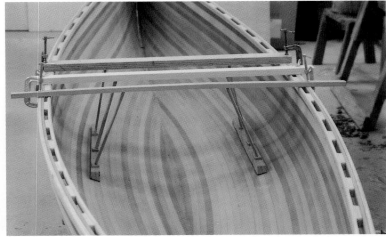

When these pieces have been shaped to fit the hull properly, draw a pencil line around them on the inside of the hull. Set up the clamping system before mixing up epoxy so you don't have to do it when time is short. Then mix up a small batch of epoxy, paint some on the bottoms of the risers, thicken the remainder of the epoxy with wood flour and colloidal silica, and apply it to the bonding surfaces of the risers also. Position them in the hull according to the penciled outlines and clamp them in place. Scrape up excess squeezed out epoxy with a putty knife or screwdriver.

Risers sealed with epoxy. Masking tape was applied to the inside of the hull about 1/8 in. away from the seat supports, all the way around. The tape helps control the spread of the epoxy and leaves nice, straight edges on the fillets I want to make around the bases of the risers.

The fillets have been applied, tooled, and the tape peeled off. As soon as the fillets have been tooled, remove the tape. That allows the edges of the fillets, which may have been lifted during tape removal, to lay back down against the hull.

Transfer the measurements to the frame, and cut off the extra wood. Based on the difference between the top and bottom side measurements, you can estimate the bevel angle that the ends of the frame need to have, and saw those also.

Measuring for seat frame width. The two sticks clamped together provide a measure of how wide the underside of the frame needs to be.

Check the seat frame for fit.

Use a small angle grinder (with a 24-grit disk) to finish shaping the ends of the seat frame.

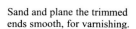

Measure the width of the upper side of the seat frame. The piece of wood spanning the seat supports is 3/4 in. thick: the same thickness as the seat frame.

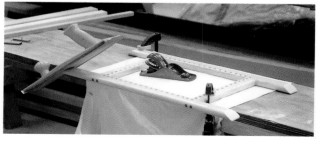

Sand and plane the trimmed ends smooth, for varnishing.

One seat frame, tailored to fit.

Establishing seat location. The canoe will handle best when it is properly trimmed. In a solo canoe like this one, the paddler's center of gravity is *the* determining factor affecting trim. The seat (placed loose in the boat) is moved as necessary to make the canoe set level. Then, the location of the front edge of the seat is marked on the risers. A light-colored grease pencil leaves a readily visible mark without denting the wood.

Seat location markings on the risers. Mark the placement of screws on the seat frame.

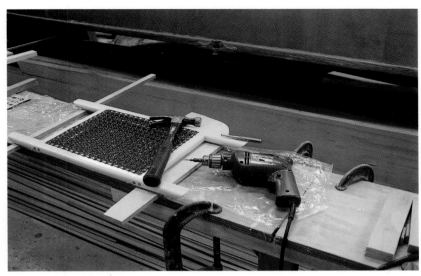

Drill holes for wood screws.

Seat installed. Drill holes into the risers using the ones in the seat frame as pilot holes. I used #10 wood screws to anchor the seat, though smaller ones would have worked.

A pair of seat supports were used in this canoe because the seat needed to be about 3 in. off the hull bottom. Some solo canoe designs specify seat placement as low as 1-1/2 in. above the hull bottom. For these low-set seats, it is simpler and easier to use a single riser placed on the centerline of the hull. A piece of cedar 1 in. wide by 1-1/2 in. high by 20 in. long was used for the riser in the following photo.[3]

A Wee Lassie solo canoe with a single seat riser. The aft end of the riser is placed under the forward edge of the thwart, according to the designer's instructions. The best location for the seat has been identified (note the yellow line on the riser, near the seat). The crosswise grooves being filed in the tops of the riser provide space for the lacing under the seat frame, which is flipped upside down in this photo. This seat is to be fastened to the riser with two screws. It is neither necessary nor advantageous to anchor the ends of the seat frame to the hull.

Seats that are hung from the inwales are fastened in place by 3/16 in. or 1/4 in. carriage bolts that go through the inwales, spacers made of wood or pipe, and the seat frame, and are snugged up with nuts and washers under the seat.

To hang seats from the inwales, a jig made of wood scraps assists in determining where to mark the seat frame ends for trimming, and how long to make the spacers that are part of the suspension system. As indicated for the solo canoe, the hull needs to be level lengthwise and from side to side before concentrating on the seat. The jig is used to hold measuring sticks in position where the seat belongs and, later, to support the seat while spacers are fitted into place.

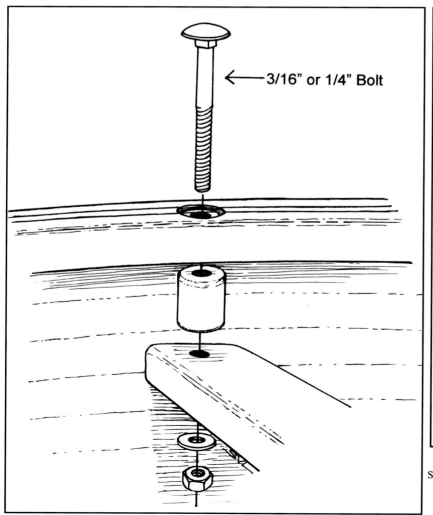

3/16" or 1/4" Bolt

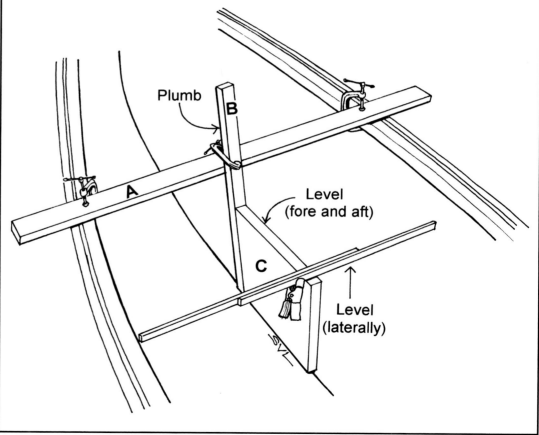

Plumb

B

A

Level (fore and aft)

C

Level (laterally)

Seat suspension assembly.

120

Opposite page bottom right: Seat jig. First, clamp Crosspiece A to the gunwales so that it is perpendicular to the centerline of the hull. Upright B and Block C are held together by tacks or screws. Two screws are suggested, so one of them can be backed out for leveling of Block C. Clamp Upright B so it is plumb. Block C needs to be level along its upper edge, even though the hull bottom may not be level at this location. Shim up one corner of Block C or plane one corner down until the upper edge is level. Keep in mind that Block C also serves to support the seat at the correct height for installation, so it may be necessary to make adjustments to get the desired seat height. Once that is done, use the "sliding stick measuring device" to find out hull width where the ends of the seat frame will rest. Level the sticks and see that they are square with Block C. This tells you how wide the seat frame needs to be to fit the hull. To find the cutting angle needed to match the seat frame ends to the hull sides, place the seat frame across the gunwales with the width markings on the frame lined up with the inside of the hull. Trace the angle of intersection with the inside hull on the top of the seat frame. Estimate the angle of tilt to the hull sides, and cut the frame ends off with the Dozuki saw.

With the seat frame trimmed to size, set it on top of Block C of the seat jig, and level the seat. Now it's time to make the spacers that fit between the inwales and the seat.

The spacers can be made of 3/4 in. dowel, 3/4 in. square wood stock, or 1/2 in. (outside diameter) thick-walled copper tubing. Although I like the copper tubing, most builders use wooden spacer blocks; both work well enough. Cut the wood stock or tubing to appropriate lengths to fit. Drill holes lengthwise down the centers of the wooden spacers. Make the holes slightly larger than the size of the bolts. Be prepared to bevel the spacer ends; that is usually necessary. If copper pipe is used for spacers, solder a brass washer onto each end to give the tubing a more substantial bearing surface against the inwales and seat frames.

With spacers in position for installation, drill holes for the carriage bolts the same way as shown for thwart installation. Make the recesses for the bolt heads first, and then drill down through the inwales, through the spacers, and through the seats if the drill bit will reach that far. You may need to take the seat

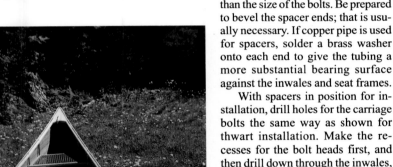

A tandem canoe with seats suspended from the gunwales. Since this canoe was constructed with the strips running level from end to end, it was very easy to level the seats using the strips as guides. The copper spacers oxidize to a brown color that matches the color of the cedar almost perfectly.

out to drill the bolt holes in the frame. Make the holes 1/16 in. larger than the bolt diameter to ease the placement of the bolts during installation. After the seats are secured in position, there should be no more than 1/4 in. of bolt length extending below the nuts. If the bolts are too long, take them back out and cut them to length with a hacksaw, and file the sharp edges smooth.

Decks

The decks are a favorite place for builders to exhibit their craftsmanship and creativity. Because of their highly visible placement in the canoe and their more-or-less flat surfaces, the decks seem to invite treatment as a decorative item. However, the decks are more than merely decorative; they strengthen the ends of the craft, they provide good places to attach hardware, and they often are used for handles when carrying the boat. (That is a good reason to make them sturdy.) These practical uses do not detract from one's ability to make them beautiful examples of good craftsmanship. In fact, even if the builder prefers the subtlety of decks made from single pieces of hardwood stock of the same species as the inwales, the decks are impossible for a viewer to ignore, so this is a good place for the builder to concentrate attention on quality construction and finish work.

It should be pointed out that despite the advantages of putting decks on a canoe, one can get along without them. The alternative is to install carrying thwarts near the ends of the canoe. These thwarts are usually about 6 in. long. Because they are so short, they will usually be placed within 12 in. of the ends of the canoe. That allows the thwart to stabilize the end of the canoe in addition to serving as a handle. Carrying thwarts may be installed the same way as other thwarts, or else fitted between the inwales (instead of below them, as usual for thwarts) and fastened with screws going through the gunwales into the ends of the thwarts. If you go with the latter, fashion the ends of the thwarts to allow for some means of keeping the thwart from turning when you pick the canoe up. There needs to be room for two screws at each end, or else a lip that hooks underneath the inwales.

There are nearly unlimited ways to make decks that are both practical and good looking. Two of the most popular general deck designs are shown in the next illustration. The way I made the decks for the Wee Lassie II differs significantly from the solid wood type, and is covered in the next chapter, because it goes beyond what is needed for a simple, functional deck.

Solid wood decks are usually made of hardwood. A softwood may be used, as long as it is of good quality; that is, free of any defect that might cause it to split. I used 3/4 in. thick yellow cedar for the breasthooks in a tandem canoe and have not had any problems with them. Most hardwoods are stronger than most softwoods, though, and are preferred by builders for that reason. Also, it is hard to resist the temptation to use special pieces of highly figured maple, or whatever else you may be hoarding, for such prominent placement in the canoe. Might as well give in to temptation; there is hardly any better way to display that fine wood!

Deck stock may be of one solid piece of lumber, 3/4 in. to 1 in. thick, or it may be of two or more pieces joined together lengthwise with a spline. It may even be joined to form a shallow V-shape, so the center part of the deck is raised slightly. If multiple pieces of wood are used for the decks, the pieces should be joined so the lengthwise orientation of the grain is parallel to the gunwales. This produces a chevron pattern in the wood grain along the centerline joint in the decks.[4] If a single piece of wood is used for each deck, then the lengthwise grain of the wood is aligned with the centerline of the canoe.

The following illustration gives an overview of the process of fitting breasthooks and decks.

Beginning with the example at the top of the illustration, start by placing cardboard over the area that will be occupied by the breasthook, and with a sharp pencil, trace the shape of the inside hull onto the underside of the cardboard. Trace the inside edges of the inwales also, but then adjust the lines outward to correspond to the inner edges of the hull. At this point, the inwales are installed in the canoe, but not cut to their finished lengths yet. The total length of the breasthook is about 12 inches. Draw the curve of the inboard edge on the pattern and cut the pattern out. Make adjustments to the pattern until it matches the shape of the inner hull, except if the hull sides aren't quite straight, make the edges of the pattern straight anyway. Make a separate pattern for each end of the canoe. Then, trace the pattern onto the breasthook blank and cut it out, staying a little outside the lines, and ignoring the cut outs for the inwales. Place the breasthook over the inwales on the canoe and check to see if the breasthook fits the inside of the hull, where the inwales aren't. If the fit is poor and the hull can't be flexed to fit the shape of the breasthook without gaps or bulges in the hull along the sheer, then work on the edges of the breasthook until it fits fairly well.

The next steps are to cut the inwales to length and make the notches for the inwales in breasthook. The inwales extend 3 in. into the breasthook, when finished. Measure back from the stems and mark all the inwale ends an equal distance to give the desired inset in the breasthooks. Cut the inwales off. This is accomplished with the least risk to the inside of the hull by using a hacksaw blade mounted in a frame that holds one end of the blade inside the saw handle, with the blade end extending beyond a clamp that grips the blade about halfway along its length. (The Nicholson tool company makes this type of hacksaw frame.) Place the breasthook back in position, and carefully trace the edges of the inwales onto the underside of the breasthook. Cut the notches for the inwales out. Be conservative; don't make the notches quite at full depth. Do the final stages of fitting by hand in order to get the best possible results. Avoid removing too much wood and leaving a visible mistake by working down the edges of the underside of the breasthook first, and shaving off only enough of the upper edges to let the piece settle snugly into place.

Then, drill holes for screws. Three screws per side will suffice. One long screw that goes through the outwale, the end of the inwale, and into the breasthook, plus two shorter screws nearer the stem need to have suitable holes drilled for them. Test fit the unit complete with screws, and once the breasthook fits satisfactorily when screwed in place, back the screws out, apply epoxy to all the joining surfaces, and run the screws back in. Clean up excess epoxy before it cures.[5]

Fitting decks that are sandwiched between the inwales is a simpler proposition. Make a pattern by placing cardboard over the gunwales and tracing the outline of the inwales onto the bottom of the cardboard. Draw the desired shape of the inboard edge of the deck onto the cardboard and cut the pattern out. Modify the pattern until it fits between the inwales nicely. Transfer the pattern onto the deck blank, and cut out the shape of the deck, keeping a little to the outside of the lines. Hand work each deck to fit tightly between the inwales. Drill holes for screws on even intervals, three or four screws per side, depending on the length of the deck. After the deck has been fitted, apply epoxy as for the breasthook installation and replace the screws.

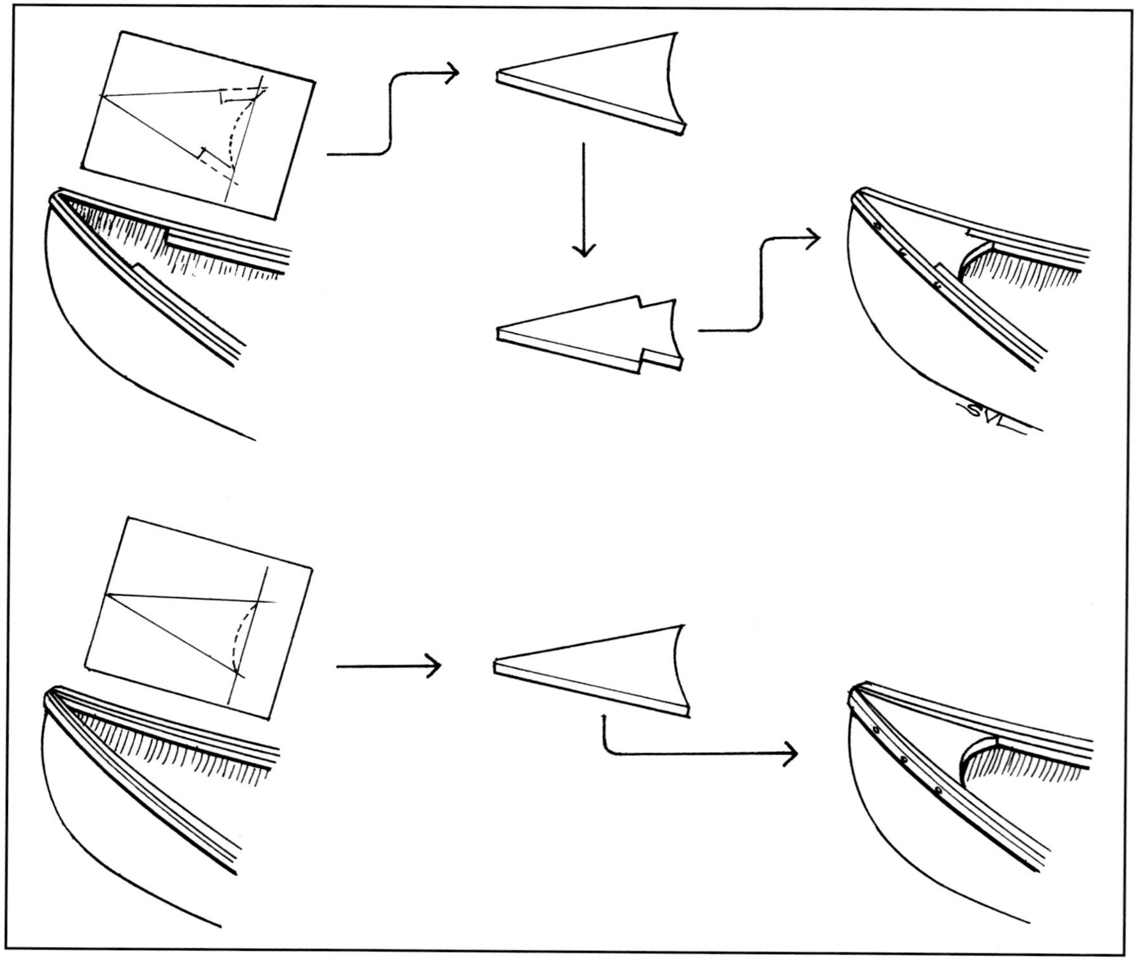

Making and fitting breasthooks and decks. The upper row illustrates the process of making a breasthook, which differs slightly from the deck, illustrated in the second row.

Chapter Ten

Details and Fancy Stuff

For many builders, a simple, elegant boat is the best kind of boat. A strip canoe does not require any extra adornment to be beautiful. On the other hand, there are a lot of things you *can* do to a strip canoe. There are so many options, in fact, as to make even the most modestly creative individual's eyes light up with possibilities. As a word of caution, it is not too difficult to overdo a wood strip boat. The pattern of the strips provides quite a lot of interest, so exercise restraint in decorating such a craft; too much "makeup" tends to be distracting and cheapen the overall appearance.

The features covered in this chapter are items that add something to the utility of the craft, and in some cases also to appearance. So far I've not experimented with features that are added *strictly* for visual effect, such as painting patterns on the hull, gluing on cutout veneer shapes, or burning designs into wood, although it would be great fun to do so. Those possibilities are there for the crafts people who are intrigued enough to try them. This discussion will focus on special features that contribute something to serviceability.

Attachments for Bow and Stern Lines

Most canoeists consider bow and stern lines and consequently, places to attach them, essential. With good reason, too; how else to secure a hold on your canoe for towing, tying up, lining, or pulling the thing off a rock? Whatever means of attachment is employed, it needs to be strong enough to perform under the worst conditions the canoe is expected to experience. See the illustration for some alternatives to consider.

Line attachments. A and B are variations of the bow eye. C is a U-bolt with a ring. D is simply a hole drilled through a 3/4 in. thick solid wood deck. E features a stem band that holds a ring. F is a hole that goes through the hull behind the inside stem. The hole is lined with plastic or metal pipe.

Each of these possibilities offers a little different "look." They all have one noteworthy feature in common, though. For maximum strength, the fasteners that hold them in place go *through* the deck or hull, or else the hole for the rope does. Examples A, B, C, and E are fastened by threaded shanks and nuts (with washers) inside the boat. In E, the screws on top of the deck and the first screw below the painter ring go through the parts they are attached to. The other screws in the stem band are wood screws.

If you decide to install hardware rope attachments, the fasteners holding the hardware need to have a marine-grade sealant applied to the threads before insertion. The idea is to exclude water from the holes, so there is no opportunity for decay to start in the wood. There are many sealants on the market. They vary in adhesive quality, with price usually related directly to improvement in adhesion. For our use, adhesion in not necessary; we only need a good seal. A couple of the more readily available sealants that are suitable are BoatLIFE® Marine Silicone Sealant and Life-Calk Sealant.

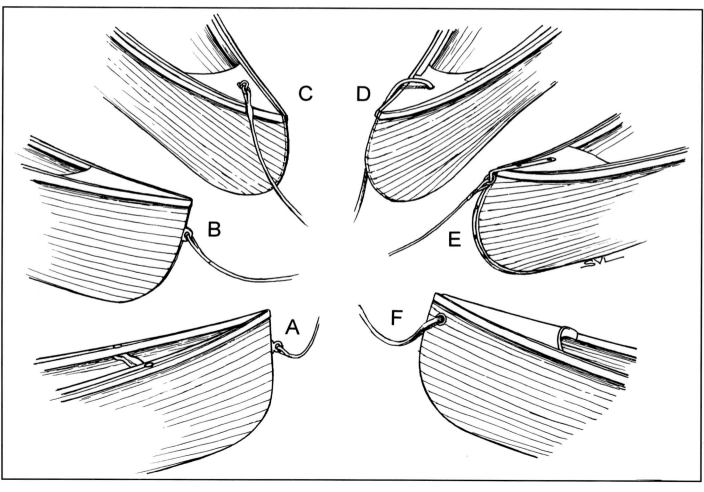

Through Hole

For the Wee Lassie II shown in the photo series, I made through holes in the hull for ropes.[1] These are probably the strongest of all the rope attachments. There are no parts sticking out to catch on things, and since I use plastic pipe, there is less weight added than with metal hardware.

Measuring to determine how far inboard to make the hole. Ideally, the pipe should just touch the back of the inside stem when the pipe is glued in place. Sight down along the stem while holding the measuring tape about where you want the hole to be (or use calipers) to measure distance needed to clear the inside stem. Then add the outside radius of the pipe to that distance to get the distance from the outer stem to the location of the middle of the pipe. Mark that location on both sides of the boat. The pipe used here is 3/4 in. Schedule 40 PVC pipe.

Drill small pilot holes at the markings for the center of the pipe.

Using a hole saw the right diameter for the pipe, cut holes in the hull. The small pilot holes help hold the drill in position. The pipe will go through the end of the canoe at an angle to the hull surface, so drill at your best estimate of that angle. Here, a 7/8 in. hole saw is being used to make the holes for the 3/4 in. pipe.

Place a long finishing nail or heavy wire through the pilot holes. Now measure the distance from the back of the inside stem to the wire. This should equal the outside radius of the pipe. If not, drill new pilot holes to get the right spacing.

Slip the pipe through the holes. Using a sharp pencil, trace a line around the pipe at the hull surface.

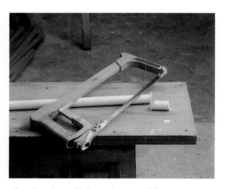

Cut the pipe off along the traced lines.

Sand and file the pipe ends until they are flush with the hull surface, when trial fitted in the boat. This may require checking the fit frequently. It's worth it to fit carefully now, before gluing the pipe in place. Once the pipe is glued into the hull, it's much harder to finish the ends of the pipe without dinging the adjacent hull surface.

Everything needed for making a hand-caned seat. The seat frame has holes drilled at 3/4 in. intervals around the seat perimeter, and is varnished. Three different spools of lacing are shown here, but only one of a single color is really needed. The wooden pegs are for temporarily securing the lacing while caning is in progress. The pegs are 1 to 2 in. long with the lower 3/4 in. whittled down to fit in the holes around the seat. The tube contains petroleum jelly, used for lubricating the caning. A lubricant is necessary to prevent the lacing from melting from the heat of friction as new lengths of lacing are pulled through existing courses of caning.

When the pipe fits as well as you can make it, sand the outside of the pipe. Slip it into the holes, mix up a small batch of thickened epoxy (match the color of the wood), and glue the pipe in place. You will probably need to use a syringe to get the epoxy into the little spaces around the pipe. If there is some epoxy left over, put it in the joint where the pipe touches the inside stem, to really anchor the pipe firmly in place. Be sure to clean up excess epoxy before it hardens.

Hand-caned Seats

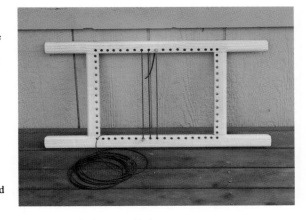

On the long sides of the seat, mark the middle holes with pegs. Turn the seat so the aft edge is at the top. Cut about 16 ft. of lacing off the spool. Begin stringing the seat by pulling about 4 in. of one end of the lacing down through the middle hole of the side away from you and securing it with a peg. Bring the lacing straight across the seat to the opposite middle hole, and pull the lacing down through it. Look closely at the lacing; it has one side that is slightly arched, and one side that is flat. The arched side should be up. Twist the lacing under the seat frame to get the lacing turned right side up, if it isn't already. Peg the long end of the lacing in the second hole. Then, bring the long end either left or right to the next hole, and pull it up through that hole. Bring the lacing across the seat and down through the corresponding hole on the other side. Move the pegs as needed to keep the lacing orderly. (It does not need to be tight at this stage.) Once again, move to the next hole, bring the lacing up through that hole, across the seat to the opposite hole, and down through that one. Continue in this fashion until one half of the seat (excluding the extreme corner holes) is done.

For a truly classy and luxurious touch, put hand-caned seats in your canoe. They look terrific, and they are every bit as nice to sit on as they look. They have enough give to be comfortable, enough substance to provide good support, they allow for ventilation so you stay dry, and they don't get unbearably hot or cold when exposed to the elements. In addition, if you use plastic lacing instead of natural cane, the seat will last a very long time.[2]

The lacing material I use is Tandy's Dura-Flex Vinyl Corded Lace. This lacing is sold at leather shops. They have another type of lacing that is available in more colors, but it is all plastic (no filaments in its core), and a less substantial lace besides, so it may be apt to stretch. The vinyl corded lace is very well suited for caned seats. It is sold by the spool (100 yds. of lace) and is made in several colors. The medium brown lace makes a very attractive seat. For purposes of illustrating this book I used a combination of blue, green, and brown lacing, and it turned out respectably well. When I am using just one color for seats, I generally can cane 1-1/2 seats with a spool of lace. In order to complete two seats, you will need two spools, with lots left over for another project. I've used another brand, called Pyrolace, with very good results. It is no longer available in my area, but if you find it, it is equal to Dura-Flex in quality.

After stringing one half of the seat, start in the middle and string the second half in the same way. If you run short of lacing, just peg the end in place at the last hole the lacing would reach, and cut a new piece to start with in the adjacent hole. Make sure that there is about 4 in. of extra length, for knotting the lacing, wherever an end is pegged off. If you are caning a trapezoidal seat, you will need to skip some holes on the angled sides to keep the runs of lacing parallel to each other. Thread lacing through all the holes on the front and

back sides of the seat; as you work your way toward the ends of the longest of these sides, you will be threading the lace through some holes on the lateral sides of the seat. Choose holes that allow you to maintain even spacing between the runs of lacing. (See the last photo in this section for an example of this style of seat.) In those instances where you skip some holes in stringing the lacing, don't carry the lacing across the skipped holes on your way to the ones you want to use. Rather, cut the lacing and peg it in place where it goes down through the seat frame. Then peg another length in the hole that you need to come up through.[3]

Starting at the upper right-hand corner, string lacing back and forth across the seat, right over the first course. Do not weave the lacing yet; that is a couple of steps away. All of the holes will be used (except the very corner ones) for this course, regardless of the seat shape.

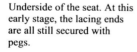

Underside of the seat. At this early stage, the lacing ends are all still secured with pegs.

The third course of lacing is executed the same way as the first course, except that you should start one hole to the side of where you started the first time. This course is laid right over the first two.

By this time, there are plenty of tails hanging out. But, there are also quite a few handy places to tie to. Use half hitches to tie off ends anywhere there is another length of lacing in the same hole suitable for securing to.

Two knots secured and trimmed. For a neat, professional-looking job, tie all the knots so the tails point the same way, and trim them to a uniform length. Where you are able to knot the ends of the lacing, the pegs can be removed. Wherever you have ends, but nothing to tie to, leave the pegs in place. Keep in mind as you weave the next courses of lacing that you need to create anchor points for those loose ends, and manage your weaving to provide them. As you move on with the caning process, tie off the ends of the lacing as soon as possible, thus minimizing the number of pegs to work around. Often, as weaving proceeds, knots will be tied adjacent to each other, almost layered over each other.

Before beginning the fourth course of lacing, straighten the first three layers of caning so the lacing is evenly spaced, and arrange the third course of lacing so the strands are all a little to right of the strands of the first course underneath. Next, peg a length of lacing in the same hole you started with for the second course. (You may want to switch to 12 ft. lengths of lacing at this point, for greater ease of handling.) The process of weaving begins as you thread the lacing over the top canes and under the bottom canes. Run lacing for the fourth course just below the strands in the second course. Continue this weaving scheme as you work your way across the seat. Put a little petroleum jelly on your fingers as you weave the caning in order to lubricate it. That reduces friction by permitting the lacing to slip through the existing caning layers easily.

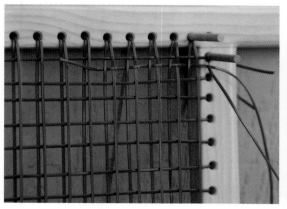

It's finally time to use those corner holes. Begin with the upper right corner. (The seat should have the aft edge at the top, as in previous steps.) For this step, you want to go under the horizontal pairs of canes and over the vertical ones. Be especially attentive to lubricating the caning, and also to twisting, since the lacing will have to be pulled out to untwist it. From now on, arriving at a certain hole at the opposite end of a run is fairly unimportant, except that the two diagonal courses should mirror each other. In other words, whatever strategy you use in the pattern of the first diagonal course should be repeated when the second course is woven. For now, concentrate on weaving the lacing straight diagonally, maintaining the correct "over-under" sequence.

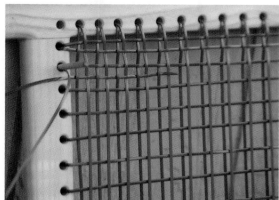

Start back across the seat, going over the top canes and under the bottom ones. Continue weaving back and forth across the seat, maintaining this same order. Now it's time to tighten up the weave, so give the lacing a pull before you thread it down through the hole at the end of a run.

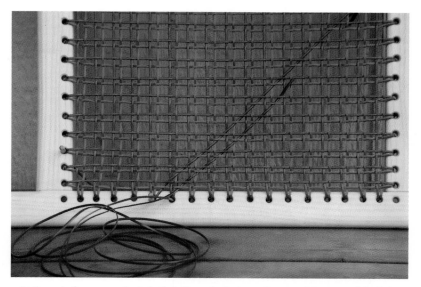

At the end of a run, use the hole that allows the lacing to lie as straight as possible. Bring the lacing up through the next hole to the right, and again, thread under the horizontal pairs and over the vertical pairs of canes, parallel to the first run.

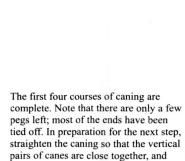

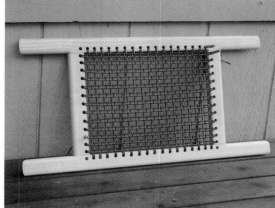

The first four courses of caning are complete. Note that there are only a few pegs left; most of the ends have been tied off. In preparation for the next step, straighten the caning so that the vertical pairs of canes are close together, and the same for the horizontal pairs.

The lower right corner is filled in. On the sides, you will probably have to "double up" two runs to the same hole, or skip a hole to get the caning to run straight, or nearly so. (Photos showing that to come.) This will look peculiar now, but later will hardly be noticeable.

All courses of caning complete.

To fill in the rest of the first diagonal course of caning, start one hole to the left of the first run on the lower edge of the frame, and weave back up to the upper right corner. Thread down through the corner hole, up through the next hole to the left, and carry on as before. Starting this way gives you something to tie the loose end of lacing pegged in that corner to. All four corners should have two strands of lacing through them for the best appearance when the seat is finished.

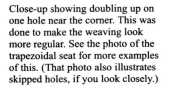

Close-up showing doubling up on one hole near the corner. This was done to make the weaving look more regular. See the photo of the trapezoidal seat for more examples of this. (That photo also illustrates skipped holes, if you look closely.)

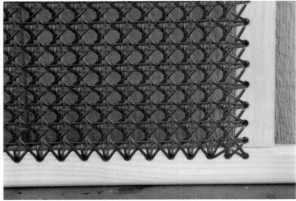

Underside of the seat, showing knots and multiple layers of lacing.

For the last course of caning, the second diagonal course begins very like the first. The only difference is, starting at the upper left corner, now you weave *over* the horizontal pairs of canes and *under* the vertical pairs. Fill in the lower left corner first. Whatever holes you skipped or doubled up on when you did the first diagonal course, duplicate that now as you weave the opposite direction.

Finishing off the seat with binder cane. This is purely cosmetic, but is worth the little bit of extra work to make the seat look really finished. Ideally, the binder cane should be a little wider than the regular lacing. If you have access to the wider material, use that. Otherwise, the regular lacing will work. Cut a piece of lacing about three times as long as the side to be bound. Thread the ends down through the corner holes. Adjust the lacing so the loose ends are about equal in length. Pull the lacing tight and peg the corners.

Finished seat. Ash frame with multicolored caning.

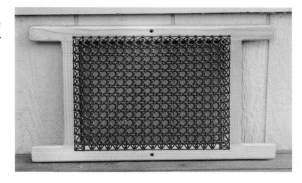

Bitter cherry frame with brown caning.

Starting from a corner, take the free end of lacing and thread it up through the neighboring hole, over the binder on the top of the seat, and back down the same hole. Then, bring the end to the next hole and do the same thing. Repeat this until you run out of length or get within three holes of the other end. Tie off, and do the rest of the binding with the remaining free end of the lacing.

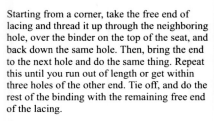

Oak frame with brown caning.

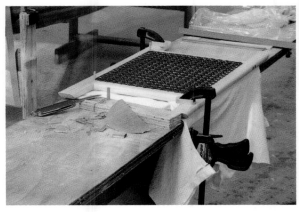

To make softwood pegs for the corner holes, saw 1 in. long pieces from leftover strips. Split the pieces down to approximate size with a knife. Sand the rest of the way down to size. Lightly tap the pegs into place and mark them where they are flush with the seat frame. Then, drive the pegs out and cut them off a little long. Sand the tops of the pegs smooth, and then drive them permanently into place, using another scrap of wood to pad the tops of the pegs from direct blows from the hammer. Varnish the tops of the pegs, and your new seat is done!

129

Bulkheads

If you want built-in flotation chambers in your canoe, a couple of bulkheads will need to be installed in the ends of the craft. Bulkheads provide other benefits besides sealing off air chambers. They add a lot of extra support to the hull, they prevent dirt and debris from collecting at the stems, they can hide a bad job of fiberglassing at the stems, and if you put deck plates in the bulkheads so you have access to the air chambers, they can provide you with dry storage space in the boat. There are plenty of good reasons to make and install bulkheads, as you can see. Nevertheless, they are optional. A reasonably well-built strip canoe does not require extra support at the ends of the boat. Also, if you have done a nice job of fiberglassing along the stems, you might prefer to show it off instead of hiding it.

There are two main variations in bulkhead design.

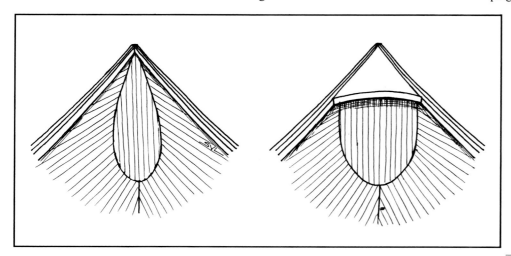

Bulkheads. The main differences between the two are the angle at which they are set into the hull, and the amount of space sealed off. The example at left is tilted so that the edges seat against the hull all the way around. The one on the right is positioned more vertically, so the upper edge of the bulkhead seats against the underside of the deck. This closes off more space, which in turn offers greater flotation if the canoe becomes swamped.

The concept of sealed-air chambers in a boat is a good one, but we need to consider what the term "sealed" really means. If the chamber is truly sealed, the air inside is permanently trapped within a fixed volume. That means it can not expand or contract in response to temperature changes, no matter how much it wants to. Now, visualize your canoe on top of your vehicle on a sunny midsummer day, in a parking lot while you have lunch in an air-conditioned restaurant. The hull of the canoe will get hot in the sunshine and the air pressure inside those chambers will grow. If the air chambers are small, the changing pressure will not be sufficient to overcome the strength of the materials forming the chamber. However, if the air chambers are large, the rising pressure inside could indeed become a problem. To guarantee the integrity of the boat, the air chambers should be vented to allow air pressure to equalize. My recommendation is to vent air chambers that attach to the decks, if they are located 8 in. or more inboard from the stems. The teardrop shaped bulkheads enclose such a small volume of air that they need not be vented.

All it would really take to vent the air chambers is a tiny hole through each bulkhead. As long as the edges of the hole were sealed with epoxy or varnish, a 1/16 in. hole would allow air pressure to equalize while excluding water, except that which gets into the chamber as vapor.

In wooden boat building, one of the least wise things to do is to allow a poorly ventilated part of a boat to collect moisture. If there is a way for water to get in, you need to have a way to get it out. Water that goes in as vapor on a hot day will condense when the weather cools off, and your chances of getting it out through a 1/16 in. hole are not great.

How much of a problem this is for you depends on how well the inside of the air chamber is sealed with epoxy. If all of the interior surfaces, including the underside of the deck, are coated with epoxy (not just varnish), then moisture in the air chambers is not a concern. On the other hand, if any part of a surface is not sealed with epoxy, a larger hole permitting better drainage and ventilation is indicated. One way to provide for these things is to put deck plates in the bulkheads, as shown in the following photo series. Another way is to make smaller holes and put plugs in them. For adequate air exchange, a 1-inch hole would be minimum. Some of the available types of plugs include transom plugs (available at power boat and sailboat supply stores) and threaded PVC pipe plugs. Some of the

Make a paper or cardboard pattern. The bulkheads for this canoe are to be of the type to join with the bottom of the deck. Station 6 from the mold is about the right size and shape to trace a bulkhead pattern from. This first pattern is only a preliminary, so it doesn't have to be perfect. If you are making the narrower bulkheads that fit against the hull all the way around, measure the distance to be spanned (lengthwise of the bulkhead) and cut out an elongated teardrop-shaped pattern to about the right size. The rest of the pattern making process is the same from here on as for the wider shield-shaped bulkheads.

The preliminary pattern is taped to the hull, and dividers being used to trace actual hull contours onto the pattern. Tape the pattern to the hull so that it is placed where the bulkhead is to be. Notice that this pattern is a little small; that is all right. If it was too large, it would have to be trimmed so the pattern would fit into the hull at the desired location. Lock the dividers at any convenient measure of width. Use a felt tip pen to mark where the inboard tip of the dividers touches the pattern. Move the dividers all around the edges of the pattern, marking at short intervals. The idea is to make a dotted line on the pattern that corresponds to the actual shape of the hull. The decks on this canoe will be flat, so to mark the upper edge of the bulkhead pattern, a long straightedge is placed across the gunwales, and a line traced along the straightedge directly onto the pattern.

transom plugs have brass hardware and are not unattractive. There may even be bottle stoppers that would serve the purpose; as long as what you use stays put if and when you "submarine" the boat.

The first step in fabrication of bulkheads is to make patterns.

The dots along the edges of the preliminary pattern are connected by a solid line.

Draw a line connecting the dotted markings. Cut out the new pattern along this line.

Make a new, more precise pattern. Tape the preliminary pattern to a new piece of cardboard. Using the dividers, still locked at the same width, transfer the hull contours from the preliminary pattern to the new one. Move one tip of the dividers along the solid line and make a series of markings on the new cardboard where the outer tip touches.

Trial fit the new pattern in the hull. Trim the pattern if necessary to make it fit.

Trace around the new pattern onto the bulkhead material and cut it out. The tool of choice for this is a jigsaw with a fine scroll blade. The plywood used here is 3 mm doorskin plywood. It is to serve as a backing for cedar strips. If the plywood is to be used by itself for bulkheads, use 1/4 in. thick plywood with at least one nice face. I like to use up scrap strips by making them part of the bulkheads and decks, so the plywood I glue the strips to doesn't need to be particularly stout. There are vertical lines penciled onto the plywood to assist in lining up strips while gluing the strips to the plywood.

The stern bulkhead backing is wedged into position. Note the narrow gap along the edge of the bulkhead. Gaps that narrow can and will be filled with epoxy, so don't worry about them. You will find that even using the thin plywood it will be necessary to bevel the edges of the plywood to make it fit into the hull well. Spend some time on this when you are well-rested, and check the fit frequently. It is easy to change the fit (usually for the worse) substantially by taking off a little too much in just the wrong place. A surprising amount of analysis goes into fitting the bulkheads. I used a couple of different files and sandpaper wrapped around a wood block to do the last stages of the fitting.

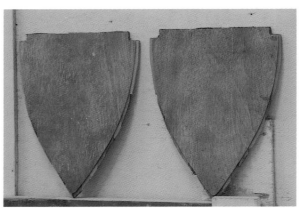

The strips are trimmed about 1/4 in. away from the plywood backing. Leave some extra wood to work with along the margin, because the edges will be beveled to fit the inside of the canoe. Be careful not to tear the strips while trimming; it helps to lay the bulkhead stripped face down on a work bench and cut near the edge of the bench with a fine-toothed jigsaw.

Select the wood strips you want to use and arrange them as you like over the backing material. When the strips are all organized, set them aside. Place plastic under the plywood and wrap plastic around any wood pieces to be used in clamping. Spread thickened epoxy on the plywood backing. (I needed 1-3/4 oz. of mixed epoxy, before adding colloidal silica and wood flour, to get complete coverage on two bulkheads.) Then, put the strips on the plywood. It is helpful to tack the middle strip to the work surface at each end so it doesn't skate around in the wet epoxy. The other strips can then be pressed up against that one to hold them straight. Clamp the strips down to the plywood and let the epoxy cure.

Bevel the bulkhead edges to fit inside the hull. Trial fit frequently, as when fitting the bulkhead backing material.

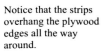

Notice that the strips overhang the plywood edges all the way around.

Gaps of up to 1/16 in. can be filled with epoxy without negatively affecting the appearance. After the bulkheads have been properly fitted, sand them smooth. Use the same sequence of sanding steps that you did on the hull in preparation for application of epoxy and fiberglass. Next, apply epoxy to both the front and back of the bulkhead, and fiberglass to the stripped side. For photos of that process, see the next section on how to make a strip deck. I fiberglassed the bulkheads and decks at the same time, so the photos for both are grouped together.

After the bulkheads have been fiberglassed, sand them smooth (on both sides).

Cut out the hole. Cut slowly and carefully with a fine-toothed scroll blade.

If you want to install deck plates or provide for drainage and ventilation using smaller openings, now is the time to cut the holes. In this brand of deck plate, the outer edge of the lid is the same diameter as the hole required for installation of the ring. Figure out how high you want to place the deck plate on the bulkhead, center it, and draw a pencil line around the lid. This will be the cutting line.

Checking for fit. The deck plate should drop right into the hole. This is a good time to drill holes for the screws. Either wood screws or machine screws are satisfactory. I drilled the screw holes later, after the bulkheads were installed, but for easier access this would have been a better time to do it.

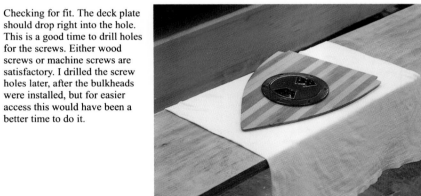

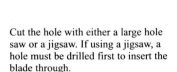

Cut the hole with either a large hole saw or a jigsaw. If using a jigsaw, a hole must be drilled first to insert the blade through.

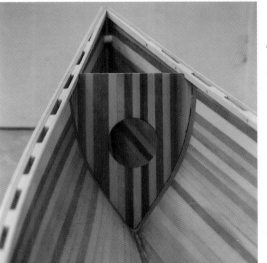

Preparing to fillet the joint between the bulkhead and the hull. The hull must be sanded, at least in the vicinity of the joint, in order to get a good bond. Masking tape was placed on the hull sides 1/8 in. away from the bulkhead. Here, the bulkhead is already glued in position with thickened epoxy on the back side of the bulkhead. I did not want the bulkhead to shift out of position while filleting the stripped face, so I ran a bead of filleting putty around the back of the joint first (with the bulkhead just pressed into place), and allowed it to cure. Not only does that serve to anchor the bulkhead in place, but it increases the area of contact between the bulkhead and the hull, which improves joint strength by distributing stresses over a larger area.

Applying a bead of filleting putty with a syringe. Make the bead as uniform as possible. As can be seen here, the bead of putty can be small and tidy-looking if the joint is closely fitted. I have better control if I start at the inwale and draw the syringe down toward the keel line.

Left and below: Tool the fillet, working in the direction that gives you the best control and smoothest results. If epoxy builds up on the bottom of the tool, wipe it off on a paper towel and continue.

Switch sides of the canoe and add a long bead to the other side the same way. Allow the fillet to cure to the point where it can be tooled without the epoxy sticking to the tooling utensil. Since a small fillet like this doesn't have much mass to generate heat (which speeds curing), it will take a while. This fillet took about 30 min. from the time of application to reach a "toolable" condition.

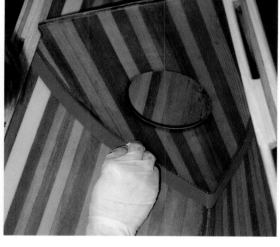

Cut a small oval tooling utensil out of a used graduated cup. Anything that will form the radius you want for tooling and last for the duration of the work will do. Epoxy doesn't soften the coated paper, and the tool can be thrown away after one use.

The finished fillet, with the tape removed. As soon as the tooling is done, peel up the tape. Then go away and let the fillet cure.

Coat the entire air chamber with epoxy or varnish. The goal is to seal all the surfaces and make them smooth. I used Clear Coat epoxy because it is a more durable coating, and there is no reason to be concerned about breakdown of the epoxy by sunlight, since there will be no exposure to sun once the deck is on. If you plan to vent the air chamber by drilling a small hole through the bulkhead, do that before putting the deck on, so you can get to the bulkhead with the drill. Place the hole where sand won't get into it; a good place would be near the upper edge, perhaps next to one inwale. Seal the edges of the hole to prevent water from wicking into the wood there.

Screw the deck plate into place. Short wood screws were used here.

Strip Decks

After the inside of the canoe has been varnished, put the deck plates in. Drill holes for screws if that is not already done. Apply a bead of non-adhesive caulk (you may want to remove the deck plates someday) around the back of the flange that seats against the bulkhead, connecting all the screw holes. You are after a water-tight seal against the bulkhead, and exclusion of water from the screw holes in the wood. A silicone sealant, such as BoatLIFE® Marine Sealant is ideal. Do *not* use a polyurethane sealant with a plastic deck plate. This type of caulk dissolves some plastics.

I find that once the hull has been constructed, there are a lot of short pieces of strips left over, and some of them are really choice wood. Rather than use these pieces for kindling, I like to make decks and other parts with them. It is very satisfying to take these strips showing outstanding color and grain pattern, and make pieces for the canoe that actually improve its utility or appearance. Decks can be more quickly and easily made using solid lumber. However, utilizing new lumber for that still leaves us with all these beautiful strips that are too short to build another boat with. Some models of canoes are more suited to fitting out with fancy decks than others, so the builder must evaluate applicability for him- or herself. If you do decide to make strip decks, this section illustrates one way to do it.

Prepare to trace the shape of the area between the inwales on the plywood backing for the strip deck. This 3 mm door skin plywood is adequately strong for this purpose as long as one plans to support the decks with bulkheads underneath. If not, use thicker (1/4 in.) plywood. Using a sharp pencil, reach up under the deck and trace a line along the inside edge of each inwale onto the plywood.

Cut the curved edge of the plywood backing material and check for fit. Here, the bulkhead backing is also being trial fit. These two pieces need to join together well. Sand any ragged edges off the plywood.

Drawing the inboard curve of the deck with a trammel bar. First, cut the plywood on the outside edge of the lines traced along the inwales. This thin plywood is apt to tear and chip if you cut against the grain, so be aware of grain direction while cutting; I used a jigsaw with a fine-toothed blade for this. The curve to be traced onto the plywood can be as evenly round or elliptical as you like. (For that matter, you could leave this edge straight.) I used a short rule to figure out what the radius of the curve needed to be to get the curve shaped the way I wanted. Then, a thin scrap of wood was drilled at each end with the holes spaced the radius distance apart. A nail was driven into one hole as a fulcrum point, and other hole is for the point of a pencil. If you draw the curve on your decks this way, save the trammel bar. You will want it later.

Strip alignment markings on deck and bulkhead backings. Mark the centerline of the deck also.

Arranging strips on the plywood. Trim the strips to convenient lengths, but leave them at least 1/4 in. long on each end, so they overlap the cutting lines.

Mark lines for positioning strips. Since I want the strips to lie parallel to the outwales, a line is being marked on the plywood by sliding the combination square along the outwales, with the pencil tip at the end of the rule.

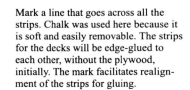

Mark a line that goes across all the strips. Chalk was used here because it is soft and easily removable. The strips for the decks will be edge-glued to each other, without the plywood, initially. The mark facilitates realignment of the strips for gluing.

Strips being edge-glued together. The work surface is covered with plastic to prevent accidental bonding. The strips are held tight together by small blocks of wood nailed to the work surface, while plastic-wrapped lengths of wood are clamped to hold the strips flat.

Trim down to the centerline with a plane.

Marking the cutting line across the ends of the strips, on the centerline. Orient the panel of strips so it lines up with the reference marks, and then place a straightedge over the centerline. Mark the centerline as precisely as possible with a sharp pencil.

Sand the cut straight. Due to differences in the grain of the strips, it may be difficult to get the cut exactly straight with the plane. Check by placing a straightedge against it. Sand the humps out with a sanding block and a medium-grit paper.

Clamp the panel of strips to the work bench and begin trimming with a utility knife. Trim to within about 1/16 in. of the cutting line.

Place the first panel of strips on the plywood backing, on the canoe, and double-check the alignment, etc. Once you are satisfied that things are straight, the right width, and so forth, use the first panel as a guide for marking the matching panel. Here, the first panel is set on top of the untrimmed matching panel, and the positions adjusted to make the strips meet at the centerline.

Cut the centerline joint as for the first panel of strips, and trial fit the matching panels on the canoe.

With the strip panels aligned as desired, clamp them to the plywood backing.

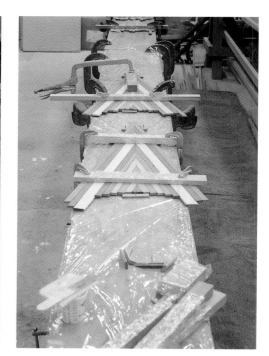

Gluing the strips to the plywood backing. Mix up a batch of thickened epoxy (these decks required 2-3/4 oz. of resin, plus fillers, for complete coverage) and spread it on the plywood. Only one strip panel can be opened at time, so spread epoxy on one side, tip the first panel into its position on the plywood, open up the second side, and repeat the process.

Turn the works upside down and clamp the pointed end of the assembly. Next, place wide masking tape along the edges of the plywood as shown. This tape holds the strip panels in proper position, and serves as a hinge in the next step.

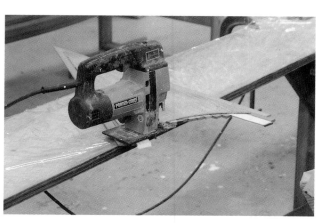

Clamp the strips flat against the plywood. The pointed ends of the decks are wedged between two blocks to close up the joints there. Make sure the wood pieces used as clamps are wrapped with plastic.

After the epoxy has cured, carefully cut the strip ends off along the inboard edge of the plywood.

Clamp the deck onto the gunwales and mark lines for trimming the three corners. Take the deck back off the hull and trim the corners and edges of the deck. Plane the edges of the long sides of the deck as needed to match the curve of the hull.

Preparing to seal the wood with epoxy. The easiest way to do this is to lay the pieces flat on a plastic-covered bench and brush the epoxy on one face at a time, letting one side cure before coating the other side. However, if you are in a hurry, you can hang the pieces up and coat both sides at once. Here, eye screws for hanging the pieces are threaded into cracks between strips.

Sand the decks flat and smooth. The decks will be highly visible, so workmanship counts. Fill gaps and finish up by dampening the wood and resanding with 220-grit paper, taking special care to sand out deep scratches.

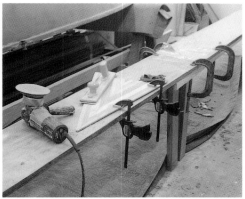

Decks and bulkheads hang while the seal coat of epoxy cures. Clear Coat epoxy was brushed onto the stripped sides of the pieces, with them lying flat on the bench. Then the pieces were hung up, and the plywood sides were coated. The runs that developed were sanded out after the epoxy cured. (This can be avoided by leaving the pieces flat during the curing time, allowing the resin to level rather than form runs.) The seat frame and thwart have fresh varnish on them.

One deck, fitted, sanded, and ready for application of epoxy and fiberglass.

Fiberglass cloth laid over bulkheads and decks. If possible, cover each part with just one piece of cloth. I did not have large enough scraps of cloth to do that, so the decks each have two pieces of cloth, overlapped by 1/2 in. down the centerline.

Saturation coat of epoxy applied to fiberglass cloth on decks and bulkheads. Clear Coat resin was used here. Trim the extra cloth along the edges of the wood when the epoxy has cured to a rubber-like state.

Before applying the final coat of epoxy, sand the deck flat. This deck has a double layer of glass cloth down the centerline (where the cloth from the two halves of the deck overlap), and I got down to the fiberglass there while sanding. Since I was using the thin epoxy resin, I actually applied two more coats to bury the cloth.

Cloth trimmed from the edges of all the pieces, and a second coat of resin applied. For these pieces, especially the decks, I favor application of four or five coats of Clear Coat resin over fewer coats of a higher-building resin. The thinner resin is clearer, less inclined to trap air bubbles, levels better, and the work can lie flat, eliminating the problem of resin running off.

Bonding a glue strip to the underside of the deck. These 3/8 in. by 1/4 in. ash strips were added for two reasons. I wanted to strengthen this edge of the deck by adding more support, and also to make a wider glue surface to bond the coamings to later. The ash strips were soaked and then bent on a jig to get them to assume this shape without breaking. (See the first photo in the section on coamings.) When the strips were dry, they were glued to the decks with thickened epoxy. Sand the joining surface of the deck edge for maximum adhesion. The twine helps hold the ash in the proper curve while the epoxy sets. The glue that squeezed out of the joint on the other side (not visible here) was tooled into a fillet rather than scraping it off and discarding it.

Sand or file resin drips from the edges, then lightly sand the whole underside of the decks and seal with a second coat of epoxy (no fiberglass cloth).

Preparing the deck for installation. The bulkhead has already been bonded into the hull, and the air chamber coated with a final application of epoxy. Trim the glue strip ends so they just fit between the inwales. Round over the edge that has the plane against it in this photo, and sand the joining parts. A block with sandpaper wrapped around it is ideal for sanding the deck edges, which will be glued to the inwales. There is no need to sand the epoxy coated plywood backing except at the very edges, and where the upper edge of the bulkhead will attach to the deck.

The outwales are masked off and a bead of filleting putty applied around the edge of the deck. The tape is about 1/8 in. away from the joint to allow for a fairly narrow fillet. This blue masking tape, called Long Mask (made by 3M Company), is a higher quality tape than the tan stuff in office supply stores. It doesn't tear when you peel it off a surface, it conforms to curves fairly well (better than most masking tapes), leaves a clean edge when peeled away, and doesn't leave adhesive behind, even if it is left on a surface in the sunshine for a few days. It is more expensive than ordinary masking tape, but I recommend it. Long Mask is carried by hardware stores and auto paint suppliers. The tan tape in the photo showing the deck clamped for gluing is Fine Line tape, which is even better than Long Mask in many respects. However, it is harder to find and is almost twice as costly as Long Mask.

Before gluing the deck onto the hull, first mask off the surfaces where you don't want stray epoxy, in this case, the outwales. Get out the clamps you need, plus scrap strips, and do a practice run on clamping the deck down. Then, go ahead and mix up a small batch of epoxy (I used 1-1/2 oz. of resin), brush some onto the bare wood of the inwales, add fillers to the remaining epoxy, and apply it to all the joining parts. Try to strike the balance point between not enough and too much epoxy on these parts, so you get a strong bond without ending up with messy drips inside the air chambers. Clamp the deck into place. When no more epoxy squeezes out of the joint, peel the tape off. Also, look underneath the deck and check the joint between the bulkhead and deck. If there is excess glue where it ought not be, clean it up now, because this is a tough spot to work in later when the epoxy has cured.

Shaped fillet along deck edge. The epoxy firmed up quickly, so a dowel ended up being the tool of choice because of the amount of pressure needed to work the fillet. The 3/8 in. dowel was just the right diameter for a fillet of this size. A wooden dowel is porous and epoxy tends to stick to it, so to offset this problem, the dowel was dipped in water before applying it to the fillet. The epoxy that did build up on the dowel was wiped off periodically. The dowel is dipped in water as often as needed to get a smooth fillet surface. As soon as tooling was done, I removed the tape. As usual, I used the faster-curing regular System Three epoxy resin for this filleting putty. The regular resin does not react to water on its surface, but Clear Coat does. If I were to use an implement with water on it on Clear Coat, it would leave milky spots on the epoxy. Be mindful of the properties of the epoxy you are using when making decisions on handling techniques.

The ash glue strip is screwed to the inwale using small #4 x 1 in. screws. I used a steel screw for strength, and because corrosion resistance will not be important here. When the coamings are glued in place, these screws will be buried in epoxy.

141

One more step in deck installation, that was impossible to photograph, was filleting of the joint between the upper edge of the bulkheads and underside of the decks, and also along the upper edge of the inwales, under the decks. In order to do this, the canoe was turned upside down, and I crawled underneath with a headlamp to do the work. These fillets were done the same as any other, only with less space and light to work. Though inconvenient, I thought it worthwhile to reinforce those joints.

Coamings

The addition of coamings to the decks of a canoe gives a traditional appearance to the craft, and also can provide a little drier climate inside the boat by adding a means of deflecting water that might otherwise run in off the decks. Coamings are details rarely found on canoes that are not hand crafted to custom specifications. In reality, most canoes don't accumulate enough spray on the decks for it to be a problem, partly because most canoes have fairly small decks. Therefore, coamings are mostly added for aesthetic reasons. There are a few canoe models that have extensive deck coverage, however, and these definitely benefit from the presence of coamings for water exclusion.

Decks of solid lumber look nicely finished either with or without coamings. In contrast, strip decks, which have a layered appearance due to the strips being bonded to plywood, look decidedly better if finished off with coamings.

The ash stock used for coamings for the Wee Lassie II was 1-1/8 in. wide x 3/16 in. thick x 16 in. long. To bend these pieces to conform to the shape of the deck edges, it was necessary to treat the wood with water to make it more flexible. The idea is to wet the wood fibers (all the way through), then bend the wood pieces over or around a jig, clamp them, and allow them to dry in the desired shape. There are two ways to do this. The simplest way is to just soak the wood until it's good and wet and clamp the pieces to the jig to dry. This is the slowest way to do it, due to the time it takes for the water to penetrate the wood, and then for the wood to dry out again. However, it requires less equipment than the other way, which is to steam the wood.

Steaming involves placing the wood pieces in a semi-closed chamber, like a cardboard tube or plastic pipe with a rag stuffed snugly in one end, and connecting a tea kettle or other source of steam to the other end (and plugging around the conduit that goes from the kettle to the pipe). Steam the wood pieces for about 20 minutes, or until they are flexible, and then quickly clamp them to the jig.[4] The advantages to this method are that the water vapor permeates the wood more quickly, and the bent wood dries much faster. Steamed stock will be dry in 24 hours, while soaked wood requires days to dry.

Coaming stock and glue strips are clamped onto jigs to dry. The curve for both of these jigs is the same as the curved edge of the decks. That being the case, the same trammel bar used for marking the cutting line on the plywood deck backing was used for these two jigs. All of the ash pieces being bent here are of small dimensions, and soaking them for 12 hours in a tub of cold water was sufficient to get the desired degree of flexibility. While coaxing the pieces to conform to the jig, exert enough pressure to effect a bend, but allow the wood to flex gradually, and expect water to seep out of the wood. Use clamps with padded grips, or place wooden pads over the pieces before clamping so as to avoid denting the wet wood. These pieces were placed on an upper shelf in the shop for a week to dry.

Using the coaming stock as a guide for marking the inwale for a notch. First, cut one end of the coaming stock off square (if it's not square already). Then, hold the bent stock against the deck as it will fit when installed, except with the lower corner resting on top of the inwale. Using a sharp pencil, draw around the corner, on the inwale.

A simple jig for bending coaming and glue strip stock. Start with a length of 2 x 6 or 2 x 4 lumber, and trace the curve of the deck edge onto the wood. Cut along this line as smoothly as possible, and save the scraps. Glue and screw the scraps to the main piece as shown. This affords an excellent grip for clamps.

Notch marking on inwale.

Carefully cut the notch in the inwale. The first cut was made with the Dozuki saw, and then the edge of the file was used to clean out the notch. The end of the file was wrapped with masking tape to prevent gouging the inside of the hull. After making the first notch, flip the coaming end-for-end, and mark and cut the notch in the opposite inwale. Do not cut the coaming stock to length yet.

Marking the length of the coaming piece. Wedge one end of the coaming in a notch, and pull the coaming into the curve of the deck. Mark the location of the opposite notch, plus 1/16 in., on the coaming stock. Use a square to mark the cutting line on the coaming. Cut the piece to length.

Check the coaming for fit. It may take some effort, but by pulling the coaming into the curve of the deck very tightly, the free end should pop into its notch. If it doesn't, re-cut the end. Avoid taking off too much, as you want the fit to be tight.

After achieving a good fit, sand the coaming smooth. It is much easier to shape and sand the edges before installation.

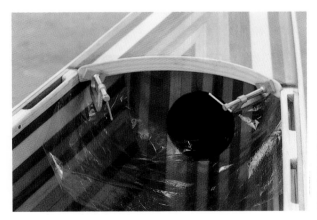

Glue the coaming into place with thickened epoxy. The plastic taped into the hull under the glue joint is to keep epoxy from where it's not wanted. The top of the deck appears pale in this photo because it has been sanded.

Keels

Whether or not to put a keel on a strip canoe is an excellent question to raise if you want to spark a spirited discussion among builders and canoeing enthusiasts. That is because advocates on both sides have several good points in their favor. Those who support the addition of a keel can tout extra protection and strength for the hull bottom, straighter tracking while under way, and better resistance to effects of wind. Those who prefer to go "keel-less" like better maneuverability, absence of projections that can hang up on rocks, and lighter weight.

The keel is a piece that is added to the hull after most of the rest of the construction is done. In fact, it is no problem to add a keel even after the canoe has been completely finished. This is a significant point to keep in mind.

When I built my first canoe, I fully intended to give it a keel, because all the canoes I had paddled up to that time that I liked, had keels. However, the designer of the canoe I built made the interesting assertion that good handling in a canoe is primarily a function of good hull design and paddler proficiency. The designer further pointed out that a keel could always be added, and recommended that the canoe be used for a while without a keel. If the builder was dissatisfied, then go ahead and install a keel later. With some skepticism, I decided to heed his advice. The end result was that I never have put a keel on that canoe, because it handles very well without one. I think that is probably true of most well-conceived designs. A couple exceptions would be in the cases of canoes used mainly on lakes that frequently experience wind, and some solo canoe designs that are very broad relative to their length. Other than that, it probably costs about as much to have a keel as you gain in benefits.

If you determine that a keel is essential, ash makes good keel stock, because it resists wear and is flexible. As with most features on a canoe, there is more than one variation on the theme. A popular type of keel is 3/4 in. to 1 in. deep, 7/8 in. wide at the base (where it joins the hull), and 1/2 in. wide at the outer edge. A keel of that width at the edge can be fitted with a 3/8 in. wide stem band (also called half oval) running along its length, if desired. The length of the keel will be determined by the shape and length of the hull bottom. The keel gradually tapers down in depth to a fine point at each end, so as to blend smoothly into the shape of the hull. Once you have visually evaluated the shape of the hull bottom and decided on an appropriate keel length, mark that length on the keel piece and cut it. In order to preserve the 1/2 in. wide outer edge while tapering the ends of the keel piece down to a point, cut the bevel from the wider base. Begin the taper 16 in. from the ends. To save time, saw or grind the bulk of the excess wood away and finish cutting the long bevel with a plane.

The keel is glued to the hull with thickened epoxy. First, position the keel on the hull bottom, clamp it, and temporarily fasten the ends of the keel to the hull with screws driven through the keel into the hull. (Remember that the joining surface on the hull must be sanded epoxy for a good bond, so attend to that if the canoe has already been finished.) With the two ends screwed to the hull, sight along the keel to check for straightness. If you want to compare to a tautline, drill a hole for a finishing nail in the keel near each of the two screws. Insert a long finishing nail in each hole, and stretch a tautline between them. When the keel is straight, apply masking tape to the hull along the base of the keel on both sides. Arrange a way to clamp the keel firmly against the hull bottom so it conforms to the hull as desired. One way to do this is to drive screws from the inside of the hull up into the keel. If you use this method, line up the screws on the centerline of the hull. When everything is in order, take the keel off the canoe and apply epoxy as usual. That is, brush unthickened epoxy onto the base of the bare wooden keel and then apply thickened epoxy. Clamp or screw the keel back in place and clean up the joint. The keel should have at least one coat of epoxy on its outer surfaces before finishing with varnish. The screw and nail holes can be filled with pieces of dowel glued into them.[5]

Stem Bands

If you anticipate that the canoe you are putting so much energy into may be banged around a bit after launching, you may want to add stem bands for extra protection. Stem bands are narrow strips of metal (either brass or aluminum) that are fastened to the leading (and trailing) edges of a canoe hull. Their purpose is to shield vulnerable areas from impacts and abrasion that can damage the fiberglass covering the hull. Canoes with keels usually have a metal strip running all the way from one stem to the other, along the keel. Since the stem band is fastened with screws, its application may be restricted somewhat by the construction of the canoe. There must be solid wood to turn the screws into. If your canoe has no keel, the stem bands would have to end where the stems do, and those need to be constructed with wooden inner and outer stem pieces.

Stem band stock is purchased as a continuous length of 3/8 in. wide metal strip, often listed in catalogs as "half oval," and the screw holes are drilled by the builder. (Other widths are available, but this is most suitable for canoes.) The band is bent to conform to the profile of the canoe. Suggested screw spacing is 5 in. apart for 1/8 in. countersink screw holes. When making sharp bends, don't allow a screw hole to be at the bending point, because the stem band may break. The last screw hole should be 1/2 in. from the cut end of the stem band; that may involve drilling additional holes.

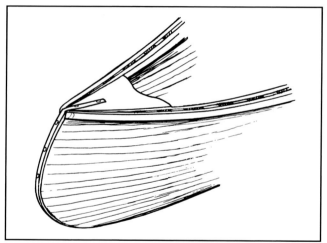

A stem band, for protection of the leading edge (and keel, if present).

The stem band does not need to be glued onto the boat. Choose 1/2 in. #4 countersink screws of appropriate color to match your stem band metal, and drill holes in the boat for the screws as you actually install them, one by one. If you are using brass screws, which are relatively soft, you may want to thread the holes with a steel screw before turning a brass screw in. That reduces the risk of twisting off a brass screw in its hole. As mentioned earlier in this chapter, put a little sealant on the screw threads before inserting them, to prevent water from getting into the holes. Once the screws are all in place, file off any protruding corners.

Foot Braces

One occasionally hears of foot braces installed in canoes. Some commercially manufactured tandem canoes have foot braces mounted in them, and a number of users of solo canoes have elected to add foot braces to their own boats. Having never paddled a tandem canoe with foot braces, I can't say whether they make a positive contribution to the utility of the craft or not. I *can* say that paddling either from a kneeling position with good knee pads, or sitting on the seat with one foot ahead of, and the other foot under the seat are comfortable enough that foot braces seem unnecessary to me.

In contrast, a foot brace in a solo canoe that has the seat located at about the waterline is a decided improvement. The paddler's feet are able to rest in a more comfortable position, and the foot brace provides a more solid connection with the boat for pushing against while paddling. A simple foot brace for a solo canoe of this type can be easily made with a minimum of materials.[6]

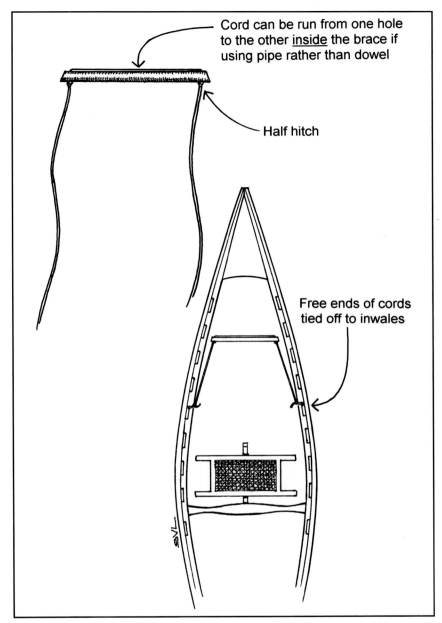

Cord can be run from one hole to the other <u>inside</u> the brace if using pipe rather than dowel

Half hitch

Free ends of cords tied off to inwales

Foot brace for solo canoe. The brace itself is a 16 in. piece of 1 in. diameter dowel, bamboo, or plastic pipe. A hole is drilled through each end, so a length of cord can be threaded through. Leave the free ends of the cord long enough to permit adjustment to suit the proportions of the paddler. Knot the cord next to the foot brace so it doesn't slide on the cord.

Chapter Eleven

Finishing

A common feature of wood strip canoes that is somewhat unique among canoes in general is that the finish work is usually done in such a way as to show off the internal structure of the strip hull. The great majority of commercially manufactured canoes are finished with a pigmented gel coat or marine paint. It could be argued that aluminum canoes do indeed show the internal structure of the hull, but then, there really isn't any finish applied to an aluminum canoe. While paint is a practical and attractive finish, and in many ways superior to varnish, most strip boat builders do elect to use varnish. A clear finish affords necessary protection while permitting the appreciation of the beautiful pattern of the wood strips that form the core of the hull.

The choice of varnish as opposed to paint is mostly a matter of aesthetic preference. However, application of one of these finishes is a must. The most obvious effect of finishing may be on the canoe's appearance, but there are other, more important reasons to bother yourself with this final step. The bare wood components of the canoe must be sealed away from moisture if they are to provide you with the duration of service you expect. Also, the epoxy that is such an integral part of the hull is subject to deterioration by exposure to ultraviolet light. That means sunlight will, given sufficient time, damage unprotected epoxy. You cannot afford to let this happen. Fortunately, this kind of deterioration is a gradual process, and some types of epoxy are substantially more resistant to breakdown than others.

With the need for finishing established, a return to the question of painting versus varnishing is warranted. Paint is a tougher, more abrasion resistant coating than varnish, so from a utility standpoint, it is the more sensible choice. Paint is also easier to apply, providing you use a good quality paint. And if you are dissatisfied with the appearance of your fiberglass job, paint is noted for its ability to hide such things. Marine paints are manufactured in a broad range of good colors, so a decision to paint rather than varnish can still result in a really beautiful boat. The preparation of the hull for paint is the same as for varnish. Also, the treatment between coats is the same. The chief differences are that primer is recommended for application over epoxy and under the first coat of paint; and that paint builds up faster than varnish, so fewer coats of paint are needed to get the same smooth surface quality.

Epoxy can prove to be a difficult material to partner with a finish. In fact, the chemical composition of epoxy is somewhat infamous for creating problems with marine paints and varnishes, usually evidenced by a failure of the finish to dry properly. Therefore you need to either consult your epoxy supplier for recommendations for compatible paints and varnishes, or do your own testing. If you have some of a finish already on hand that you'd like to try, you should apply it to a small area of the hull to see if it will work before covering the whole hull with it. After all, there is a risk you might have to strip it back off.

Polyurethane paints perform well over epoxy, particularly when used with an appropriate primer. Paint products have become more and more sophisticated over recent years, to the point where specific combinations of products, called paint systems, must be used together to get the expected results. For example, a two-part polyurethane enamel paint that is peerless when applied over a two-part primer may be a disaster if applied over a one-part primer. The two-part enamel will lift the one-part primer from the hull surface. A paint system that has worked well for me over System Three's epoxies is Interlux® Brightside Polyurethane Enamel, with Brightside Primer. Both products are one-part products, requiring no mixing of ingredients. Coverage and leveling quality of the paint are very good when applied with a brush. (I have not tried spraying

it.) There are other brands that will work; this just happens to be one I have experience with.

Varnish, though not as tough as paint, has remained the most popular finish among strip boat builders. Part of the attraction for building a wood strip canoe is the distinctive appearance of the finished hull. Varnish highlights the beauty of the wood, while at the same time protecting the epoxy from the harmful effects of sunlight. Varnishes suitable for this application must be specifically labeled as marine varnish, with ultraviolet light blocking agents. There are several varnishes on the market (which vary considerably in price) that meet these criteria. Of more importance than price is the compatibility of the varnish with the epoxy you've used. Epoxy suppliers can tell you what varnish is known to work with their epoxy. However, that list is not always complete; there may be other brands that also work, so some cautious experimentation on the builder's part can be worthwhile.

To experiment with a new finish, prepare the hull as you normally would, but apply the finish to only a small area, following manufacturer's instructions on handling of the paint or varnish. If the finish has not dried after three days and the temperature and humidity are within the range of tolerance, then the finish is not compatible with the epoxy. (Three days seems like an extraordinarily long time, but I have observed several instances where the first coat of varnish dried very slowly. The varnish did eventually dry, however, and subsequent coats dried in a normal length of time.) In the event that the finish does not dry properly, scrape off as much of it as you can, and wipe off the remainder with the thinner that is recommended for that paint or varnish. Do not use a chemical stripper because most, if not all of them will dissolve the epoxy as well.

Just because a finish works with one brand of epoxy doesn't necessarily mean it will work with all of them. I had a discouraging experience with a varnish that was recommended to me by a boat restorer whose work I admire. He uses WEST SYSTEM brand epoxy, and told me that he gets his mirror-bright results with Clipper Clear Urethane Varnish. I was especially interested because this is a non-yellowing varnish, which doesn't alter the natural color of the wood. I confidently applied two coats of this varnish to the interior of a new canoe built with System Three epoxy. It was easy to apply, and initially gave most pleasing results. Some two months later, I brought the canoe out into the July sunshine for the first time. After twenty minutes or so of exposure to the hot sun, I found, to my dismay, that the surface of the varnish had become quite sticky in two places. This condition spread, and over a period of time, dust became embedded in the varnish surface. It was obvious by then that this varnish would have to be removed, and the interior of the hull refinished. That's when I found out about chemical strippers dissolving epoxy. The hull was not damaged to the point of not being serviceable, but does have some blemishes that make it unfit to present as an example of my best work. The tardiness of my discovery of the incompatibility of the epoxy and varnish was an abnormal development. Compatibility problems are nearly always apparent within a few days. Still, strange things can happen. This incident illustrates the need to exercise caution when departing from known combinations. To avoid such risks altogether, follow the recommendations of your epoxy supplier.

Varnish has a reputation for being somewhat temperamental to deal with. While it is more demanding than paint, it is still well within your ability to get a fine finish with varnish, and without having to have a professionally equipped finishing shop. Most hobby builders brush varnish on, because the equipment required is much less complicated and expensive, there is less masking to do, and the exposure to harmful vapors is far less than when spraying. I prefer to apply varnish with a brush, and the information presented here will be geared for that method. Although my discussion will focus on varnish, the preparation for and application of paint is essentially the same.

Success in applying varnish is directly related to the amount of experience one has with that medium. Don't be too perturbed if the first coat of varnish you put on the hull turns out imperfectly. The hull really needs to have at least two coats of varnish, and applications of as many as five coats are common. Each additional coat of varnish provides more protection for the boat (although it does add a little weight to the canoe), and more practice for the builder in varnishing. What follows is a list of pointers on how to achieve the beautiful finish your heart desires.

1. Allow the epoxy on the hull to cure completely before varnishing. See the epoxy manufacturer's technical manual to find out how long it takes, at what temperature, to effect a complete cure.
2. Scrub the amine blush off the epoxy surface after it has cured.
3. Sand the epoxy at least lightly before the first coat of varnish and between coats of varnish so the varnish will adhere.
4. Rid the shop of airborne dust and bugs to the best of your ability. Do all the sweeping and vacuuming two or three days before varnishing, to allow time for the dust to settle. Close up the shop and fumigate it if you are plagued by large numbers of insects and spiders. By all means, don't varnish at night by artificial light with the shop doors open! If you must varnish under a tree that is shedding pollen, or some similar adversity, rig up a tent of clear plastic (so light can penetrate) over your boat. If you can seal the ends of the shelter and install a series of filters at one end and a fan to draw air through at the opposite end, so much the better.
5. Good light is essential for good varnish work. The light must be good enough for you to be able to see skips in coverage, sags, runs, and brush marks, so you can do something about it before the varnish dries.
6. Wear lint-free clothing and wipe the canoe down before varnishing with a lint-free tack rag. Cheesecloth dampened with mineral spirits makes a good tack rag. Old T-shirts make acceptable varnishing apparel. There isn't much fabric to shed lint and they have no cuffs to drag through wet varnish. I read of one fellow who always showers before a major varnish job, puts on a cap to prevent his own hair from falling in the varnish, and then proceeds with the job shirtless, to completely eliminate that lint source.
7. Seal bare wood with a thinned varnish.
8. Try to varnish while you have environmental conditions that permit the varnish to dry, but not too quickly. One of the keys to getting a varnish job that is free of brush marks is being able to finish the necessary brush work while the area being coated is still wet enough for the varnish to level out after you are done working it. If the varnish is drying too quickly, your brush marks will still be visible when the varnish is completely dry.
9. Thin the varnish sparingly, using the thinner that the varnish manufacturer recommends. If you have a choice of thinners, use the one that evaporates slowest (i.e. mineral spirits rather that lacquer thinner). That way, once you thin to the viscosity you want, the longer the mixture will stay that way.
10. Strain the varnish through a disposable paint strainer into a clean container before using it (even if the varnish is from a brand new can). Strain out about twice as much varnish as you expect to use; that makes it easier to maintain the optimum viscosity of your varnish, especially under warm conditions (above 70° F).
11. Use foam brushes that have small cells in the foam, and use a new brush for each coat of varnish. I get good results with a wooden-handled variety called Poly-Brush. These come in several sizes, ranging from 1 in. to 4 in. wide. The narrower ones are good for varnishing seats, thwarts, and gunwales, while the wider ones work well for the hull. I once splurged and bought a nice badger hair brush for varnishing. It was wonderful, the first time I used it. Unfortunately, I was never able to get the same flawless results with it again, because I could never get it completely clean. Much better to use a disposable foam brush (which also doesn't shed bristles) for varnishing and leave the bristle brushes to the painters. If you *are* applying paint, use a good quality bristle brush of the size and type you would use for house trim.
12. Be attentive to the way the varnish is working while using it. It may be necessary to thin the varnish part way through the job to regain the proper viscosity. On the bigger jobs, like varnishing the hull of a tandem canoe, be mindful of the fact that the varnish in the container you're dipping your brush into is drying along with the varnish you've put on the boat. If you begin to notice problems with the brush marks not leveling out, it's time to add thinner.
13. Wet sand with a sanding block between coats of varnish to smooth out minor irregularities in the surface. Layers of varnish will fill the low spots, while the high spots are sanded off. A few repetitions of this treatment can yield an amazingly smooth surface.

The following photos illustrate the finishing process.

Varnishing supplies. This varnish is labeled for marine use and contains UV light inhibitors. Mineral spirits, also known as paint thinner, is the recommended thinner for this varnish. Cheesecloth, at left, is for dusting off the hull just before varnishing. The two rolls of tape are Long Mask (blue) and Thin Line tape. The paint strainer is the rayon mesh type, which sheds no lint. Muslin (cotton) paint strainers are cheaper, and better than no strainer at all, but they sometimes shed a little lint. The foam brushes are 1 in. wide and 3 in. wide Poly-Brushes. The narrower brush is for gunwales, and the wide brush is for the hull. For tandem canoe hulls, 4 in. wide brushes are best, because you need to be able to apply the varnish fairly rapidly in order to avoid leaving brush marks in the varnish. The abrasive pad at right, is for raising tooth on smooth spots (low places) left on the hull after sanding. Varnish will not stick to glossy-smooth surfaces. The empty plastic container is for straining the varnish into, and the stir stick is for mixing the varnish with thinner, if needed.

Strain the varnish. Even if you are using a newly-opened can of varnish, strain it. A fresh can of varnish is usually free of crud, but partially used cans of varnish are notorious for having granules of dried varnish and small globules of gel in them.

Checking the viscosity of the varnish. Sometimes the consistency of the varnish needs to be altered to get better handling characteristics. I found a fairly accurate way to assess viscosity by observing how the varnish runs off a stir stick. For application at 65° to 70°F, the viscosity is about right if, when a stir stick is lifted up out of the varnish, the varnish runs continuously off the stick for the first 4 sec., and then 6 or 7 drips fall during the next 6 sec. If the varnish is thicker than that, I add a little thinner at a time until it's right. Don't add any more thinner than the manufacturer specifies as a maximum. That means you do need to keep track of at least approximate measures of varnish and thinner. Mixing thinner into varnish is about the only time stirring is called for, at least with the varnish I use. Otherwise, stirring merely introduces bubbles into the finish.

The first coat of varnish on the interior of the hull. The interior was done first because it needs to be finished before installing deck plates, the seat, and thwart. The application of the first coat of varnish is both thrilling and deflating. The beauty of the wood coming to life with each stroke of the brush makes this part of the project hugely satisfying. (See the next few photos for brushing techniques.) Inevitably, however, you always find that the wet varnish highlights irregularities in the epoxy surface you *thought* was smooth. When the varnish has dried, lightly hand sand with fine sandpaper (like 220-grit) and vacuum the dust out of the hull. Dust it with an ordinary rag, like an old T-shirt, and then dust it again with cheesecloth slightly dampened with thinner. Make all your wiping strokes the same direction, turning or refolding the cloth frequently to avoid re-depositing the dust you've picked up. Then, brush on the next coat of finish. After repeating this process a couple times you will see that the combination of sanding off the high spots and adding more varnish smoothes up the inside of the hull nicely. The finished appearance of the decks in this picture is deceptive; they actually have a recent coating of unsanded epoxy on them.

Interior of the hull, ready for finish. The hull has been sanded, and all the residual glossy spots scrubbed with an abrasive pad. Sanding smoothes the hull surface, creates a texture for the varnish to grip, and aids in removing the amine blush byproduct of many epoxies. If the epoxy you used for the last coat is one of the types that produces a blush, you will also need to use water (I think a little detergent helps) to completely remove this residue. If the epoxy you used was the type that doesn't produce a blush (like Clear Coat), check the literature for the epoxy before using water to clean it. Water will cause milky spots to appear on the surface of Clear Coat. These water spots can be removed by sanding, but probably the best plan is to not use water to clean the surface. Just vacuum and dust it instead. If in doubt as to

The outer hull is prepped for varnish. Patches of resin applied to bury exposed fiberglass cloth have been sanded to blend smoothly with the surrounding surfaces. This involved careful work with the dual action sander (220-grit disk), the longboard (180-grit paper), and hand sanding pad (220-grit paper). A dry rag was used to dust the hull, and then the bubble craters in the epoxy were cleared of dust with a toothbrush. Next, I masked off the undersides of the outwales, because I wanted to seal the bare wood with thinned varnish, and that is *not* what will be put on the hull. (The gunwales are to be done soon, but not now.) Also, a strip of masking tape is placed with one edge along the keel line. After both halves of the hull are varnished, there will be a visible line down the middle of the canoe bottom. Since this is inescapable, it might as well be made to look as good as possible by keeping it neat and straight; and that is the purpose of the tape.

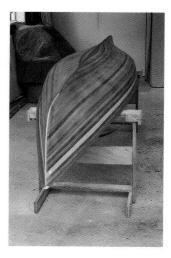

whether the epoxy surface is adequately prepared, varnish only a limited area and see if it dries. If not, you might consult your epoxy supplier for technical advice. The varnish may or may not be incompatible with the epoxy; if it turns out you prepped the hull correctly, then it's safe to assume there is a compatibility problem, and you need to switch to another finish.

Beginning the first coat of varnish on the outer hull. Start by brushing varnish onto the upper areas and work down toward the outwale, with horizontal strokes running toward the end of the canoe. If brush strokes begin at the end of the canoe, there is a strong probability of ending up with runs of varnish down along the outer stem. Laying brushstrokes parallel to the strips gives better control of the behavior of the finish, and also, if the brush marks don't all level out, they will be less noticeable if they run the same direction as the strips.

Adjust your point of view so you can see what the varnish is doing. The only way to spot unwanted behavior in the varnish is to look for highlights that give away the development of sags and runs. You can also spot skips in coverage this way. Skips in the first coat are obvious, but are far from obvious in subsequent coats. Check frequently for runs and sags and brush them out as soon as possible for best chances of a smooth finish. When you arrive at the far end of the first side, peel off the tape along the keel line. Then, you can begin the second side, or take a break. I always go ahead and do the other side to get the most mileage from my brush before throwing it away. Check the viscosity of the varnish; if you haven't had to thin it already, you probably will need to now. Take care of that before starting the second side, because if you have to stop and thin it part way through, you run the risk of having the varnish on the hull dry to the point where the next round of brush marks won't blend in.

Cover one section of the hull before moving to the next section. Let brush strokes end by overlapping the varnish laid down in the previous section. Make the first stroke along the keel line, and each successive stroke below the one before, with the last one just above the outwale. Adjust the width of the sections you cover according to how long the varnish along the edges stays wet enough for brush marks to level out. The whole strategy for the application of the varnish is based on getting the finish on without telltale brush marks left behind. This, of course, while getting complete coverage, and without excess varnish forming runs. Practice will teach you how heavily to load the brush, how long to make the strokes, and how quickly to make them to achieve this result. You will find that near the ends of the canoe, sections about 18 in. wide allow you to move along at a good pace, but as you work your way toward the middle of the hull you will have to shorten the sections up to about 12 in. That is because it takes more time to cover the distance between the keel line and outwale, and you need to be able to start the next section before your first stroke at the keel line has begun to dry.

When the coat of varnish is complete, peel the tape off the outwales. This is done while the varnish is still wet. Put tape on before every coat, and peel it off after each coat is applied. If you try to conserve tape and work by leaving the same tape on for all the coats, the tape will end up stuck to the boat, and will have to be cut off.

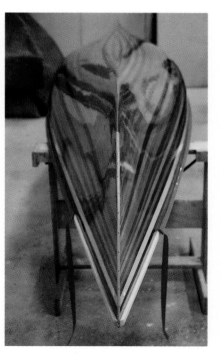

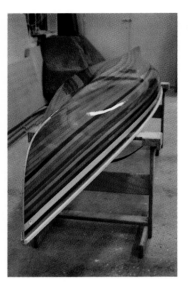

First coat of varnish
on the Wee Lassie II.

The first coat of varnish on the gunwales, coamings, and decks. The varnish was thinned to the maximum extent recommended by the manufacturer to promote the penetration of the varnish into the wood. Remember to varnish the bare wood inwales up under the decks. The gunwales of a canoe are subject to quite a bit of wear, so apply at least three coats of varnish for adequate protection. The varnish for the last two coats is thinned only as needed to get good brushing qualities.

Preparing the gunwales for varnish. Sand the gunwales as needed to make them smooth with evenly rounded corners. I mask the hull just below the gunwales as much to protect the hull from marring with the sanding block as to catch varnish drips. The sanding block has 60-grit paper wrapped around it for tough spots, and the scraper is for epoxy stains, but most work was done with an 80-grit disk and 120-grit disk folded in half.

Wet sanding equipment and supplies. To smooth the exterior of the hull to perfection, wet sand with a sanding block after the second coat of varnish, and subsequently after every second coat. (Varnish does not build up very quickly, so there is not much to be gained by wet sanding between each coat.) The sanding block has 400-grit wet-or-dry paper on it. Other items are a sanding lubricant, in this case Behlen's Wool Lube,™ an abrasive pad such as Scotch-Brite, a bucket of plain water, and a sponge. The gunwales need to have a couple coats of varnish on them before wet sanding the hull, so sanding residue doesn't get trapped in the pores of the wood.

Spread a film of sanding lubricant on the sandpaper. This keeps the paper from clogging up with varnish particles.

Use a Scotch-Brite pad to raise some tooth in the low spots and remove any traces of wet sanding residue. Next, dust the hull as usual and wipe with cheesecloth dampened with thinner. Mask and brush on the next coat of varnish.

Squeeze water from the sponge onto the hull while sanding. Keeping the surface wet allows the sanding block to run smoothly over the hull. The tendency of varnish to clog sandpaper makes it nearly impossible to sand without resorting to this method, or using an abrasive pad, which is ineffective for leveling the ridges and valleys.

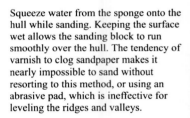

A Wee Lassie solo canoe with five coats of varnish. It was wet sanded after the second and fourth coats.

Exterior of the hull wet sanded and rinsed with clear water.

Wee Lassie II with varnish work complete and all parts installed.

Some builders like to varnish the outer hull above the waterline to retain the visual impact of a strip canoe, but paint the hull below the waterline for better protection there. Most of the wear and tear on the outer hull is below the waterline anyhow, so this is a good way to meld aesthetics with practicality.

To finish a canoe this way, the first step is to mark the waterline on the hull. Find a flat, smooth, level floor to set the canoe on, right side up. Then brace the canoe so that it is level and stable. Cut a block of wood, such as a piece of 2 x 4, to a length of about 5 inches. With the block standing on its long edge, tape a felt tip marker or dark pencil to the upper edge of the block. The block is sized to place the tip of the marker or pencil at a height of 4 inches. Then, set the block on the floor and mark the 4 in. waterline on the outside of the hull by sliding the block along the floor with the tip of the marker against the hull. The line marked at 4 in. is actually an arbitrary location. The builder can vary the position of that line according to his or her preference.

Then, put the canoe upside down on sawhorses and place masking tape along the marked line. Do the varnish work first, from the taped line to the gunwales. As soon as a fresh coat of varnish is on the hull, peel the tape off to leave a smooth, clean edge on the varnish. Replace the tape before the next coat. Put all the coats of varnish on the outer hull, and after the last coat is

thoroughly dry, put tape along the marked line again, but position it so the varnish is protected while you paint the hull bottom. Offset the masking tape slightly, so that the paint overlaps the edge of the varnish. That eliminates potential gaps in the protective finish. Primer the bottom of the boat, and after the coating has begun to set, peel the tape off. Tape before each coat of paint, and remove it when the paint is still soft enough to form a smooth edge, but not run. It will take fewer coats of paint than of varnish to finish to the same thickness on the bottom of the boat.

While the lower limit on the number of coats of finish you apply to your canoe is two, the upper limit is what your time, patience, and standards dictate. As you add more coats, you gain more expertise, and your canoe gains more protection. On the other hand, finishing does involve an investment in time, and the canoe will pick up a little weight with each application of finish. Up to about the sixth coat, I usually figure the benefits of more varnish outweigh the costs. After that, if the last coat of varnish still isn't up to snuff, my mind set shifts to the position that the canoe will need a new coat of varnish in a year or so anyway as routine maintenance; I can try for the perfect varnish job then. Actually, there is something to be said for an imperfect finish. That is, when it gets scratched, it's a lot easier to take it as a matter of course. So do the best job of finishing that you can; but also, it is healthy to regard paint and varnish as expendable.

Chapter Twelve

Launching

Canoe conveyance. Note foam padding on the gunwales and also under the buckles on the tiedown straps.

After that last coat of varnish or paint has dried, pause to let the reality of having finished sink in. Walk around the canoe and admire the shape of the hull, which (if your canoe is finished bright) is accentuated by the pattern of the strips. Start thinking of your canoe as a boat, waiting for you to use, rather than a project. The launching day marks the official transition from project to vehicle.

Preparing the canoe for launching doesn't take long, fortunately, because it tends to intensify the anticipation of getting out on the water, and many of us do not wait well in that frame of mind. There are a few things to look to, however.

One is that you have a suitable means of getting your canoe to the water. A vehicle that has a pair of crossbars over the roof is highly desirable, because it provides good stability for the canoe, good places to anchor tiedowns to, and raises the canoe up high enough to get it out of your field of vision while driving.

Padding for the gunwales is a good idea. While you should not have to constantly pamper the canoe, there is no sense in marring the finish when it can be so easily and inexpensively protected. The perfect accessory for gunwale protection is foam pipe insulation. The insulation comes in a few different diameters, so you can make your selection according to the dimensions of the gunwales on your canoe. (If the cross bars on the overhead racks of your vehicle have no padding, you can also put pipe insulation around them.) Cut the insulation into about 6 in. lengths, open up the slit along the sides, and slip the insulation onto the gunwales where you expect the crossbars to rest.

Good tiedowns are a must. I prefer a pair of 10 ft., 1 in. wide nylon straps with "self-binding" buckles for fastening a canoe to the supporting crossbars of an overhead rack. They are easy to use, are strong and dependable, and are less apt to mark the finish than rope, because the straps distribute their pressure over a wider surface area. Also, get some 1/4 in. rope (or larger) to tie the ends of the canoe to the vehicle with. The crosswise tiedowns should be sufficient, but why not give yourself and your canoe additional security in case your primary system fails?

In most (if not all) localities, some type of personal flotation device (PFD) is required for each person aboard. Check to see what you need to comply with the laws in your area. PFDs come in two main varieties: throwable (boat cushions) and wearable (life vests).

Normally, bow and stern lines are attached before launching time. These should be at least 6 ft. long, with floating rope (polypropylene) being the top choice among the many rope options available.

When you have assembled the necessary equipment and secured the canoe for hauling, notify all your friends and neighbors, especially the ones that helped fiberglass and lent you tools, of the imminent launching. (You may even decide to make a christening event of it, not just a launching!) And then, you're all off to a body of water that is worthy of your new canoe.

At the launch site, size up the potential hazards before blithely toting your canoe to the water. Footing conditions (good or bad), submerged rocks, decrepit docks, and abrupt drop-offs underwater are potentially useful features, but are just as apt to be nuisances. If nothing else, it would be embarrassing to crash with friends looking on, so choose your route with care.

Now for the moment you've been waiting for. Liberate your canoe from it's bindings, and with or without ceremony, carry it to the water.

A perfect launching spot. To preserve the integrity of the varnish job, set the canoe in water deep enough to float it. For such a lightweight craft, 3 in. of water is usually ample. However, for ease of launching, and especially picking the canoe out of the water, wading out into deeper water can considerably shorten the distance of the required lift. Launching from a dock keeps the feet dry, but also necessitates lowering the canoe to a point below the feet. That puts a person in a rather awkward position. Even so, seasonal temperatures may make it much the preferred alternative. *Photo courtesy of Janet Van Leuven-Kern.*

Wee Lassie II at first official launching. Its finished weight, at 13 ft. 3 in. long, is 34 pounds.

Take up your paddle and step aboard. Feel how alive the canoe is in its element. A few strokes of the paddle, and you're skimming along over the water. Delight in the quick response of the canoe to your paddle: yet another benefit of having a lightweight boat. Practice cruising on a straight course; practice all your maneuvering strokes; learn how this particular craft reacts to your guidance. Get to know your new partner.

Confirming the Wee Lassie II's billing as a fast cruising canoe. Propelled by a person wielding a double-bladed paddle, this canoe covers the water at a good clip.

This first launching marks the beginning of a potentially long and pleasant association, laced with excitement and also mesmerizing tranquillity, as the boat carries you into realms best appreciated from a paddler's perspective. Paddling provides a relief from the other rigors of the day in a way that can only be derived from being on the water in a human-powered craft. The interplay between water, canoe, and canoeist is so immediate as to be wholly absorbing. A wood strip canoe of one's own making is a most fitting vehicle for the mind as well as body in restoring balance to a sometimes topsy-turvy world.

Use your canoe absolutely as often as possible; don't allow a concern over minor dings (which you are quite capable of fixing yourself) deter you from enjoying your boat. You will certainly extract more of the real value of a strip canoe by using it than by putting it on display. Some minor accidents are to be expected, but these impart a certain "character" to the craft, which over time disturb you no more than the distinctive features of your friends' countenances. And indeed, the more you use your canoe, the more you will come to regard it as your friend. So indulge in the exhilaration and freedom of paddling your wood strip canoe to reap the richest rewards of building and owning such a craft.

Appendix

Sources of Plans

Here are the names of some of the better-known strip boat designers and plans distributors. These individuals and companies advertise fairly regularly in boat building magazines, or else have published books featuring their plans. This source list is not complete. There are active designers whose names or reputations are not yet known to me. New names arrive on the scene periodically, so readers can find other designers by looking through the advertisements in current issues of magazines like *WoodenBoat*, *Boatbuilder*, and *Messing About in Boats*. As in any field of creative endeavor, fresh ideas abound among boat designers. If you are considering building your first strip canoe, I suggest obtaining plans from an established designer for the greatest assurance of success. After building that first canoe, you will be in a better position to determine whether an unfamiliar designer's plans are suitable to your needs.

Henry "Mac" McCarthy
Feather Canoes, Inc.
1705 Andrea Pl.
Sarasota, FL 34235
Phone: 941-355-6736, 941-953-7660
Full size plans for solo canoe models Wee Lassie and Wee Lassie II, a sailing canoe, and two tandem canoes.

Ted Moores
Bear Mountain Boat Shop
275 John St.
Peterborough, ON K9J 5E8
Canada
Phone: 705-740-0470
Full-size patterns for canoes and kayaks. Send $3 for information.

David Hazen
See *The Stripper's Guide to Canoe-building* for plans for seven tandem canoe models (one including optional modifications for square stern) and two kayak models.

Gil Gilpatrick
See *Building a Strip Canoe* for plans for two solo canoes, five tandem canoes, and one square-sterned canoe.

Eric Schade
Shearwater Boats
22 Soundview Drive
Stamford, CT 06902
Phone: 203-359-6431
Full-size patterns for a tandem canoe and four models of kayaks.

Rob Macks
Laughing Loon Custom Canoes and Kayaks
833 W. Colrain Rd.
Greenfield, MA 01301
Phone: 413-773-5375
Plans for three models of kayaks. Send $5 for color catalog.

Nick Schade
Guillemot Kayaks
10 Ash Swamp Rd., Apt. M
Glastonbury, CT 06033
Phone: 860-659-8847
Plans for eight kayaks.

J. D. Brown, John Hartsock, and Bob & Erica Pickett
See *Rip, Strip, and Row!* for plans for a cosine wherry.

Glen-L Marine Designs
9152 Rosecrans Ave.
Box 1804 DB8
Bellflower, CA 90706-2138
Phone: 562-630-6258
Plans for many kinds of boats, including strip canoes. Send $5 for catalog.

The Newfound Woodworks, Inc.
RFD #2 Box 850
Bristol, NH 03222
Phone: 603-744-6872
Plans for canoes and kayaks. Send $3 for study plans and other information.

Sources of Strips and Kits

Flounder Bay Boat Lumber
1019 3rd Street
Anacortes, WA 98221
Phone: 800-228-4691 Dept. X
Milled strips, kits, epoxy, fasteners, and finishes.

The Newfound Woodworks, Inc.
RFD #2 Box 850
Bristol, NH 03222
Phone: 603-744-6872
Milled strips, kits, and epoxy. Send $3 for information.

Nick Schade
Guillemot Kayaks
Apt. M, 10 Ash Swamp Rd.
Glastonbury, CT 06033
Phone: 860-659-8847
Kayak kits. Send $2 for catalog.

Sources of Epoxy, Fiberglass, and Associated Supplies

Here are some of the companies that sell top-quality boat building epoxies. My experience is mostly with System Three's products, but the other two companies' products are well known and accepted among professional builders. These products are available through local distributors, and it may be more economical to purchase from them. Call the companies for the names of suppliers nearest you.

System Three Resins, Inc.
P.O. Box 70436
Seattle, WA 98107
Phone: 206-782-7976, 800-333-5514
Epoxy, fiberglass, all related equipment and supplies, plus manual on use and handling of epoxy.

West System
Gougeon Brothers, Inc. Dept. 77
P.O. Box 908
Bay City, MI 48708
Phone: 517-684-7286
Epoxy, fiberglass, all related equipment and supplies, plus technical manual.

Matrix Adhesive Systems
Phone: 888-627-3769
Distributed by:
The Newfound Woodworks, Inc.
RFD #2 Box 850
Bristol, NH 03222
Phone: 603-744-6872

Sources of Hardware

Jamestown Distributors
Phone: 800-423-0030
Two locations:
P.O. Box 348
Jamestown, RI 02835
Phone: 401-423-2520
and
1236 Trask Parkway
Seabrook, SC 29940
Phone: 803-846-9500
Brass, silicon bronze, and stainless fasteners, as well as other hardware, tools, and supplies. Free catalog.

The Wooden Boat Shop
1007 Northeast Boat St.
Seattle, WA 98105
Phone: 206-634-3600, 800-933-3600
Stem bands, bronze screws, and bow eyes. Free catalog.

Northwoods Canoe Shop
336 Range Rd.
Atkinson, ME 04426
Stem bands, bronze carriage bolts, and other hardware.

West Marine
(many stores nationwide)
P.O. Box 50050
Watsonville, CA 95077-5050
Phone: 800-538-0775
Bow eyes, transom plugs, deck plates, silicon bronze and stainless fasteners. There is a $5 charge for the catalog.

Sources of Tools

Here is a small sample of the many suppliers of tools. Most of the tools needed for building a wood strip canoe can be found at the nearby hardware store or building supply outlet. A few of the tools may be somewhat harder to locate. Readers are encouraged to look first at local businesses, especially woodworkers' supply stores if you are privileged to have one within a reasonable distance. If you are not so favorably placed, then the listed suppliers can help you gear up for your project.

Grizzly Industrial, Inc.
(three locations)
P.O. Box 2069
Bellingham, WA 98227
Phone: 800-523-4777
Bead and flute router bits, Forstner bits, brad point drill bits, scrapers, spokeshaves, and many power tools.

MLCS Professional Woodworking Products
P.O. Box 4053BB
Rydal, PA 19046
Phone: 800-533-9298
Bead and flute router bits. Free catalog.

Trend-Lines
135 American Legion Hwy.
Revere, MA 02151
Phone: 800-366-6966 (to request catalog)
Brad point drill bits, adjustable countersinking drill bits, and Forstner bits. Price of catalog is $2.

The Wooden Boat Shop
1007 Northeast Boat St.
Seattle, WA 98105
Phone: 206-634-3600, 800-933-3600

Forstner bits, brad point drill bits, tapered drill bits for wood screws, and spokeshaves. Free catalog.

Woodcrafters
212 NE Sixth Ave.
Portland, OR 97232
Phone: 503-231-0226, 800-777-3709

Dozuki saws, brad point drill bits, spokeshaves, scrapers, and a combination bead and cove router bit. No catalog available; however, phone orders accepted. Inquire for item availability and price.

Sources of Other Supplies

These "miscellaneous" supplies may be locally scarce. It is advisable to check first because prices may be lower locally, and also the cost of shipping heavy items like cans of paint will be high. West Marine deals in high-quality products, but is not an inexpensive distributor. Other places to look for plastic buckles and nylon webbing are rafting supply stores and fabric shops.

West Marine
(many stores nationwide)
P.O. Box 50050
Watsonville, CA 905077-5050
Phone: 800-538-0775

Marine sealants; marine paints, primers, and varnishes; masking tape, nylon webbing, plastic buckles, and rope. There is a $5 charge for the catalog.

The Woodworker's Store
(several locations)
4365 Willow Drive
Medina, MN 55340
Phone: 800-279-4441

Natural rattan cane, reed spline, pre-woven rattan cane, tools, and information on how to apply cane (pre-woven or not).

Tandy Leather Company
(many stores nationwide)
Advertising Dept.
P.O. Box 791
Fort Worth, TX 76101

Vinyl corded lace. Write to this address for a list of store locations. Many of these stores serve as mail-order outlets. There is a charge for the complete catalog.

Sources of Information

For the most current information on what is sold by whom, readers are invited to survey the following periodicals. Not only are there advertisements for plans, tools, and supplies, but also interesting and educational articles on boats and boat building techniques. There are other maga-

zines that sometimes have articles of interest to hobby boat builders, but these three are densely packed with good stuff.

Boatbuilder
Subscription Dept.
Box 420235
Palm Coast, FL 32142-0235

This journal is published bimonthly, in odd-numbered months. Subscribers also receive, at no additional cost, *The Complete Guide to Boat Kits & Plans*, which is published annually. The magazine is about boat design and construction, and yet is written in language readily understandable to a lay audience. Subscription rate is $30/year in the United States and Canada.

WoodenBoat
Subscription Dept.
P.O. Box 54767
Boulder, CO 80323-4767

This glossy magazine is devoted to wooden boats of all types and sizes, whether powered by wind, motor, or human. Boat design, construction and finishing techniques, and building materials are regularly covered. The articles are very readable, and the photography is terrific. Publication is bimonthly, in odd-numbered months. Subscription rates are $27/year in the United States and $32/year in Canada.

Messing About in Boats
29 Burley St.
Wenham, MA 01984-1943

This magazine contains articles on various small boat designs, boating adventures and events, and construction. The tone is informal and entertaining, with many accounts of experiences shared by readers. Publication is twice per month, at $24/year in the United States and $36/year in Canada.

Notes

Chapter Two

1. Additional suggested reading is David W. Carnell's excellent article, "Safe Boatbuilding." The article is short, concise, easy to read, and packed with information on exposure to vapors, wood dust allergies, and hazardous solvents. As a career chemist, the author is well qualified to write on this topic. This article has appeared two times; once in the Vol. 10 No. 3 issue of *Boatbuilder* (1992), and *The Complete Guide to Boat Kits and Plans*, 9th Edition (1995), published by *Boatbuilder*.

Chapter Three

1. There are situations where decay resistance in hull material may be important. If for some reason you expect the canoe to be banged hard enough on a rock to puncture the fiberglass (permitting water to penetrate), and timely repairs are not possible, spruce would not be a good choice for the wood strip material because it has a low resistance to decay. Also, fiberglass applied with polyester resin is less effective in sealing out water (due to its permeability to water vapor), and is more brittle and more likely to crack. If you elect to use this type of resin in your fiberglass layup, a more rot resistant wood for the hull is recommended. Most experienced strip boat builders agree with Ted Moores, who in *Canoecraft* (p. 62) states that epoxy resin is far superior to polyester resin for this application.

2. See *Featherweight Boatbuilding*, page 8.

3. From *Canoecraft*, p. 63.

4. From *Building a Strip Canoe*, p. 57, and *Canoecraft*, p. 61.

5. From "Building Bob's Special" by Ted Moores, in *Build a Boat: A Beginner's Guide to Simple Boat Construction*.

6. *The Gougeon Brothers on Boat Construction*, and *Canoecraft*, respectively.

7. For more information on different fibers and their application in boatbuilding, see *The Gougeon Brothers on Boat Construction*, p. 91-92.

8. For comparison of polyester vs. epoxy resin based on first-hand experience, see *Canoecraft*, p. 62, and "Safe Boatbuilding," by David W. Carnell, in *Boatbuilder* magazine.

9. *The Gougeon Brothers on Boat Construction*, p. 82.

10. See *The Epoxy Book*, p. 16-17, or *The Gougeon Brothers on Boat Construction*, p. 44-46 for more information on properties of fillers.

Chapter Four

1. The subject of canoe design is well covered in *Canoecraft*, by Ted Moores and Merilyn Mohr, Chapter 3; and also in *Song of the Paddle, an Illustrated Guide to Wilderness Camping*, by Bill Mason, Chapter 10.

2. Examples are David Hazen, with *The Stripper's Guide to Canoe-building*, Gil Gilpatrick, with *Building a Strip Canoe*, and "Mac" McCarthy, with *Featherweight Boatbuilding*.

3. One such author is Ted Moores, of Bear Mountain Boat Shop, who co-wrote *Canoecraft* with Merilyn Mohr.

4. A list (current as of this writing) of distributors and independent designers appears in the Appendix.

5. See *Canoecraft*, "Pipedreams to Paper," Chapter 4, and *Building a Strip Canoe*, "Other Designs."

Chapter Five

1. The T-beam strongback is described in *Rip, Strip, and Row! A Builder's Guide to the Cosine Wherry*, by J. D. Brown; and in *Canoecraft*, by Ted Moores and Merilyn Mohr. Instructions for the T-beam and box beam strongbacks appear in *The Stripper's Guide to Canoe-building* by David Hazen. The box beam strongback is presented in excellent detail in "Building Bob's Special" by Ted Moores, published in *Build a Boat: A Beginner's Guide to Simple Boat Construction*. And finally, the open frame strongback is advanced in *Building a Strip Canoe*, by Gil Gilpatrick.

2. An illustration showing how to make any needed adjustments is in Hazen's book, *The Stripper's Guide to Canoe-building*; see the chapter entitled "Make the Jig."

3. You can easily make a serviceable fence to use with a hand-held circular saw for cutting plywood. From the long side of a full sheet of 1/2 in. (or thicker) plywood, saw off a 4 in. wide strip. Now, you have an 8 ft. long, 4 in. wide strip of plywood with one factory-cut edge to use as a fence. Clamp this strip to the sheet of plywood you need to cut up, with the factory-cut edge placed so you can slide the saw along it. Offset the plywood fence from the cutting line by whatever distance is necessary to locate the saw blade on the cutting line.

4. From instructions for construction of the Wee Lassie canoe, by Henry "Mac" McCarthy.

5. For more information on laminating wood, see *The Gougeon Brothers on Boat Construction, 4th Ed.*, Chapter 9.

6. For photos and detailed instructions on steam bending hardwood stock, see *Canoecraft*, p. 90-92, or "Building Bob's Special," p. 91-92

7. Suggested and illustrated in *Canoecraft*, page 93.

Chapter Six

1. See *The Stripper's Guide to Canoe-building*, the chapter titled, "To Make a Kayak."

2. This hull stripping pattern is a standby of Gil Gilpatrick's, described in his book, *Building A Strip Canoe*.

3. Ted Moores presents this stripping pattern in *Canoecraft* and in "Building Bob's Special," in *Build a Boat: A Beginner's Guide to Simple Boat Construction*.

4. This pattern was developed by "Mac" McCarthy; see *Featherweight Boatbuilding*, or "Strip Building a Double-Paddle Canoe," in *WoodenBoat* magazine.

5. See *Featherweight Boatbuilding* for more ideas.

6. Photos and detailed instructions for this method may be found in *Canoecraft* and "Building Bob's Special," by Ted Moores.

7. Recommended in *Rip, Strip, and Row!*.

8. David Hazen, in *The Stripper's Guide to Canoe-building*.

9. Hull bottoms done this way can look very good. For photos of this type of bottom stripping pattern, see *Featherweight Boatbuilding*, pages 25-27.

Chapter Seven

1. Gil Gilpatrick shows his canoes, built without wooden stems, specifically designed for whitewater and extended river tripping in his book, *Building a Strip Canoe*.

2. This method of installing outer stems is described in detail by Ted Moores. The most complete discussion is in *Build A Boat: A Beginner's Guide to Simple Boat Construction*, the

article "Building Bob's Special." It is also covered, though not as thoroughly, in *Canoecraft*.

3. This outer stem construction originally from instructions for building the Wee Lassie canoe, by "Mac" McCarthy.

Chapter Eight

1. "Mac" McCarthy describes specific problems with a canoe fiberglassed only on the outside on pages 64-65 of his book, *Featherweight Boatbuilding*.

Chapter Nine

1. For more specifics, see *Canoecraft*, p. 75.
2. *The Stripper's Guide to Canoe-building*, p. 55.
3. From instructions for building the Wee Lassie canoe, by "Mac" McCarthy.
4. See *Canoecraft*, the chapter titled "Material Matters," for more ideas, detailed instructions, and illustrations for finely crafted hardwood decks featuring masterful joinery.
5. For photos showing how to fit breasthooks, see the chapter titled "Wood Work" in *Building a Strip Canoe*.

Chapter Ten

1. Suggested in the instructions for the Wee Lassie canoe.
2. Gil Gilpatrick must be given proper credit for his presentation of these most excellent seats in his book, *Building a Strip Canoe*.
3. For a series of photos on trapezoidal seat caning, see the chapter titled "Seats" in *Building a Strip Canoe*.
4. The time begins when steam is observed escaping from the end of the chamber opposite the tea kettle. The actual time required for steaming depends on the dimensions of the wood pieces, and how dry they are to begin with.
5. For photos and more specific directions, see *Canoecraft*, the chapter titled "Character Development."
6. These foot braces are popular for use in Wee Lassie and Wee Lassie II solo canoe models. Foot braces described here are based on a version shown in *Featherweight Boatbuilding*.

References

Brown, J. D., John Hartsock, and Bob & Erica Pickett. *Rip, Strip, and Row! A Builder's Guide to the Cosine Wherry.* Larkspur, California: Tamal Vista Publications, 1985.

Carnell, David W. "Safe Boatbuilding." *Boatbuilder* 10, no. 3 (1992): 22-28.

Editor, in reply to reader's inquiry regarding ventilating air chambers. *Boatbuilder* 15, no. 2 (1997): 3.

Gilpatrick, Gil. *Building a Strip Canoe.* Freeport, Maine: De Lorme Publishing Company, 1985.

Gougeon Brothers, The. *The Gougeon Brothers on Boat Construction, 4th Ed.* Midland, Michigan: The McKay Press, Inc., 1985.

Hazen, David. *The Stripper's Guide to Canoe-building, 4th Ed.* Larkspur, California: Tamal Vista Publications, 1976.

Mason, Bill. *Song of the Paddle: An Illustrated Guide to Wilderness Camping.* Minocqua, Wisconsin: NorthWord Press Inc., 1988.

McCarthy, Henry "Mac." *Featherweight Boat building: A WoodenBoat Book.* Brooklin, Maine: WoodenBoat Books, 1996.

McCarthy, Henry. Instructions for building a Wee Lassie canoe. Sarasota, Florida: Feather Canoes, Inc.

McCarthy, Henry. "Strip Building a Double-Paddle Canoe." *WoodenBoat* 100 (1991): 92-99.

Mac Naughton, Thomas A. "Scantling Rules for Sheathed-Strip Construction." *Boatbuilder* 8, no. 4 (1990): 32-37.

Moores, Ted. "Building Bob's Special." *Build a Boat: A Beginner's Guide to Simple Boat Construction*; by the editors of *WoodenBoat* magazine (1996): 84-113.

Moores, Ted, and Merilyn Mohr. *Canoecraft: A Harrowsmith Illustrated Guide to Fine Woodstrip Construction.* Camden East, Ontario: Camden House Publishing, 1983.

The Epoxy Book: A System Three Publication. Seattle, Washington: System Three Resins, Inc., 1992.

Photo Courtesy of Janet Van Leuven-Kern.